Cisco Unified Communications Manager 8: Expert Administration Cookbook

Over 110 advanced recipes to effectively and efficiently configure and manage Cisco Unified Communications Manager

Tanner Ezell

BIRMINGHAM - MUMBAI

Cisco Unified Communications Manager 8: Expert Administration Cookbook

Copyright © 2012 Packt Publishing

All rights reserved. No part of this book may be reproduced, stored in a retrieval system, or transmitted in any form or by any means, without the prior written permission of the publisher, except in the case of brief quotations embedded in critical articles or reviews.

Every effort has been made in the preparation of this book to ensure the accuracy of the information presented. However, the information contained in this book is sold without warranty, either express or implied. Neither the author, nor Packt Publishing and its dealers and distributors, will be held liable for any damages caused or alleged to be caused directly or indirectly by this book.

Packt Publishing has endeavored to provide trademark information about all of the companies and products mentioned in this book by the appropriate use of capitals. However, Packt Publishing cannot guarantee the accuracy of this information.

First published: March 2012

Production Reference: 1170312

Published by Packt Publishing Ltd.
Livery Place
35 Livery Street
Birmingham B3 2PB, UK.

ISBN 978-1-84968-432-3

www.packtpub.com

Cover Image by David Gimenez (bilbaorocker@yahoo.co.uk)

Credits

Author
Tanner Ezell

Reviewers
Michael Ciulei
John Schreiner
Victor Rosa
Justin O'Sullivan

Acquisition Editor
Rukshana Khambatta

Lead Technical Editor
Dayan Hyames

Technical Editors
Veronica Fernandes
Vishal D'souza
Sonali Tharwani

Project Coordinator
Leena Purkait

Proofreader
Lydia May Morris

Indexer
Hemangini Bari

Production Coordinator
Nilesh R. Mohite

Cover Work
Nilesh R. Mohite

About the Author

Tanner Ezell has over five years of experience working with Cisco's Unified Communications platform, along with custom application development in the same field. He currently works as a Consultant with a Cisco partner that specializes in Unified Communications and Contact Center. He spends most of his time designing and implementing UC solutions as well as custom applications and Contact Center scripts. He has a passion for understanding the underlying technology that makes the solutions possible. When he is not working, he enjoys bicycling around the bay area and spending time outdoors on beautiful Northern California days.

> I would like to thank my family and my dear friends who have been supportive of this challenging process from the beginning. I cannot thank the contributors, editors, and reviewers enough for the dedication, input, and honest feedback.
>
> I would also like to thank my colleagues, who are a wealth of information, and an uninterruptable source of laughs and good times.
>
> Lastly, I would like to thank my Editor and Project Coordinator who have graciously put up with seemingly endless delays, and offered me this opportunity to grow in ways that will continue to benefit me and my career.

About the Reviewers

Michael Ciulei has more than 11 years of experience in the IT field, as an IT and Telephony Specialist, with a focus on network design and implementation. He is currently a Cisco CCNP Voice Engineer, with a specialization in Advanced Wireless LAN. He has a Bachelor of Engineering degree in Informatics and Computer Science from Tibiscus University, Timisoara.

John Schreiner is a Captain in the United States Marine Corps and the Lead Voice Instructor and Curriculum Manager for the Communication Training Centers. He serves as the Director for Communication Training Center-2, training marines on the East Coast in the latest commercial technologies (Cisco, Microsoft, REDCOM, Harris, and so on). He has experience with both military tactical voice systems and commercial voice systems. He also instructs on security and advanced networking.

John holds CCNP, CCNP Voice, CCNA Security, CCDA, CISSP, and various other certifications.

> I'd like to thank my amazing wife, Jacki, who has an impressive tolerance for my Cisco endeavors.

Victor M. Rosa has been in the computer industry for over 25 years. He is experienced in the design and implementation of large IP and multiprotocol networks, encompassing complex wide area network designs, campus local area networks, IP Telephony and Data Center technologies. In the past 10 years, he has planned, implemented, and supported many networks, utilizing both Layer 2 and Layer 3 techniques. In the past five years, he has worked with companies such as HP, Bank of America, and Cisco Systems. He is currently a Networking Consultant for the largest privately owned enterprise in South Carolina, serving the health care industry, pharmaceuticals, and state government agencies. He is certified in two major network technologies: Microsoft and Cisco in the area of Cisco IP Telephony, holding a CCNP Voice and is currently pursuing a CCIE in Routing and Switching.

www.PacktPub.com

Support files, eBooks, discount offers and more

You might want to visit `www.PacktPub.com` for support files and downloads related to your book.

Did you know that Packt offers eBook versions of every book published, with PDF and ePub files available? You can upgrade to the eBook version at `www.PacktPub.com` and as a print book customer, you are entitled to a discount on the eBook copy. Get in touch with us at `service@packtpub.com` for more details.

At `www.PacktPub.com`, you can also read a collection of free technical articles, sign up for a range of free newsletters and receive exclusive discounts and offers on Packt books and eBooks.

`http://PacktLib.PacktPub.com`

Do you need instant solutions to your IT questions? PacktLib is Packt's online digital book library. Here, you can access, read and search across Packt's entire library of books.

Why Subscribe?
- Fully searchable across every book published by Packt
- Copy and paste, print and bookmark content
- On demand and accessible via web browser

Free Access for Packt account holders

If you have an account with Packt at `www.PacktPub.com`, you can use this to access PacktLib today and view nine entirely free books. Simply use your login credentials for immediate access.

Instant Updates on New Packt Books

Get notified! Find out when new books are published by following `@PacktEnterprise` on Twitter, or the *Packt Enterprise* Facebook page.

Table of Contents

Preface	**1**
Chapter 1: Call Routing, Dial Plan, and E.164	**5**
Introduction	5
Implementing local route groups with device pools for E.164 call routing	6
Implementing E.164 route patterns and partitions	8
Implementing E.164 called and calling party transformations	12
Implementing least cost call routing using Tail End Hop Off	17
Implementing calling restrictions with line blocking partitions and calling search spaces	20
Implementing short dial numbers	26
Implementing time-of-day call routing	28
Implementing Forced Authorization Codes	32
Implementing Client Matter Codes	35
Chapter 2: Call Admission Control	**37**
Introduction	37
Implementing location-based call admission control	37
Implementing regions for call admission control	43
Implementing the Resource Reservation Protocol	45
Enabling Automated Alternate Routing	48
Implementing Automated Alternate Routing	50
Chapter 3: Media Resources and Music On Hold	**55**
Introduction	55
Configuring software conference bridges	56
Configuring IOS conference bridges	58
Configuring transcoders	59
Configuring media termination points	60
Configuring media resource groups	62
Configuring media resource group lists	63

Table of Contents

Implementing unicast Music On Hold	65
Configuring multicast Music On Hold	69
Adding custom media files for Music On Hold	72

Chapter 4: Tracing and Troubleshooting Tools — 73
Introduction	73
Configuring user permissions for the Real-Time Monitoring Tool	73
Collecting traces using the Query Wizard	76
Configuring the e-mail server for the Real-Time Monitoring Tool	81
Creating custom alerts in the Real-Time Monitoring Tool	82
Configuring custom alert actions	86
Capturing packets	88
Analyzing the Dial Plan with the dialed number analyzer	93

Chapter 5: Device and Unified Mobility — 101
Introduction	102
Configuring physical locations	102
Configuring device mobility groups	103
Configure device pools for device mobility	103
Configuring device mobility info	104
Enabling device mobility	106
Configuring mid-call feature access codes	108
Configuring Session Handoff	109
Enabling Intelligent Session Control	110
Implementing mobility access lists	111
Configuring remote destination profiles	113
Configuring remote destinations	115
Implementing Mobile Voice Access	118
Enabling Enterprise Feature Access	122
Adding the Mobility softkey	123

Chapter 6: User Management — 125
Introduction	125
Enabling LDAP synchronization	126
Configuring an LDAP Directory	126
Enabling LDAP authentication	129
Configuring custom LDAP filters	131
Configuring credential policies	132
Configuring default credential policies	135
Assigning credential policies	138
Configuring user roles	141
Configuring user groups	143
Assigning user groups to end users	145

Chapter 7: User Features — 147
- Introduction — 147
- Implementing direct transfer to voice mail — 148
- Implementing Meet-Me conferencing — 151
- Implementing call park — 154
- Implementing directed call park — 156
- Configuring the Intercom feature — 158
- Configuring Malicious Call Identification — 163
- Adding a custom ringtone — 166
- Adding a custom background image — 169
- Configuring dual mode for iPhone — 173

Chapter 8: Advanced Features — 177
- Introduction — 178
- Enabling the Extension Mobility service — 178
- Configuring the Extension Mobility phone service — 179
- Configuring phone devices for Extension Mobility — 180
- Configuring device profiles for Extension Mobility — 183
- Configuring Extension Mobility service parameters — 189
- Enabling the Cross Cluster Extension Mobility services — 191
- Configuring the Cross Cluster Extension Mobility phone service — 192
- Configure users for Cross Cluster Extension Mobility — 193
- Preparing certificates for Cross Cluster Extension Mobility — 194
- Creating a template for Cross Cluster Extension Mobility devices — 197
- Configuring Cross Cluster Extension Mobility parameters — 198
- Configuring intercluster trunks for Cross Cluster Extension Mobility — 199
- Configuring the intercluster service profile for Cross Cluster Extension Mobility — 200
- Configuring monitoring and recording — 202
- Configuring geolocations and filters — 205
- Implementing logical partitioning — 207
- Configuring hotline service parameters — 209
- Configuring a hotline device — 210
- Configuring barge for devices and users — 213
- Configuring privacy for devices and users — 216

Chapter 9: Securing Unified Communications — 221
- Introduction — 221
- Configuring phone security profiles — 222
- Configuring devices for secure tone — 224
- Configuring Certificate Authority Proxy Function — 227
- Configuring digest authentication — 229

Table of Contents

Implementing endpoint hardening	230
Implementing a secure conference bridge	232
Implementing secure Meet-Me conferences	233
Configuring VPN for Cisco IP phones	234
Configuring application users for secure communication	236

Chapter 10: Serviceability, Upgrades, and Disaster Recovery — 239

Introduction	239
Configuring alarms	240
Configuring traces	242
Configuring SNMP versions 1 and 2	244
Configuring SNMP Version 3	247
Applying patches and upgrades	250
Configuring a backup device	253
Configuring a backup schedule	255
Performing a manual backup	256
Restoring from backup	258

Chapter 11: Bulk Administration Tool — 261

Introduction	262
Introducing the Bulk Administration Tool	262
Enabling the Bulk Provisioning Service	264
Creating and using a custom file	265
Bulk provisioning phones	268
Bulk provisioning users	269
Bulk provisioning user device profiles	271
Bulk provisioning gateways	273
Bulk provisioning Forced Authorization Codes	275
Bulk provisioning Client Matter Codes	276
Bulk provisioning call pickup groups	277
Bulk provisioning access lists	278
Bulk provisioning remote destination profiles	279
Bulk provisioning remote destinations	280
Bulk provisioning mobility profiles	282
Exporting data	283

Index — 287

Preface

Cisco Unified Communications Manager 8: Expert Administration Cookbook is filled with many advanced recipes to effectively and efficiently configure and manage Cisco Unified Communications Manager.

This book intends to serve as a quick reference for consultants and administrators to quickly address and resolve common problems while providing design insights. Coupled with clear instructions and plenty of screenshots, this book will help in implementing new features and improving the existing architecture. This practical cookbook will help familiarize the readers with various aspects and conventions of Cisco's Unified Communications Manager solution.

What this book covers

Chapter 1, Call Routing, Dial Plan, and E.164, will expose you to call routing with an emphasis around local route groups and E.164. You will learn how to implement least cost routing, Tail End Hop Off, and various call routing technologies available.

Chapter 2, Call Admission Control, focuses on call admission control features, the components that make them up, as well as how to reroute calls when enough bandwidth is not available.

Chapter 3, Media Resources and Music On Hold, focuses on the multimedia aspects of the platform; you'll learn how to set up Music on Hold and upload custom audio files. You'll also learn how to configure media-related devices and their functions such as Media Termination Points and Transcoders.

Chapter 4, Tracing and Troubleshooting Tools, will expose you to some of the most common tools used to debug and troubleshoot issues on the platform, including the Real-Time Monitoring Tool.

Chapter 5, Device and Unified Mobility, focuses specifically on mobility for devices and end users. You'll learn to configure single number reach, two state dialing, and how to configure mobility-related features.

Chapter 6, User Management, will teach you how to manage end-user permissions, roles and user groups, and how they might apply to end users and administrators alike. You'll learn about LDAP integration and authentication as well as how and when to apply filters.

Chapter 7, User Features, focuses on commonly requested and demanded features for users, including Meet-Me conferencing, directed call park, as well as user niceties such as custom ringtones and backgrounds.

Chapter 8, Advanced Features, explains advanced features of Unified Communications Manager, specifically focusing around extension mobility, call recording, and monitoring along with the introduction of geolocations and logical partition.

Chapter 9, Securing Unified Communications, provides common configuration information for securing a Unified Communications Manager cluster. It also includes configuration for phones and conference resources over SRTP.

Chapter 10, Serviceability, Upgrades, and Disaster Recovery, aims to cover configuration of alarms and tracing, along with configuration of the three versions of SNMP. It also covers the backup and restore process for the Unified Communications Manager publisher.

Chapter 11, Bulk Administration Tool, introduces the Bulk Administration Tool. We will learn to generate CSV files with and without the `bat.xls` spreadsheet, as well as cover the fields required for some of the most common items that are bulk provisioned including devices, user device profiles, analog gateways, and mobility users.

What you need for this book

- Cisco Unified Communications Manager 8.5
- Cisco IP Communicator 8

Who this book is for

If you are a Cisco Unified Communications Administrator or Engineer looking forward for advanced recipes to perform important administration tasks, then this is the best guide for you. This book assumes familiarity with the basics of Cisco's Unified Communications Manager architecture.

Conventions

In this book, you will find a number of styles of text that distinguish between different kinds of information. Here are some examples of these styles, and an explanation of their meaning.

Code words in text are shown as follows: " The pattern \+[^1] will match any E.164 number that does not start with a one."

Any command-line input or output is written as follows:

```
dial-peer voice 200 voip
service CCM
incoming-called number 13400
destination-pattern 13400
session target ipv4:192.168.1.5
codec g711ulaw
dtmf-relay h245-alphanumeric
novad
```

New terms and **important words** are shown in bold. Words that you see on the screen, in menus or dialog boxes for example, appear in the text like this: " Add a new route list that will serve as the link to the local route groups (**Call Routing** | **Route/Hunt** | **Route List**)."

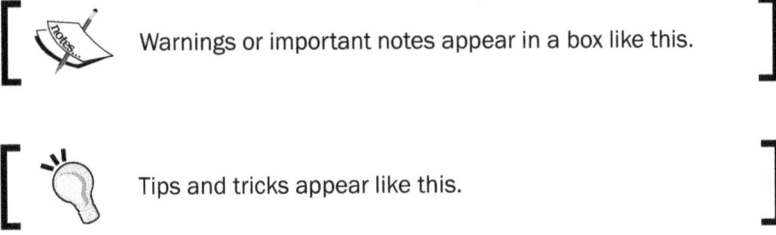

Reader feedback

Feedback from our readers is always welcome. Let us know what you think about this book—what you liked or may have disliked. Reader feedback is important for us to develop titles that you really get the most out of.

To send us general feedback, simply send an e-mail to feedback@packtpub.com, and mention the book title through the subject of your message.

If there is a topic that you have expertise in and you are interested in either writing or contributing to a book, see our author guide on www.packtpub.com/authors.

Customer support

Now that you are the proud owner of a Packt book, we have a number of things to help you to get the most from your purchase.

Errata

Although we have taken every care to ensure the accuracy of our content, mistakes do happen. If you find a mistake in one of our books—maybe a mistake in the text or the code—we would be grateful if you would report this to us. By doing so, you can save other readers from frustration and help us improve subsequent versions of this book. If you find any errata, please report them by visiting `http://www.packtpub.com/support`, selecting your book, clicking on the **errata submission form** link, and entering the details of your errata. Once your errata are verified, your submission will be accepted and the errata will be uploaded to our website, or added to any list of existing errata, under the Errata section of that title.

Piracy

Piracy of copyright material on the Internet is an ongoing problem across all media. At Packt, we take the protection of our copyright and licenses very seriously. If you come across any illegal copies of our works, in any form, on the Internet, please provide us with the location address or website name immediately so that we can pursue a remedy.

Please contact us at `copyright@packtpub.com` with a link to the suspected pirated material.

We appreciate your help in protecting our authors, and our ability to bring you valuable content.

Questions

You can contact us at `questions@packtpub.com` if you are having a problem with any aspect of the book, and we will do our best to address it.

1
Call Routing, Dial Plan, and E.164

In chapter 1 we dive straight into the dial plan with recipes on E.164 globalization, call routing, and call restrictions. We will cover:

- Implementing local route groups with device pools for E.164 call routing
- Implementing E.164 route patterns and partitions
- Implementing E.164 called and calling party transformations
- Implementing least cost call routing using Tail End Hop Off
- Implementing call restrictions with line blocking patterns and calling search spaces
- Implementing short dial numbers
- Implementing time-of-day call routing
- Implementing Forced Authorization Codes
- Implementing Client Matter Codes

Introduction

In this chapter, we will focus on implementing local route groups, device pools, route patterns, and various other call routing technologies with a specific focus on building an E.164 compatible dial plan. All the recipes in this chapter require administrator access to the **Unified Communications Manager** (**UCM**). It is strongly recommended you get comfortable performing these recipes in a lab environment before implementing them into production.

Even if you're not interested in E.164, the recipes in this chapter can be applied to building any style of dial plan while utilizing some of the feature benefits to make dial plan management easier than before.

Implementing local route groups with device pools for E.164 call routing

To simplify call routing and dial plan management, local route groups provide a logical way to process calls according to settings specific to the device pool of the originating device.

Getting ready

This recipe assumes you have a gateway or trunk device configured.

How to do it...

To implement a local route group for use with a device pool, perform the following:

1. Add a new route list that will serve as the link to the local route groups (**Call Routing | Route/Hunt | Route List**).
2. Click on **Add New** to add a new route list.
3. Type in a name and select a Call Manager Group in the drop-down with which the route list will be associated:

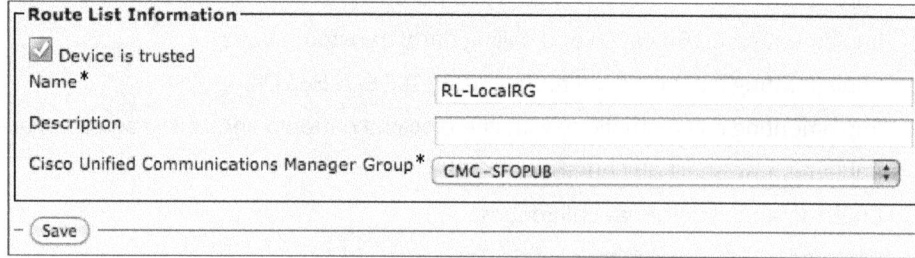

4. Click on **Save**.
5. Once the page reloads, click on **Add Route Group** and a new page will open.
6. Select **Standard Local Route Group** from the **Route Group** drop-down menu then click on **Save**. You will be returned to the **Route List** page:

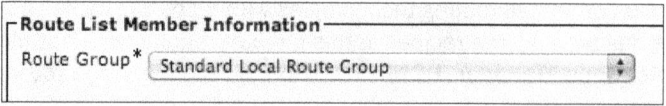

7. Finally, click on **Save** to save the Route List.
8. Add a new route group containing the gateway or trunk (**Call Routing | Route/Hunt | Route Group**).

9. Find and select your gateway or trunk under the **Find Devices to Add to Route Group** section. Then click on **Add to Route Group**. You should now see the device in the **Selected Devices** list:

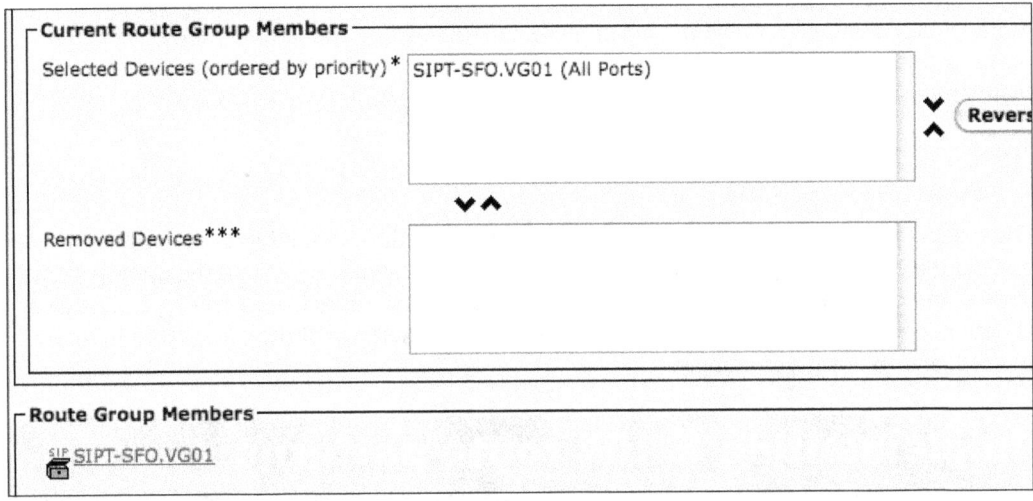

10. Click on **Save**. The device will show up under **Route Group Members**.
11. Assign the route group you created in the previous step to the device pool by navigating to the device pool (From the menu, **System | Device Pool**) configuration page and selecting the route group from the **Local Route Group** drop-down under the **Device Pool Settings** section:

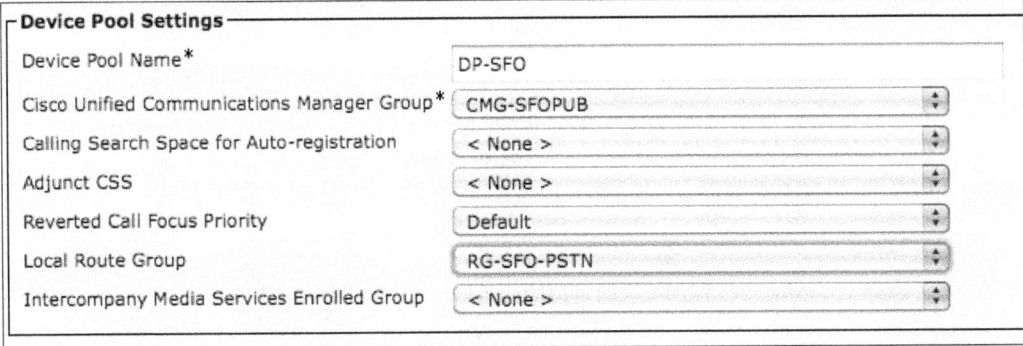

12. Click on **Save**.

 These changes will not take effect until you *reset* the devices in the device pool.

Call Routing, Dial Plan, and E.164

How it works...

Prior to the introduction of local route groups in CUCM, dial plans relied on route patterns pointing to specific gateways and route lists in site-specific partitions. By utilizing local route groups with device pools we can simplify call routing and reduce the number of route patterns needed throughout the system, thereby making the overall system simpler and maintenance easier.

There's more...

When a call is placed on the system it matches a route pattern that informs the system where to send the call, typically a route list containing trunks and gateways. When the system is told to send the call to a route list containing the Standard Local Route Group, the egress gateway is determined by information pulled from the device pool settings of the device that initiated the call, and routes it accordingly.

Implementing E.164 route patterns and partitions

An advantage of an E.164 dial plan is that it requires only a single route pattern to make it all work, though additional route patterns are still needed to allow users to dial using traditional dialing and TEHO. Here we will create the route partition to be used by the E.164 route pattern.

How to do it...

To create the route pattern to support an E.164 dial plan, we will do the following:

1. Add a new partition, which will be globally accessible, by clicking **Add New** on the **Partitions** page located in the **Class of Control** submenu under the **Call Routing** menu.

```
┌─ Partition Information ──────────────────────────────────────────────────
│  To enter multiple partitions, use one line for each partition entry. You can enter up to 75 partitions; the
│  names and descriptions can have up to a total of 1475 characters. The partition name cannot exceed 50
│  characters. Use a comma (',') to separate the partition name and description on each line. If a description
│  is not entered, Cisco Unified Communications Manager uses the partition name as the description. For example:
│       << partitionName >> , << description >>
│       CiscoPartition, Cisco employee partition
│       DallasPartition
│  Name*  ┌────────────────────────────────────────────────────────────────┐
│         │ PT-Global-E164,Clusterwide E.164 Partition                     │
│         └────────────────────────────────────────────────────────────────┘
```

2. Enter in a partition name and a description in the text box and then click on **Save**.

3. Add the E.164 Route Pattern and assign the Route List to it (**Call Routing | Route/Hunt | Route Pattern**).
4. Click on **Add New**.
5. Enter \+.! for the **Route Pattern** and select the route partition previously created in the **Route Partition** drop-down:

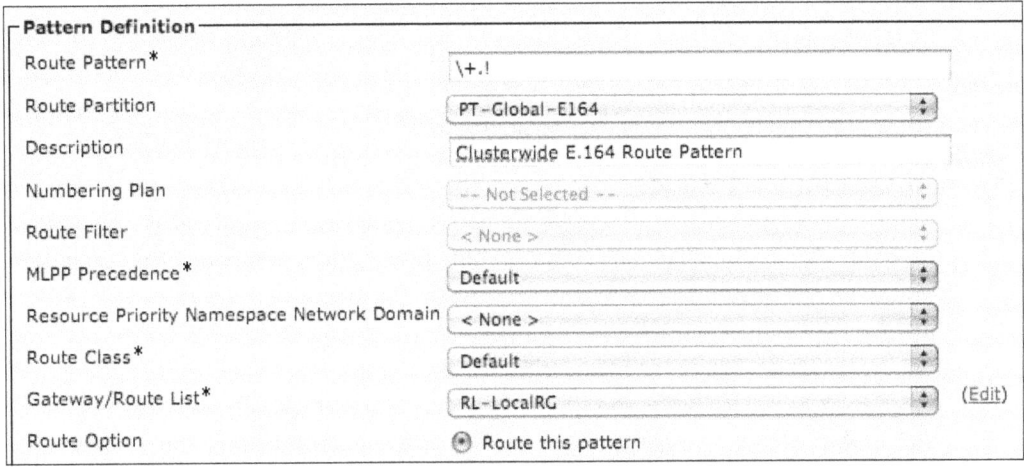

6. From the **Gateway/Route List*** drop-down, select the route list containing the Standard Local Route Group.
7. Ensure that the **Call Classification** is **OffNet** and the **Route Option** is set to **Route this pattern**.
8. Click on **Save**.

How it works...

When an E.164 number is dialed, the system will match it against the route pattern. The purpose of this pattern is to get the call to route to the local gateway or trunk where number normalization occurs, before sending the call out to the local gateway. **Call Classification** is set to **OffNet** for this pattern because we expect any calls that match this pattern to be routed out to the PSTN.

There's more...

Implementing a successful dial plan requires a few considerations from a technical perspective as well as a user experience standpoint.

Dial plan considerations and partitions

Partitions are a crucial part of both the dial plan and the implementation of calling restrictions. Having a well designed partition scheme can make management easier and it isn't difficult to implement. Some things to consider when planning your partition scheme are as follows:

- How many locations?
- Multinational?
- Will short dials (or hot numbers) be used?
- What about multinational dialing considerations?

Common system partitions

In most systems there are a few basic requirements from a partitioning perspective and at the very least we want to separate user directory numbers from system numbers. To accomplish this we might have the following partitions:

- PT-Line
- PT-System

If this is an E.164 dial plan, we want to separate the partitions from the rest of the system. That is why we also include:

- PT-Global-E164

Partitioning at a national level

In order to support a basic multinational dial plan we need partitions for dialing rules specific to each nation, for example:

- PT-US-DialPlan
- PT-UK-DialPlan

We would typically use these partitions for any patterns that reach the PSTN, including emergency and information services, as well as regular outbound calls.

Partitioning at a local level

If location specific dial rules are required, we might have partitions for each location. For example:

- PT-US-SFO-DialPlan

By doing this at the location level, we can allow for location specific short dials or dialing rules. For example, if we wanted to implement extension 4357 as a short dial to reach the local help desk, we would use a location specific partition such as that shown previously.

Chapter 1

Dial plan considerations and route patterns

It's important to define how users will access the outside world based on what they are familiar with. In many corporations, dial plan rules exist to allow local calls to be dialed first with a 9 or 91, followed by seven or ten digits; other companies may require nine or ten digits for all calls. We call this seven digit and ten digit dialing, respectively.

Regardless of which dialing method is used, the setup is the same and thanks to E.164 you only need one route pattern to support all locations.

Seven digit dialing

To implement seven digit dialing we will add another route pattern as explained earlier, which is the `9.[2-9]XXXXXX` pattern:

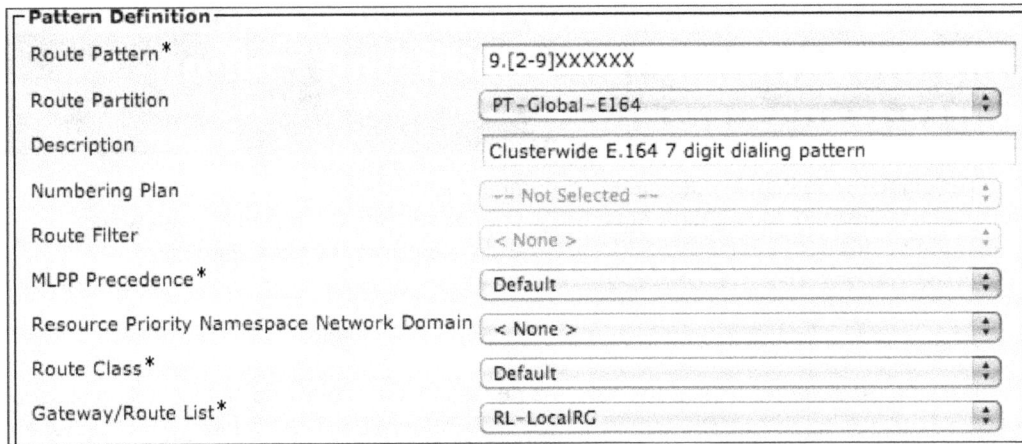

Unlike the earlier example, we want to strip the `9` off and append a plus sign. This is necessary so the call will match the `\+.!` pattern before it can be routed to the local gateway or trunk:

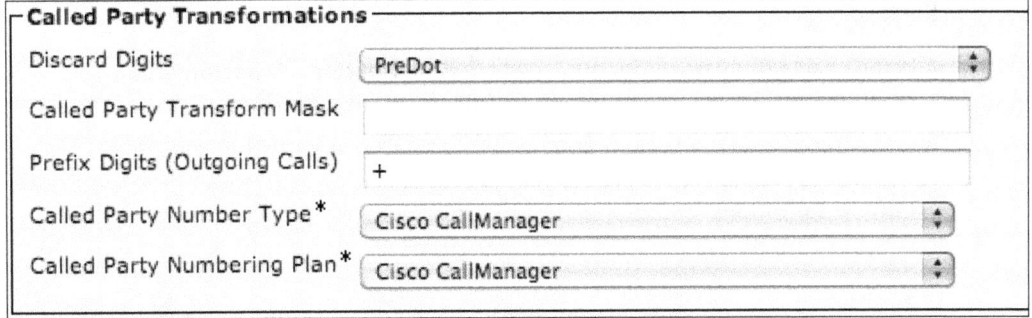

Call Routing, Dial Plan, and E.164

In situations where you are not using an E.164 dial plan but want to implement seven digit dialing, you need to only put the pattern in a location specific partition and point the **Gateway/Route List*** to the appropriate route list or gateway. In this situation, you would not prefix the plus sign.

>  Don't forget to include a pattern for non-local calls!

Ten digit dialing

To configure ten digit dialing, follow the previous steps and instead use a pattern of 9.[2-9]XXXXXXXXX.

Implementing E.164 called and calling party transformations

By using cluster-wide E.164 route patterns, number localization is no longer done on the route pattern. Instead, localization must occur prior to sending the call to the gateway or trunk device. This is accomplished with called and calling party transformations.

Getting ready

In this recipe we assume you already have the necessary partitions and calling search spaces for called and calling party transformations created. Refer to the *There's more...* section for an example partition and calling search space scheme.

How to do it...

To implement called and calling party transformation on either a gateway or trunk device, perform the following:

1. Add the calling party transformation pattern (**Call Routing | Transformation | Transformation Pattern | Calling Party Transformation Pattern**).

2. Add the transformation pattern appropriate to your environment and location:

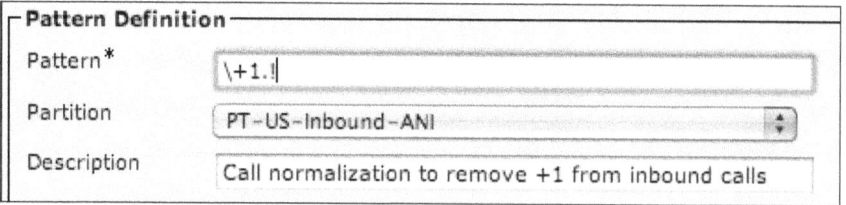

3. Prefix any necessary digits and select the appropriate digit discard field. In the case of the previous example, **Discard Digits** is set to **PreDot** with no digits being prefixed.

4. Add the called party transformation pattern (**Call Routing | Transformation | Transformation Pattern | Called Party Transformation Pattern**).

5. Add the appropriate transformation pattern and any prefix digits necessary. In this case, we again choose **PreDot** for **Discard Digits** and set **Prefix Digits** to **9**. Refer to the *There's more...* section for further explanation if required.

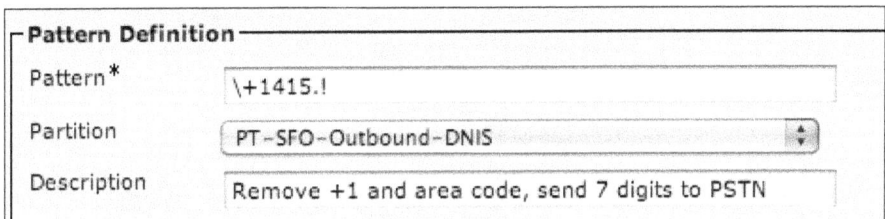

6. Navigate to the configuration page for the port or device.

7. On a MGCP controlled gateway, transformations are configured on a per port basis. The configuration page for the port is found by navigating to the configuration page for the gateway, then selecting the appropriate T1 port under the **Configured Slots, VICs and Endpoints** section as indicated in the following screenshot:

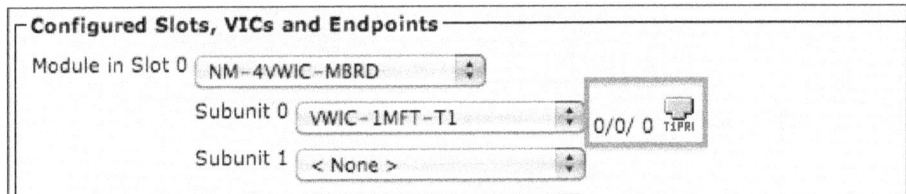

8. This is configured at the device level for trunks and gateways.

9. Next we apply the transformations to our trunks or gateways. Calling party transformations are configured under the section titled **Incoming Calling Party Settings**.

> The type of device we are configuring will determine the fields available to us. On gateway devices we see **National**, **International**, **Unknown**, and **Subscriber**. On trunk devices we see **Incoming Number**.

Call Routing, Dial Plan, and E.164

10. Select the **Calling Search Space** that contains the partitions you assigned to the called and calling party transformation patterns and apply it to all applicable fields:

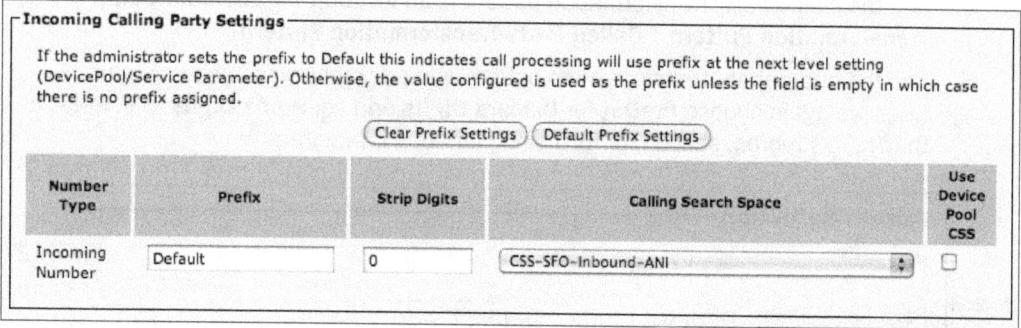

The previous screenshot is for an SIP trunk. Here we uncheck **Use Device Pool CSS** as we are not using the device pool for number transformation.

11. Finally, called party transformations are configured under different sections depending on the type of device.

On the gateways configuration page, this section is called **Call Routing Information - Outbound Calls**, and **Outbound Calls** for trunks.

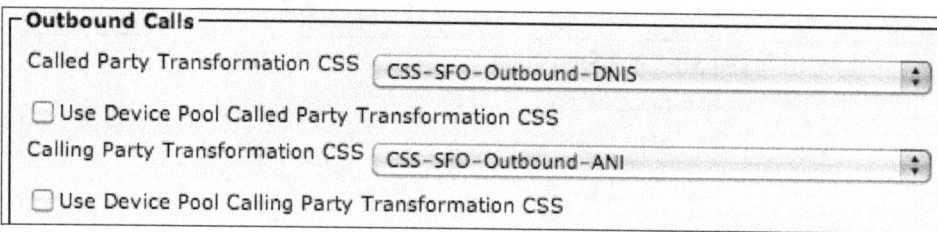

Again, we are not using the device pool for number transformation, so we uncheck boxes for both calling and called device pool transformations.

>  The calling search space selected for the **Called** and **Calling Party Transformation CSS** must contain the partitions used when creating the transformation patterns.

How it works...

When a call enters through a gateway or trunk device, the calling and called party transformations are applied depending on transformation patterns available to the calling search space used:

- **Calling party transformation patterns**: In the example from the recipe you see a calling party transformation pattern using \+1.!. As we explain in the example, we discard digits PreDot. We do this to normalize the number users see when their phone is ringing and connected, as users in the United States may not be accustomed to seeing +1 before the number.

    Alternatively, say we have an office in San Francisco where users are accustomed to seeing only seven digits for local calls and ten for everything else. We still use the \+1.! PreDot pattern to remove the +1 for calls but we add another pattern to strip the area code off. In this case that pattern would be \+1415.!, stripping PreDot with a partition of PT-SFO-Inbound-ANI, or something similar. By doing this, calls from 415 numbers will show as seven digits on the display when ringing and connected.

- **Called party transformation patterns**: Prior to local route groups and called party transformations, you would prepare the dialed number to be sent to the gateway or route list on the route pattern itself. Called party transformation patterns would then be used to prepare the dialed digits to be accepted by the gateway, trunk, or PSTN. In many cases this involves stripping the plus sign and prefixing an access code before sending it out to the gateway or trunk to route the call to the PSTN.

    How we modify the number depends on the type of gateways or trunks we are using. With MGCP gateways, we format the number so that it can be sent across to the PSTN. In some cases this means removing the plus, and appending or removing digits depending on what the carrier expects. For instance, if the carrier expects seven digits for local calls and 1 + 10 digits for long distance calls, we might strip the +1 and area code for local calls and strip only the plus for all other calls.

    For gateways and trunks, access codes are typically configured to inform the gateway or trunk to send the call to the PSTN. Typically these are 9, or 91. In this situation we would strip the necessary digits and prefix the access code appropriate to the call. For example, say our carrier requires seven digits for local and eleven digits for long distance calls; assuming we require an access code of 9 for local and 91 for long distance calls, we might implement the following called party transformations:

    - \+1.!

        Partition: PT-SFO-Outbound-DNIS

        Prefix digits: 91

    - \+1415.!

Partition: PT-SFO-Outbound-DNIS

Prefix digits: 9

Now, when a call is made to +1 415 555 1234, for example, the transformation pattern will remove +1415 and append a 9, sending the call to the gateway or trunk as 95551234 where it would match a dial peer before being sent out to the PSTN. While it is possible to do these transformations on the gateway themselves, managing them in UCM provides a central point for configuration and can help reduce dial plan maintenance.

There's more...

Calling and called party transformations are primarily used to localize the ANI displayed for calls entering the system and localizing calls for the gateway before sending it out to the PSTN.

Partitions and calling search spaces for called and calling transformation patterns

In this recipe you will see a few partitions and calling search spaces that may not immediately make sense. In order to accomplish these transformations on a per location basis we have six partitions and three calling search spaces.

The partitions and calling search spaces we use are:

- CSS-SFO-Outbound-ANI
    - PT-SFO-Outbound-ANI
    - PT-US-Outbound-ANI
- CSS-SFO-Outbound-DNIS
    - PT-SFO-Outbound-DNIS
    - PT-US-Outbound-DNIS
- CSS-SFO-Inbound-ANI
    - PT-SFO-Inbound-ANI
    - PT-US-Inbound-ANI

If you have no need to localize the ANI on a per location basis you might have a single calling search space and partition instead:

- CSS-US-Inbound-ANI
    - PT-US-Inbound-ANI

These are only some suggestions; make sure you apply the appropriate calling search spaces and partitions for your cluster.

Implementing least cost call routing using Tail End Hop Off

Least Cost Routing (**LCR**) is not strictly limited to calls destined for the PSTN, instead LCR can be used to prevent OnNet calls from being routed OffNet. In this recipe we will cover both uses.

Getting ready

Before we begin this recipe it is helpful to have some information:

- DID ranges of locations for which we are implementing LCR
- Site codes of locations for which we are implementing LCR
- Local numbers per location for Tail End Hop Off

In this recipe we will implement LCR and Tail End Hop Off for calls destined to an office in San Francisco. We will assume the following:

- DID Range for this location: +1 415 555 1000 to 1099
- Site code for this location: 11
- Local numbers for this location: 415 XXX XXXX

Call Routing, Dial Plan, and E.164

How to do it...

To implement Least Cost Routing for a location, we need to perform the following:

1. Add a new route list that will contain the route group with the gateway or trunk device local to the location for which we are implementing LCR, as well as the Standard Local Route Group:

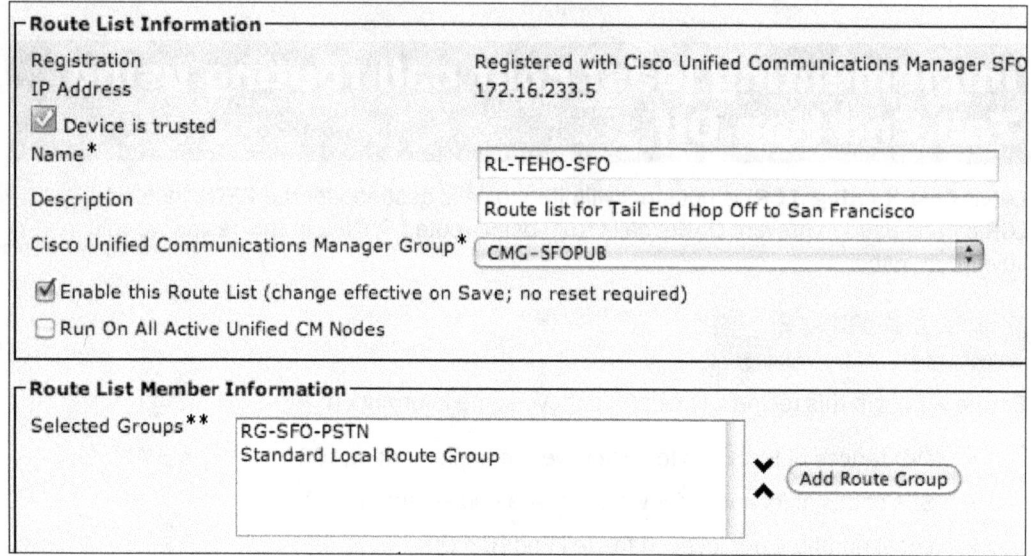

 The order here is important. Ensure the local route group is above the Standard Local Route Group in the list.

2. Add a new route pattern to send local calls to our new route list. Key fields to note here are **Route Pattern**, **Route Partition**, and **Gateway/Route List***:

Chapter 1

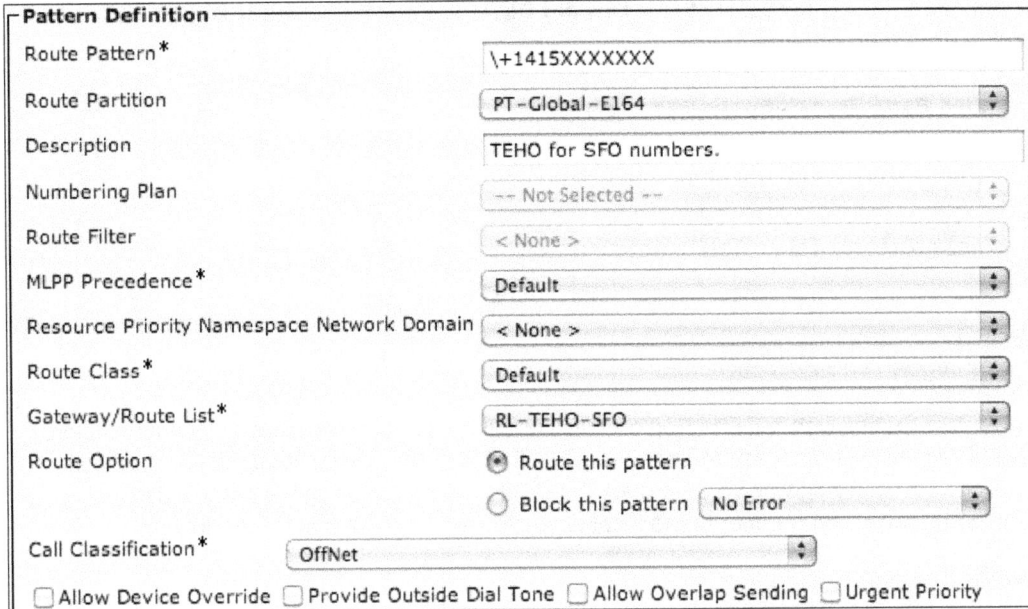

 Here we have unchecked **Provide Outside Dial Tone** as it is unused, but feel free to leave it checked.

3. Next add a translation pattern (**Call Routing | Translation Pattern**, then click on **Add New**) that is responsible for converting E.164 numbers to their internal extensions.

   ▫ Here the **Translation Pattern** must match only the DID range for the location. For our recipe the pattern is \+1415555.10XX. For the partition use something that is globally accessible, for example **PT-Global-E164**:

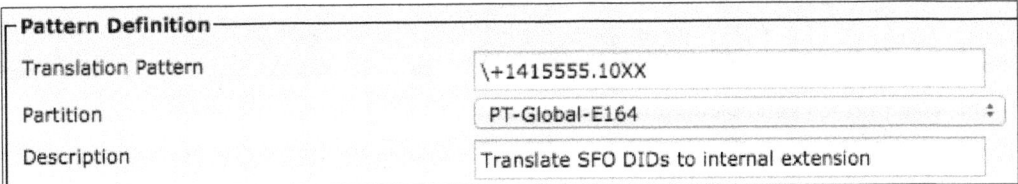

For our pattern, it is necessary to set **Discard Digits** to **PreDot** and **Prefix Digits** to the site code—12 in this recipe.

Called Party Transformations	
Discard Digits	PreDot
Called Party Transform Mask	
Prefix Digits (Outgoing Calls)	12

How it works...

Least cost routing with Tail End Hop off is accomplished by sending calls to locations where the call would cost the least. In addition to Tail End Hop Off, we can accomplish least cost routing by recognizing when a user dials the DID to another user on the same cluster by converting the E.164 number to the local extension and routing over the IP network.

There's more...

Once more we see the benefits of the logical nature of local route groups. By having localization settings at the gateway level, we don't have to worry about formatting and allow the local gateway to normalize the call as required by the PSTN. In the event that the call cannot be made through the gateway or trunk device at the local site, the call will fall back to the gateway or trunk device local to the originating caller.

Do remember that Tail End Hop Off is not legal in all countries. Check with local regulations before implementing it.

Implementing calling restrictions with line blocking partitions and calling search spaces

In this recipe we will be implementing class of service calling restrictions using partitions and calling search spaces, as well as exploring their design considerations.

Getting ready

For this recipe, preparation is key. We will need to determine the partitions, calling search spaces, and patterns to be blocked that will be appropriate to the environment. There is more information on this in the *There's more...* section of this recipe.

How to do it...

To implement calling restrictions, perform the following:

1. First, create the partitions with the necessary descriptions (**Call Routing | Class of Control | Partition**):

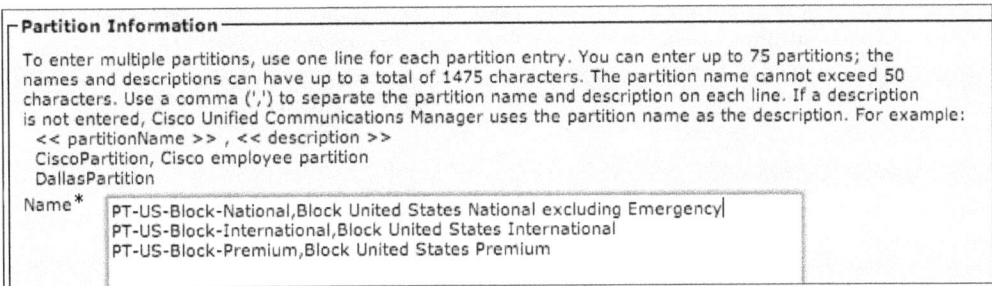

2. Next, create the calling search spaces (**Call Routing | Class of Control | Calling Search Space**):

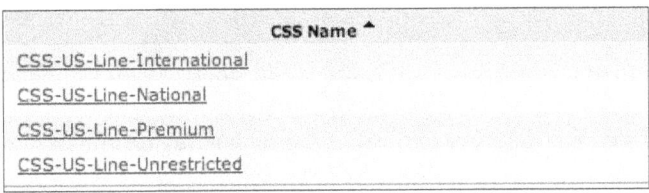

3. Finally, add the translation pattern for the blocking patterns (**Call Routing | Translation Pattern**):

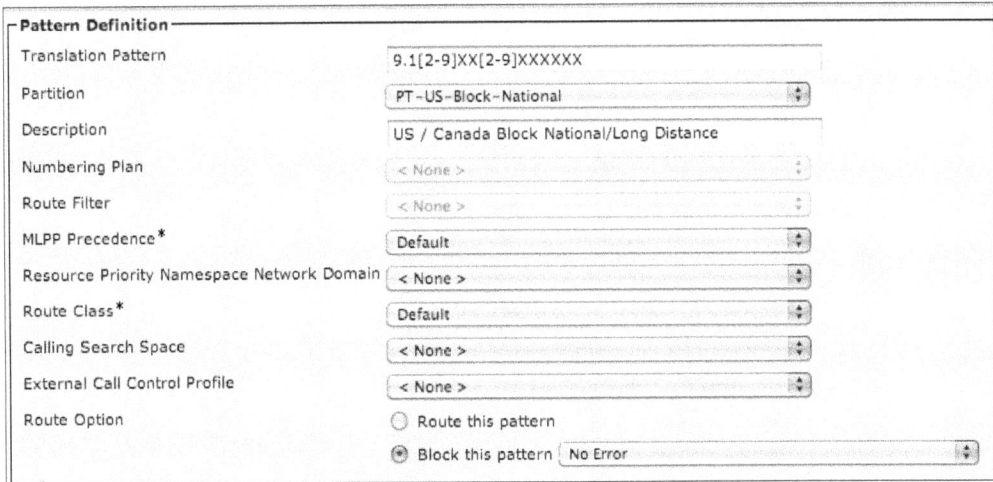

It is important to note here that we have used the **Partition PT-US-Block-National** with a **Route Option** set to **Block this pattern**.

Repeat this process for all the necessary blocking translation patterns.

How it works...

When a calling search space used for calling restrictions is applied to the directory number of a device, those settings override the calling search space patterns specified on the device, denying calls or access to certain numbers.

There's more...

While each environment is unique, there are some design considerations that apply to most. Calling restrictions is one of them.

Determining classes of restriction

In general, external calls fall in to one of these three classes:

- National/long distance
- International
- Premium

While the patterns for each category may vary according to region and requirements, these set up the foundation for our calling search spaces. Sometimes we find ourselves in need of an unrestricted calling search space. While you may choose to leave this to <none> on the directory numbers, I prefer to use an empty calling search space for clarity.

An example partition and calling search space arrangement for a US-based solution would be:

- CSS-US-Line-National
    - PT-US-Block-National
    - PT-US-Block-International
    - PT-US-Block-Premium
- CSS-US-Line-International
    - PT-US-Block-International
    - PT-US-Block-Premium

- CSS-US-Line-Premium
    - PT-US-Block-Premium
- CSS-US-Line-Unrestricted
    - No partitions selected

This setup is not overly complex and can be easily used to expand calling restrictions to suit most environments.

Patterns required for call restrictions

There are two ways in which we can implement translation patterns for call restrictions, neither of which are mutually exclusive.

Design considerations for preventing call restriction bypass

With careful consideration it is possible to bypass calling restrictions, though this is most typical for environments using E.164 call routing. In these environments it is typical for engineers accustomed to the traditional way of blocking to block digits as the user dials them. For example, if a user dials a premium number such as a 900 number, they typically do so with a 9 or 91 first, followed by the number, before hearing a message informing the user that the call was denied.

When using E.164 for call routing, this is not enough. In this type of environment there is usually a pattern for national calls, for example, `9.1[2-9]XXXXXXXXX`. It is common to strip PreDot and prefix the plus sign for final routing. While this is the most common form of dialing, it is not the only way to dial.

On second generation and later phones, which Cisco calls Type-B phones, it is possible to dial a properly formatted E.164 number directly from the keypad, such as `+19005551234`, and have it routed. Because of this capability, it is important to add blocking patterns for the E.164 compatible number.

Blocking in traditional environments

In environments that do not use E.164 call routing, calling restrictions are enforced primarily with route patterns set to **Block this pattern**, similar in setup to the translation pattern in this recipe's *How to do it...* section. Translation patterns may also be used for enforcing call restrictions.

Blocking in E.164 environments

In this type of environment, translation patterns are typically used to enforce call restrictions, though as with the traditional method, we may also use route patterns.

As mentioned in the *Design considerations for preventing call restriction bypass* section, it is possible to bypass traditional calling restrictions on Type-B phones by dialing the E.164 number directly. This is possible because of the added layer of routing associated with E.164 call routing.

To mitigate this and enforce call restrictions for these types of devices, we need to match the final number, which is in E.164 format. For example, if we want to block calls to 900 numbers we would implement the translation pattern \+1900XXXXXXX with the **Route Option** set to **Block this pattern** and a **Partition** of **PT-US-Block-Premium**.

Partitions used in call restrictions

In the previous example we have three partitions and four calling search spaces that enforce call restrictions at various levels: national, international, and premium. We include an empty calling search space to allow for unrestricted calls, called CSS-US-Line-Unrestricted for the sake of clarity, though in such cases a calling search space of <none> will suffice.

National

Represented by **PT-US-Block-National,** this class is used to prevent long distance calls or any calls on a national level that need to be blocked, such as fraud numbers. It is typically represented by the following patterns:

- For seven digit dial plans
    - 91.[2-9]XXXXXXXXX
    - \+1[2-9]XXXXXXXXX

International

Represented by **PT-US-Block-International**, this class is used to prevent international calls. It is typically represented by the following patterns:

- 9.011!
- 9.011!#
- \+[^1]

> The pattern \+[^1] will match any E.164 number that does not start with a one. For instance, the pattern will match +44 but not +1.

Premium

Represented by **PT-US-Block-Premium**, this class prevents calls to premium numbers. It is typically represented by the following patterns:

- 9.1900XXXXXXX
- \+1900XXXXXXX

Mitigating fraud

In some cases it may be a requirement to proactively prevent users from dialing commonly known fraud numbers. Typically these are standard looking numbers that when called charge per minute connected. While this list is by no means complete, it is a good starting point for common fraud numbers in the US.

- 124[26][2-9]XXXXXX
- 126[48][2-9]XXXXXX
- 1284[2-9]XXXXXX
- 134[05][2-9]XXXXXX
- 1441[2-9]XXXXXX
- 1473[2-9]XXXXXX
- 1649[2-9]XXXXXX
- 1664[2-9]XXXXXX
- 1758[2-9]XXXXXX
- 1767[2-9]XXXXXX
- 178[47][2-9]XXXXXX
- 1809[2-9]XXXXXX
- 186[89][2-9]XXXXXX
- 1876[2-9]XXXXXX
- 1976[2-9]XXXXXX

Call Routing, Dial Plan, and E.164

Implementing short dial numbers

In this recipe we will set up basic short dials on a per location basis.

Getting ready

We will need a location-specific partition for the location for which we are implementing short dials. In this recipe we use PT-SFO-DialPlan.

How to do it...

To implement short dials for a location, perform the following:

1. Add the short dials partition to the calling search space of the device for the relevant location (**Call Routing** | **Class of Control** | **Calling Search Space**):

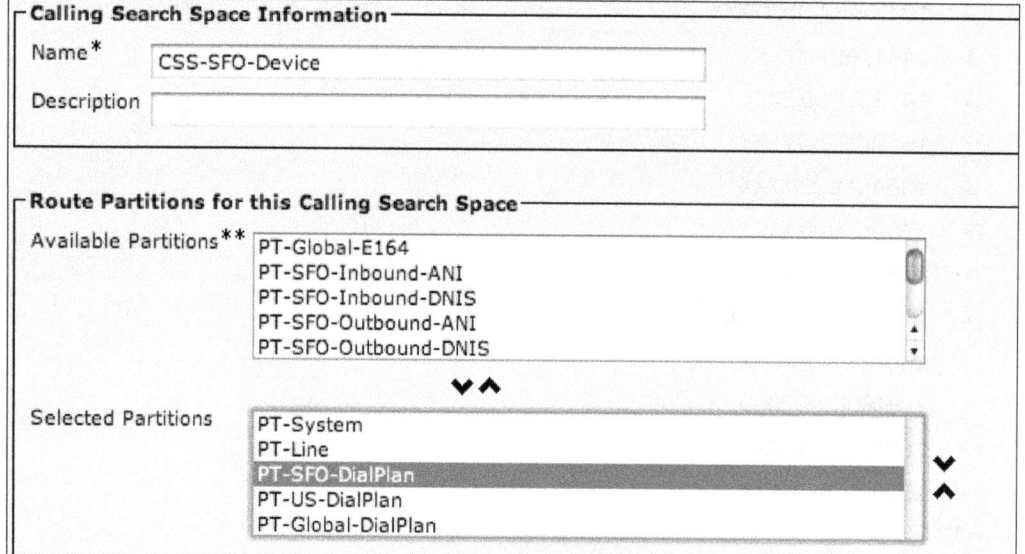

 Order is important here. Generally, short dials follow system numbers and directory numbers in the partition order.

2. Create and save a translation pattern for the short dial in an appropriate partition (**Call Routing | Translation Pattern**):

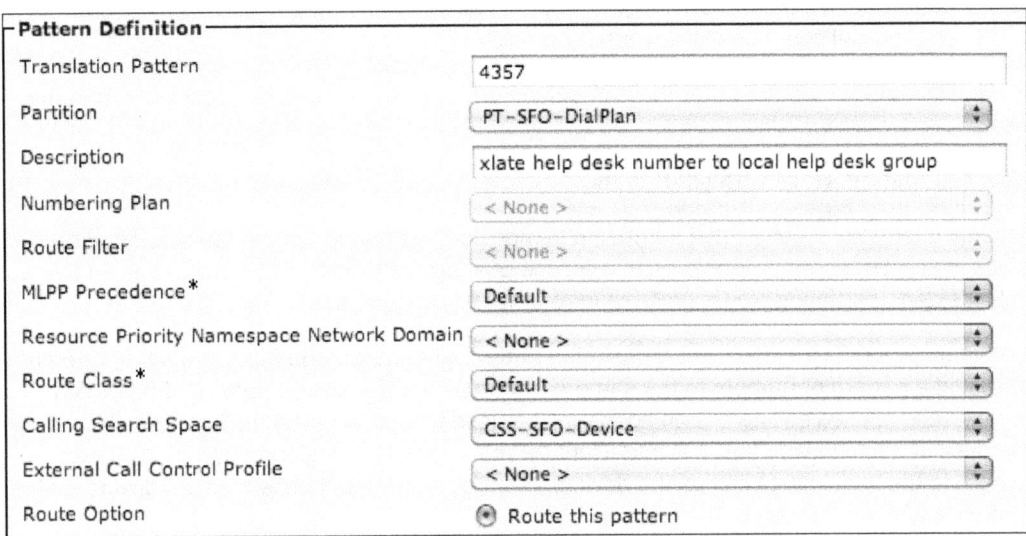

3. Fill in **Translation Pattern** and **Partition** as appropriate. Here we use `4357` and **PT-SFO-DialPlan**, respectively.

4. **Calling Search Space** is of special note. Here, we apply a device calling search space appropriate to the location, **CSS-SFO-Device**.

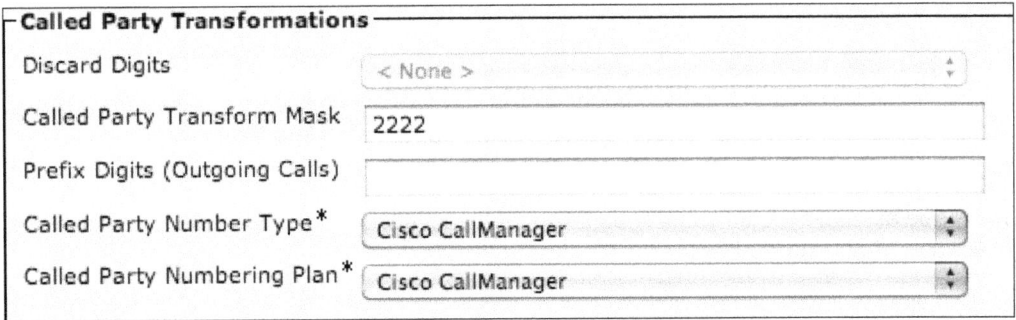

5. Finally, under the **Called Party Transformations** section, we change **Called Party Transform Mask** to the final number, `2222` in this recipe.

How it works...

When a call matches the translation pattern, the called number is translated as per our rule to 2222, and the call continues to be routed normally.

It is important to remember that the number we are translating must be accessible from the translation pattern.

How call routing works with short dials

When a user enters a short dial number, it is modified by the appropriate translation pattern and then routed normally. However, in the case of short dials, calling search spaces and, to a lesser extent, partitions play a vital role in routing the call properly.

Before a number is modified by a translation pattern and routed, the pattern will first attempt to match a pattern or number in the same partition as the translation pattern. If no match is found the applied calling search space will be used to search partitions for a match. It is because of this behavior that it is important for the short dial translation pattern to have access to the same partitions as the device, and that is why we choose to use a device calling search space appropriate to the location.

Implementing time-of-day call routing

Time-of-day routing has various uses in the typical production environment. In this recipe we will focus on implementing time-of-day routing on a location's main number.

Getting ready

For this recipe we need to know the hours and/or days we are considered open and closed, and the appropriate action to take. In this recipe we apply a standard Monday through Friday work week, opening at 8 a.m. and closing at 5 p.m.

This recipe assumes the time-of-day partition for the location is already created. In this recipe, we will use PT-SFO-TimeOfDay.

How to do it...

1. Add the time-of-day partition to your device and gateway calling search spaces (**Call Routing | Class of Control | Calling Search Space**):

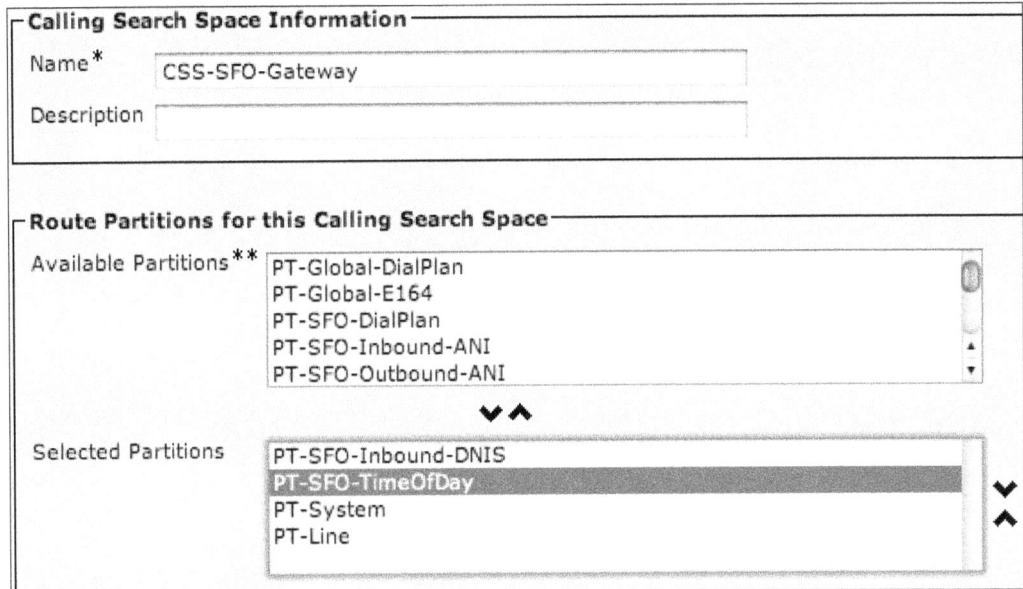

 Order is important here. Time-of-day should be before system and line partitions to ensure we don't accidentally match the wrong pattern.

2. Create a new time period and configure it with the appropriate settings (**Call Routing | Class of Control | Time Period**):
3. Click on **Add New**.

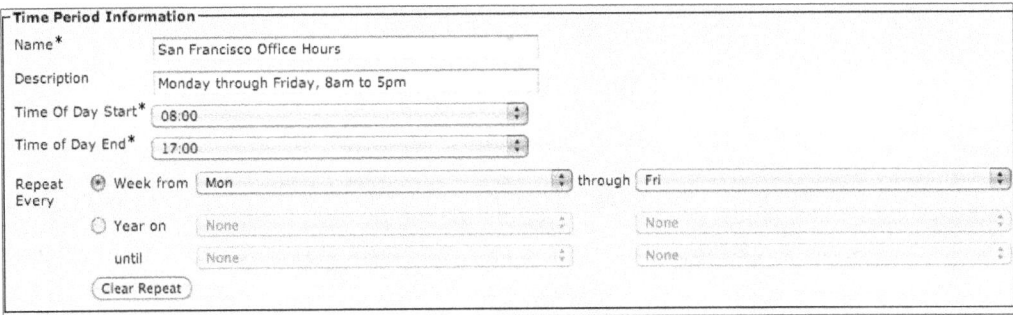

4. Click on **Save** and repeat this process for each time period as appropriate.
5. Create a new time schedule containing the previously created time period(s):

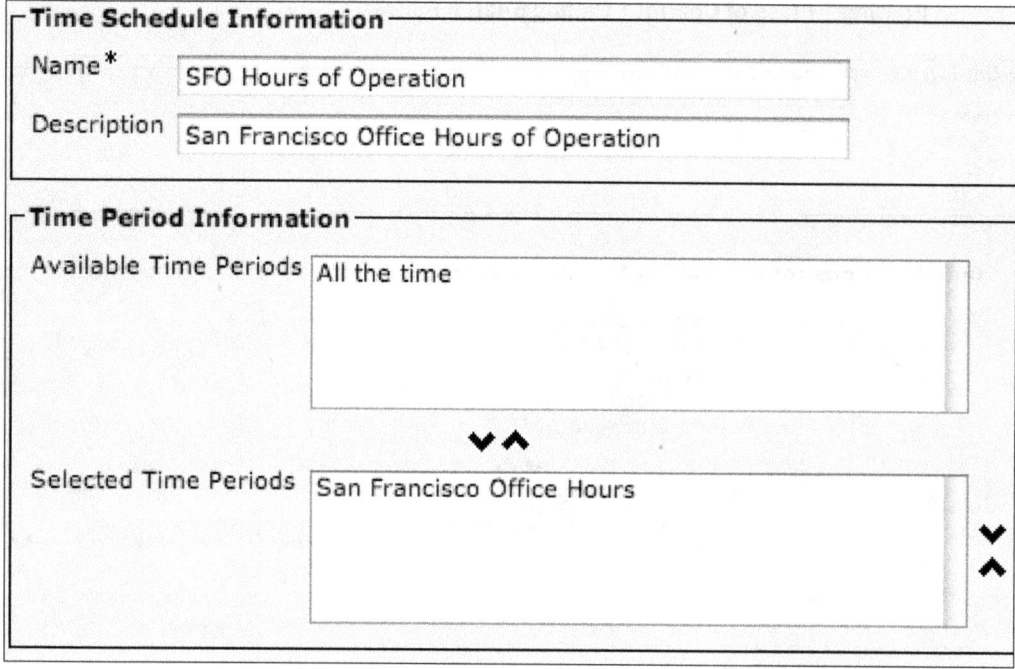

Ensure only the time periods we want are under **Selected Time Periods**.

6. Finally, apply the previously created time schedule to the time-of-day partition (**Call Routing | Class of Control | Partition**).
7. Click on **Add New**.
8. Select the appropriate time schedule from the **Time Schedule** drop-down:

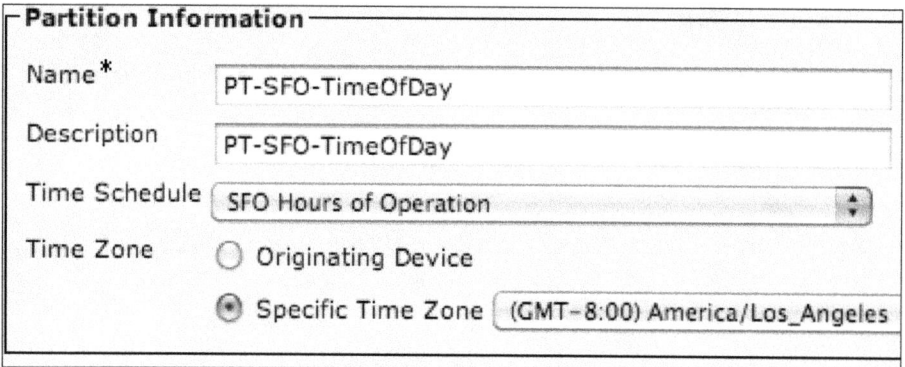

9. For **Time Zone**, select the time zone from the drop-down that is appropriate to the location.
10. Click on **Save**.

How it works...

By applying a time schedule to the partition, we are setting the foundation for time-of-day call routing. Now any patterns in the time-of-day partition will only be matched if they occur during the time period(s) we've specified.

There's more...

Time-of-day routing is a valuable feature, though it lacks flexibility.

Considerations for advanced time-of-day routing

As the complexity of time-of-day routing grows, so do the configuration requirements. CUCM lacks any means to specify gaps during time periods. For example, let's assume users take lunch from 12 p.m. to 1 p.m. with a typical 8 a.m. to 5 p.m. schedule.

If we wanted to use CUCM's time-of-day routing features, it would require the creation of two time periods for that office, one beginning at 8 a.m. and ending at noon Monday to Friday, the other beginning at 1 p.m. and ending at 5 p.m. Monday to Friday.

This can become extremely tedious when configuring time-of-day routing for offices that close at different hours depending on the day. Drawing on our previous example, say on Wednesday the office closes early at 4 p.m. This now requires six time periods as follows:

Monday to Tuesday, starting at 8:00 and ending at 12:00

Monday to Tuesday, starting at 13:00 and ending at 17:00

Thursday to Friday, starting at 08:00 and ending at 12:00

Thursday to Friday, starting at 13:00 and ending at 17:00

Wednesday to Wednesday, starting at 08:00 and ending at 12:00

Wednesday to Wednesday, starting at 13:00 and ending at 16:00

As the time-of-day routing requirements become more complex, so does the implementation. In some cases it may be more appropriate to use third party software to handle complex time-of-day routing, such as Cisco Unified Contact Center Express, Unity, and Unity Connections.

Holidays

Implementing holidays with time-of-day routing is generally not a recommended use of the provided time-of-day routing features.

Routing on holidays

If we are limited to CUCM's time-of-day routing features and must implement specific routing for holidays, we can do so. To configure time-of-day routing so that a location is 'closed' during holidays, perform the following:

1. Add each holiday as a time period, select **No Office Hours** for these and select the appropriate **Repeat Every** option.
2. Add the previously created holiday time periods to a time schedule, **SFO-Holidays** for this example.
3. Add a new partition; we'll call it **PT-SFO-TimeOfDay-Holiday**.
4. Assign the holiday time schedule to the newly created partition.
5. Assign the partition to the appropriate calling search spaces.

Note that this partition should be before any other time of day partitions in the partition order.

6. From here add a translation pattern using the previously created holiday partition as the partition and an appropriate calling search.

In general this is used for specific numbers such as the main call in number for a location.

Implementing Forced Authorization Codes

Forced Authorization Codes (**FAC**) are another method of call restriction, requiring a user to enter in a code prior to the call being connected. However, the primary use of Forced Authorization Codes is call accounting and billing.

Getting ready

We need to know which patterns will be requiring Forced Authorization Codes, and the codes themselves.

Chapter 1

How to do it...

To implement Forced Authorization Codes, perform the following:

1. Add a new Forced Authorization Code (**Call Routing | Forced Authorization Codes**).
2. Click on **Add New**.

Forced Authorization Code Information

Authorization Code Name*	John Smith - International
Authorization Code*	1234
Authorization Level*	0

---

3. For this recipe we will name it `John Smith - International` with an **Authorization Code** of `1234` and the default **Authorization Level** of `0`.
4. Click on **Save** and repeat for any additional Forced Authorization Codes.
5. Find the route pattern (**Call Routing | Route/Hunt | Route Pattern**).
6. Check **Require Forced Authorization Code** and then click on **Save**:

☐ Allow Device Override ☑ Provide Outside Dial Tone ☐ Allow Over
☑ Require Forced Authorization Code
Authorization Level* 0

How it works...

When a user attempts to use a route pattern that requires Forced Authorization Codes, he will hear a tone prior to entering the code. Once the correct code is entered, the call is routed and that call is specifically marked in call records with the Forced Authorization Code used.

There's more...

Forced Authorization Codes are primarily for billing and accounting purposes.

Design considerations for Forced Authorization Codes

Depending on requirements, we may have a situation where it is necessary to allow the management unfettered access to international calls, while requiring other employees to use Forced Authorization Codes.

Partitions for Forced Authorization Codes

If we require Forced Authorization Codes for segments of users but not for all, we need to create one partition for each group that requires their use. In the previous example, we needed only one partition, which we will call PT-FAC.

Calling search spaces for Forced Authorization Codes

For each FAC partition created, that same partition will need to exist in a calling search space. Those using Forced Authorization Codes will need to be assigned the appropriate calling search space.

Device calling search space

We may add the FAC partition to the device calling search space if we want to limit FAC based on device and/or location. Ensure the FAC partition is listed prior to any line or system partitions.

Line calling search space

We may enforce Forced Authorization Codes to a wider subset of users by using line calling search spaces. To use a line calling search space for enforcing FAC, we add the FAC partition to the end of the line calling search space partitions.

Call routing considerations with Forced Authorization Codes

How we implement Forced Authorization Codes depends heavily on the environment in which they are being deployed.

Traditional call routing

In environments with traditional call routing, using route patterns pointing to specific gateways, the route patterns' pattern will match the digits dialed by the user.

E.164 call routing

In environments where E.164 call routing is implemented because translation patterns are used to convert the dialed digits into an E.164 compatible format, the pattern we use must match this format and not the dialed digits. In the case of enforcing FAC for international calls, we would use the pattern `\+[^1]!` with an appropriate FAC partition.

We use this pattern because we assume there is a translation pattern matching `9011.!`. Converting the number into +011 will match any number E.164 that doesn't begin with the US country code of 1. This is necessary, as Forced Authorization Codes do not apply to translation patterns.

Authorization levels with Forced Authorization Codes

The authorization level is a number between 0 and 255 and works in a simple way. If the authorization level of the code entered is higher than the authorization level set on the route pattern, the call will route; otherwise the call is denied.

Implementing Client Matter Codes

Client Matter Codes are used solely for call accounting and billing purposes and are typically employed with Forced Authorization Codes.

Getting ready

We only need the list of codes to implement.

How to do it...

To implement Client Matter Codes, perform the following:

1. Add the Client Matter Codes (**Call Routing | Client Matter Codes**).
2. Click on **Add New**.

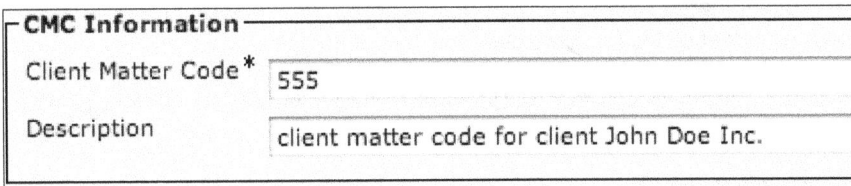

 The **Client Matter Code** may be up to 16 digits in length and is the number entered when the user hears the prompt.

3. Click on **Save**.
4. Apply Client Matter Codes to the appropriate route pattern (**Call Routing | Route/Hunt | Route Pattern**).
5. Check **Require Client Matter Code** and click on **Save**:

How it works...

When a user matches a route pattern with **Client Matter Codes** (**CMC**), a tone is heard and the system collects the CMC. Once collected, the Client Matter Code is recorded in CDR records along with the call.

There's more...

Client Matter Codes are configured much in the same way as Forced Authorization Codes. As such, they have some of the same design considerations.

Design considerations for Client Matter Codes

As with Forced Authorization Codes, if only a subset of users will be required to use Client Matter Codes, a new partition and route pattern will have to be created and configured appropriately.

Partitions

Only one partition is required to enforce Client Matter Codes for users.

Route patterns

With an E.164 dial plan, only one additional pattern may be required for each route pattern to which the Client Matter Codes will be applied. This pattern should match the E.164 compatible number and not the digits dialed by the user.

In a more traditional environment, a route pattern for each pattern per location may be required.

Calling search spaces

To enforce Client Matter Codes selectively, add the partition containing the Client Matter Code route patterns to the calling search space for each location to which they will be applied.

This may be accomplished using either device or line calling search spaces.

See also

For more information on Client Matter Codes, see the *CDR Analysis and Reporting Administration Guide* (http://www.cisco.com/en/US/docs/voice_ip_comm/cucm/service/8_0_2/car/CAR.html).

2
Call Admission Control

In this chapter, we will focus on call admission control technologies and will be covering:

- Implementing location-based call admission control
- Implementing regions for call admission control
- Implementing Resource Reservation Protocol
- Enabling Automated Alternate Routing
- Implementing Automated Alternate Routing

Introduction

In this chapter, we will be focusing on call admission control (CAC) and the technologies associated with it, including Resource Reservation Protocol (RSVP) and Automated Alternate Routing (AAR).

Call admission control is an important aspect of any unified communications deployment and its proper configuration will help to ensure call quality and resilience.

Implementing location-based call admission control

Location-based call admission control provides a mechanism for controlling the number of calls allowed between two locations. Controlling the number of calls between locations can prevent over saturating IP WAN links and degrading overall call quality.

Call Admission Control

Getting ready

To complete this recipe successfully, it is important to have a list of locations and the available bandwidth for calls and videos per location.

How to do it...

To implement location-based call admission control, perform the following:

1. Add a new Location for each location as appropriate (**System | Location**).
2. Click **Add New** to add a new location.
3. Type in an appropriate name.
4. Specify the **Audio Bandwidth** available to the location or select **Unlimited**.
5. Specify the **Video Bandwidth** available to the location, or select either **Unlimited** or **None** depending on the environment. The given setting is shown in the following screenshot:

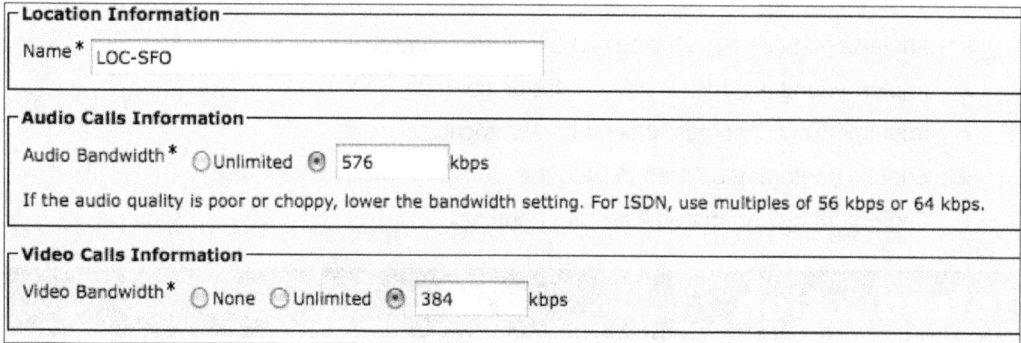

6. Click **Save**.
7. Repeat this process for each location to be added.
8. Configure the location under the appropriate device pool (**System | Device Pool**).
9. Find the device pool and open its configuration page.

10. Find and select the appropriate location from the **Location** drop-down menu under the section **Roaming Sensitive Settings,** as shown in the following screenshot:

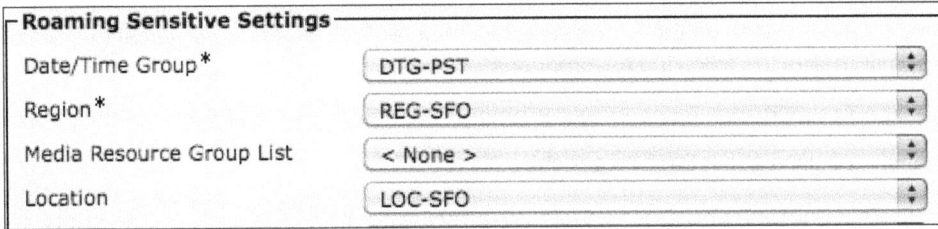

11. Click **Save**.

 You must reset the device pool before the changes will take effect.

How it works...

Location-based call admission control is a static method of calculating bandwidth available for calls between sites. This type of call admission control is known as topology-unaware.

When specifying the audio bandwidth as a fixed number, we are telling Unified Communications Manager approximately how much bandwidth is available for inbound and outbound calls to another location; we will call this *Available Bandwidth*.

When a call is made between locations, Unified Communications Manager will deduct the approximate bandwidth required for that call (based on codec used) from the available bandwidth for that site. When the call is released, the bandwidth is added back to the Available Bandwidth.

 Call admission control is not enforced between devices configured for the same location.

If enough calls are generated, such that the Unified Communications Manager determines there is no more available bandwidth, then a reorder tone will be played and the phone will display "Not enough bandwidth".

 This message can be customized by changing the **Out-of-Bandwidth Text** under the **Clusterwide Parameters** (**Device | Phone**) section for the Cisco CallManager service (**System | Service Parameters**).

How Unified Communications Manager calculates bandwidth requirements

As previously mentioned, location-based call admission control subtracts the bandwidth required for a call based on the codec selected. In order for Unified Communications Manager to do this, it makes the following assumptions:

- G.711 and G.722 calls use about 80kbps per call
- G.729 uses about 24kbps per call

In an Ethernet environment, these figures are pretty accurate including overhead but bear in mind actual bandwidth required will vary depending on the technology used; packetization, ATM, and Frame Relay for instance.

 Location-based call admission control is ideally suited for a single cluster topology but is not limited to one.

Single Cluster

Centralized call processing consists of a single call-processing agent that provides services for many sites. In a single cluster, hub-spoke type environment, location-based call admission control provides a quick and straightforward solution in helping to prevent oversubscription of IP WAN links.

Centralized vs. Decentralized

Decentralized call processing can be utilized for multiple call-processing agents distributed between locations.

This method of call admission control is best suited for centralized topologies. A decentralized topology would drastically increase the complexity and configuration required.

IP to IP based calls will not fully benefit from location-based call admission control in a decentralized topology; this can be somewhat mitigated by configuring a location in Unified Communications Manager on the trunk device.

There's more...

While location-based call admission control can help mitigate some of the problems with oversubscription, it is important to remember that there is no guarantee of bandwidth from locations.

Importance of Quality of service

Where call quality is important (everywhere!), quality of service should be used in conjunction with location-based call admission control to better ensure that bandwidth will be available for voice calls.

The importance of quality of service cannot be overstated. It is prudent to have the highest possible end-to-end quality of service implemented on the network.

An entire book could be written on best practices for quality of service, and there has been, so I won't tread there in this book. Instead, I recommend taking a look at the *Enterprise QoS Solution Reference Network Design Guide* (`http://www.cisco.com/en/US/docs/solutions/Enterprise/WAN_and_MAN/QoS_SRND/QoS-SRND-Book.html`) provided by Cisco, which is available for free online and provides a wealth of information from design to implementation as well as best practices.

Implementation strategies for location-based call admission control

Depending on the environment, there are two particularly functional ways of implementing location-based call admission control.

Using device pools

Using device pools for location-based call admission control provides a centralized and relatively configuration-free implementation of location-based call admission control. Using the device pool applies the location information to all the devices under it, though it may still be overridden by specifying the location on the device itself.

> More specific settings always take precedence over less specific settings.

Per device

Configuring location-based call admission control on a per device basis requires a bit more effort with configuration and maintenance in the long run. When configuring per device, simply assign the appropriate location for that device. Locations are most commonly configured on IP phones, gateways, trunks, and CTI devices.

Call Admission Control

Not Enough Bandwidth – synchronization issues with location-based call admission control

In some instances, particularly when a link is oversubscribed, Unified Communications Manager may lose sync with its internal algorithms, and not properly free or consume bandwidth. This results in "Not Enough Bandwidth" being displayed on end user devices.

This is particularly frustrating when everything seems normal; we are unable to see what the system believes is available or unavailable.

We can remedy the situation and resynchronize the bandwidth settings in Unified Communications Manager.

Resynchronization is recommended wherever possible after hours; even if performed initially in-hours, this will reset the available bandwidth to its maximum.

To synchronize bandwidth for a location, perform the following:

1. Find the Location affected and open its configuration page (**System | Location**).
2. Click **Resync Bandwidth** as shown in the following screenshot:

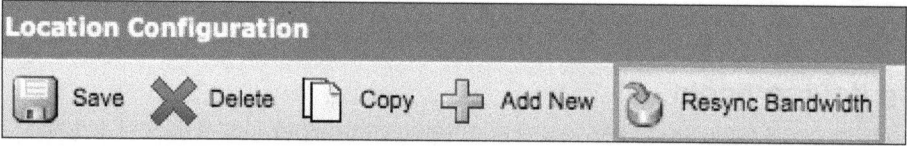

 A message appears informing us that bandwidth calculations may be skewed if calls are active between that location and another. It is for this reason that performing bandwidth resynchronization after hours is recommended, when no or few calls are active.

3. Click **Ok**.

 For more information on QoS implementation including best practices, consult *Cisco's Enterprise QoS Solution Reference Network Design Guide* (http://www.cisco.com/en/US/docs/solutions/Enterprise/WAN_and_MAN/QoS_SRND/QoS-SRND-Book.html)

Chapter 2

Implementing regions for call admission control

Regions play an important role in location-based call admission control; they specify the codec relationships between regions allowing us to choose quality or quantity of calls.

How to do it...

To configure regions for call admission control, perform the following:

1. Add a new region (**System | Region**)
2. Click **Add New** to add a new region.
3. Specify a name, for example, that shown in the following screenshot:

4. Click **Save**.
5. Repeat this process for each region to be created.
6. Next, configure region relationships between one another and within it.
7. On the region configuration page under **Modify Relationship to other Regions**, select a region.

 You can select multiple regions at once to save time!

8. Select a bitrate from the **Maximum Audio Bit Rate** drop-down. This will be applied to calls between the region we are configuring and the ones we selected.
9. For Max Video Call Bit Rate you may choose to either:
    - Specify a particular bandwidth
    - Specify none to prevent video calls
    - Use the system default or keep the setting as it is (by default it is Use System Default)

Call Admission Control

10. From the **Link Loss Type** drop-down, select the appropriate link loss type; generally system default is sufficient.

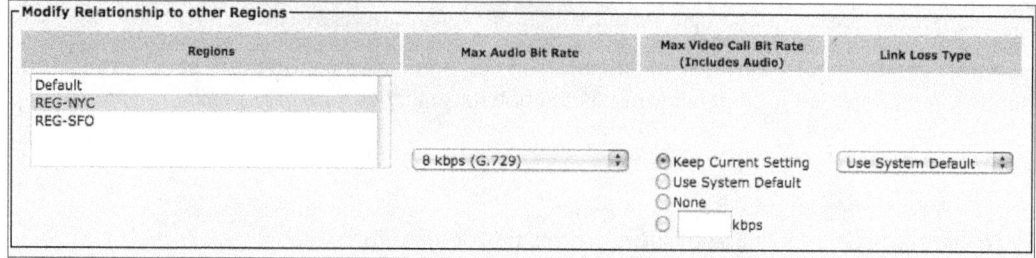

 In the previous screenshot, we are modifying **REG-SFO**'s relationship with **REG-NYC**. All calls between those regions will use **G.729** or if unavailable, a lower bitrate codec.

11. Click **Save**.
12. Repeat this process until each region's relationships are defined.

 Don't forget to set the region's relationship with itself; this will determine what codec is used locally in the region and should generally be the highest bitrate codec available.

How it works...

Regions support location-based call admission control by defining codec relationships between themselves. By defining bitrate relationships between regions we control which codec is used when talking between devices in specific regions, and consequently, the bandwidth deducted from the available bandwidth for a location influencing the number of available calls for a given bandwidth.

There's more...

In general, there isn't much to discuss in regards to regions, but there are a few specific scenarios we should watch out for.

Most specifically, this includes voicemail platforms such as Cisco Unity and Unity Connections; these typically only support one type of codec, generally G.711. This is also the case with Cisco Unified Contact Center Express, which supports both G.711 and G.729 but does not support them concurrently.

It is important to bear in mind which codecs are supported by third party platforms integrated into the system, as regions will need to be configured to accommodate them.

Implementing the Resource Reservation Protocol

Call admission control using locations based on the Resource Reservation Protocol (RSVP) has one specific advantage over standard locations-based call admission control, that is, it is topology-aware. This is particularly beneficial in the case of link failures where standard location-based CAC would be unaware of the failure and unable to compensate the actual available bandwidth, potentially leading to oversubscription and degrading call quality.

Getting ready

This recipe assumes locations already exist in the system and any associated devices are ready to be configured for RSVP.

Media resource groups and media resource lists are required to function; these are discussed in *Chapter 3, Media Resources and Music on Hold*, so the detailed steps are omitted here.

How to do it...

To implement RSVP based call admission control perform the following:

1. First, add a new Media Termination Point (MTP) device. (**Media Resources | Media Termination Point**)
2. Click **Add New** to add a new Media Termination Point.
3. Specify the **Media Termination Point Name**.

> This must match the configuration on the device exactly.

4. Specify the **Device Pool** appropriate to this device.

Media Termination Point Information	
Media Termination Point Type*	Cisco IOS Enhanced Software Media Termination P
Media Termination Point Name*	SFO_RSVP
Description	
Device Pool*	DP-SFO

5. Click **Save**.

Call Admission Control

6. Repeat for each MTP device required.
7. Once the MTP devices have been created, add them to the appropriate Media Resource Groups.

> Registration and IP Address fields on the Media Termination Point device will remain Unknown until the IOS device is configured and the **sccp** service registers to the Unified Communications Manager.

8. Next, configure locations to be RSVP enabled for each location that uses RSVP (**System | Location**).
9. Select a region from the **Location** table under the **Modify Setting(s) to Other Locations** section.
10. From the **RSVP Setting** drop-down menu, select the appropriate RSVP setting. In this recipe, we are using **Optional (Video Desired)**.
11. Click **Save**.
12. Repeat this for each location relationship for which RSVP will be enabled.
13. Once the RSVP location has been added, it will appear under **Location RSVP Settings** on the configuration page.

Location RSVP Settings	
Location	**RSVP Setting**
LOC-NYC	Optional(Video Desired)
LOC-SFO	No Reservation

14. In this example, we are modifying LOC-SFO and its relationship to LOC-NYC.

> Note that this relationship can also be seen on the configuration page for LOC-NYC.

15. Finally, configure the IOS Device. Following is the very minimum configuration to register an MTP device and enable RSVP on a Cisco IOS device.
16. Bind the sccp service to an interface, and define a call manager to register to. In the following example, `Loopback0` and `172.25.233.5` are used, respectively:

```
sccp local Loopback0
sccp ccm 172.25.233.5 identifier 1 version 7.0+
sccp
```

17. Configure the MTP profile as follows:

    ```
    dspfarm profile 1 mtp
      codec pass-through
      rsvp
      maximum-sessions software 30
      associate application SCCP
    ```

18. Add a sccp group and associate the MTP profile to it as shown:

    ```
    sccp ccm group 1
      associate ccm 1 priority 1
      associate profile 1 register SFO_RSVP
    ```

19. Finally, specify how much bandwidth is available per interface and enable RSVP on the interface:

    ```
    interface GigabitEthernet1/0
      ip rsvp bandwidth 88
    ```

How it works...

When a call is made between two RSVP enabled locations, Unified Communications Manager instructs the end points to terminate directly with the media termination points. This is required as IP phones do not support RSVP natively, and require the use of an intermediary; in this case the MTP device acts as an RSVP agent, to negotiate RSVP with another RSVP agent.

RSVP Settings

RSVP Settings define how we negotiate RSVP with another RSVP agent. Their functions are as such:

- **No Reservation**: No RSVP reservations are made between the locations.
- **Optional (Video Desired)**: Calls receive best-effort treatment. If RSVP is unable to secure enough bandwidth for audio and video, the call will proceed as audio only.
- **Mandatory**: Unified Communications Manager will not begin ringing the terminating device until RSVP has secured enough bandwidth to support the audio and/or video streams.
- **Mandatory (Video Desired)**: A video call will proceed as an audio-only call, if enough bandwidth to support the video stream cannot be secured.
- **Calculating Bandwidth**: Much like locations, RSVP uses the same 80Kbps for G.711 and G.722 and 24 Kbps for G.729 calls when calculating available bandwidth. However, when attempting to make a reservation, RSVP will request 16 KB additional bandwidth from the codec requirements. For example, a G.722 call will require 80Kbps + 16 KB of available bandwidth; this applies when specifying the interface bandwidth on the IOS device adds an additional 16 to it.

Call Admission Control

 The 16 KB reserved are immediately freed once the call is established.

- **RSVP Service Parameters**: Various settings for RSVP are located under the Cisco CallManager service, under Service Parameters. These settings affect various aspects of the operation of RSVP, including default inter-location RSVP settings, retry timer, quality of service markings, and various other settings.

RSVP settings can be located under the sections **Clusterwide Parameters (System | RSVP)** and **Clusterwide Parameters (System | QOS)**.

There's more...

It has been my experience that RSVP is not widely deployed despite its overwhelming advantage over location-based call admission control; this is due mostly to carrier support.

Carrier support for RSVP

In order for RSVP to be successful, it must be implemented end-to-end, which requires support from the carrier. Unfortunately, not all carriers will offer to support RSVP across their networks so make sure a discussion takes place with the carrier prior to implementing RSVP.

Without end-to-end carrier cooperation there is little point in implementing RSVP.

See also

For an in-depth look at Resource Reservation Protocol in a unified communications environment, check out the call admission control section of Cisco's Unified Communications Manager 8.x Solution Reference Network Design guide (http://www.cisco.com/en/US/docs/voice_ip_comm/cucm/srnd/8x/cac.html#wp1161546).

Enabling Automated Alternate Routing

Before we can configure Automated Alternate Routing, we must ensure it is enabled in the system.

How to do it...

To enable Automated Alternate Routing, perform the following:

1. First, activate the necessary services for AAR (**System | Service Parameters**).
2. Select a server from the **Server** drop-down menu. This should be a server running the CallManager service.
3. Select the **Cisco CallManager** service from the **Service** drop-down menu as shown in the following screenshot:

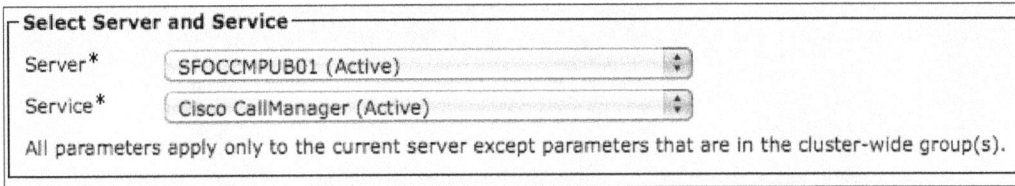

4. After selecting the CallManager service from the drop-down, and the page reloads, the associated parameters are seen.
5. Near the bottom, under the section titled **Clusterwide Parameters (System | CCM Automated Alternate Routing)**, change the **Automated Alternate Routing Enable Required Field** to **True**, as shown in the following screenshot:

6. Click **Save**.

How it works...

By default, Automated Alternate Routing is not enabled on the system. By setting the **Automated Alternate Routing Enable** flag to **True**, we inform Unified Communications Manager to enable call re-routing through Automated Alternate Routing, by calling search spaces on devices that have it configured.

Without this setting, calls would simply fail, with the **no available bandwidth** message.

Call Admission Control

Implementing Automated Alternate Routing

While not a call admission control mechanism itself, Automated Alternate Routing cannot function without one, be it location-based or RSVP. Automated Alternate Routing only takes effect when a call is denied for bandwidth reasons, and will not reroute calls if they were rejected by the gateway for any other reason.

Getting ready

This recipe assumes Automated Alternate Routing is enabled as described in the previous recipe.

How to do it...

To implement Automated Alternate Routing, perform the following:

1. First, activate the necessary services for AAR (**System | Service Parameters**).
2. Select a server from the **Server** drop-down menu. This should be a server running the CallManager service.
3. Select the **Cisco CallManager** service from the **Service** drop-down menu as shown:

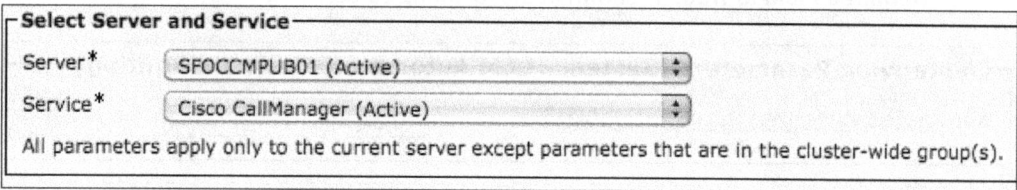

4. After selecting the CallManager service from the drop-down, the page reloads and the associated parameters are seen.
5. Near the bottom, the section titled **Clusterwide Parameters (System | CCM Automated Alternate Routing)**, change the **Automated Alternate Routing Enable Required Field** to **True**.

6. Click **Save**.

7. Next, create a calling search space that will be used exclusively for AAR (**Call Routing | Class of Control | Calling Search Space**).
8. Click **Add New** to add a new calling search space.
9. Give it an appropriate name and assign the partition containing the route patterns that AAR will use to route the calls. In this example, we use **CSS-CallForwardNoBandwidth-AAR** and **PT-Global-E164,** respectively, as shown in the following screenshot:

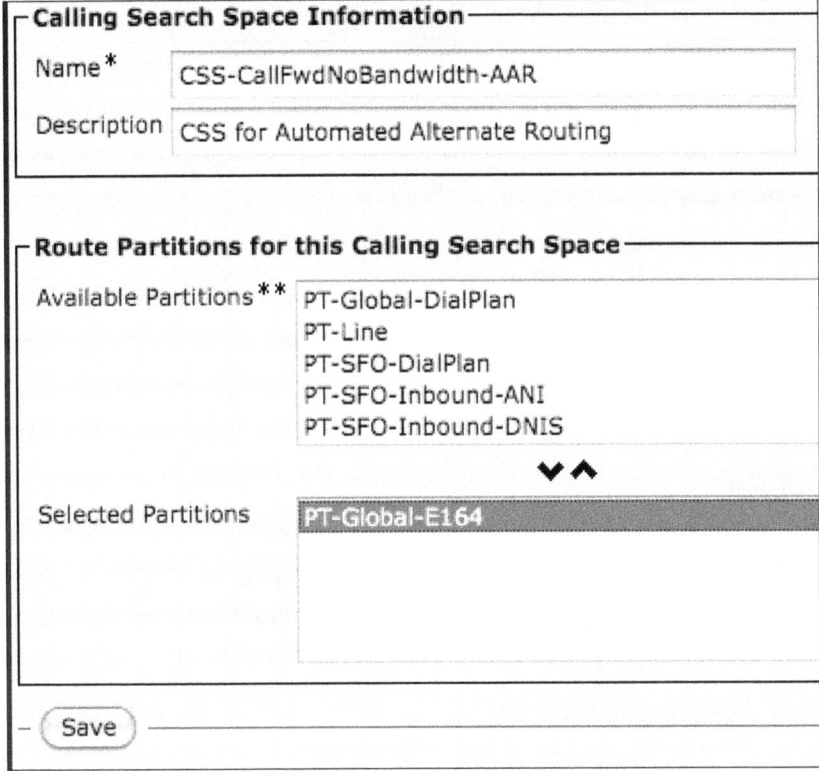

10. Click **Save**.
11. Next, we configure the AAR Group (**Call Routing | AAR Group**).
12. Click **Add New** to add a new AAR Group.
13. Give the group an appropriate **Name**.
14. Click **Save**.

After the page reloads, we are given the option to specify prefix digits for use within that AAR group. If there are multiple AAR groups on the system, we are given the option to configure prefix digits to and from the AAR group.

15. Under the section **Prefix Digits within AAR-Default**, where **AAR-Default** is the name of the AAR group previously created, configure a **Dial Prefix** as necessary. More on this shortly.

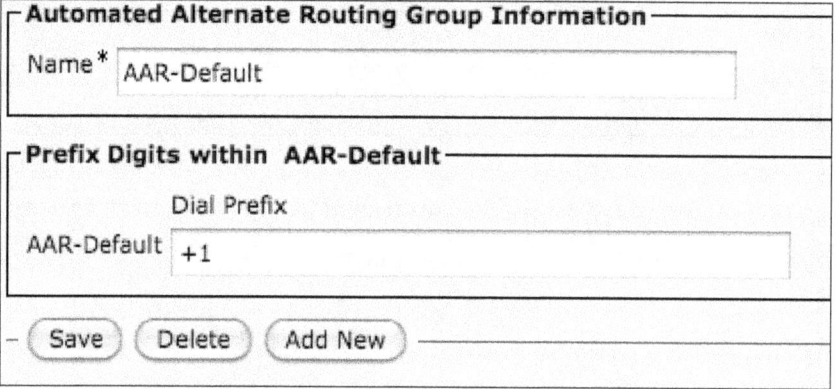

16. Click **Save**.
17. Next, we apply the AAR group to the Device Pool (**System | Device Pool**).
18. Locate the device pool and open the configuration page.
19. Under the section **Device Mobility Related Information**, specify the **AAR Calling Search Space** and the **AAR Group** as created previously.

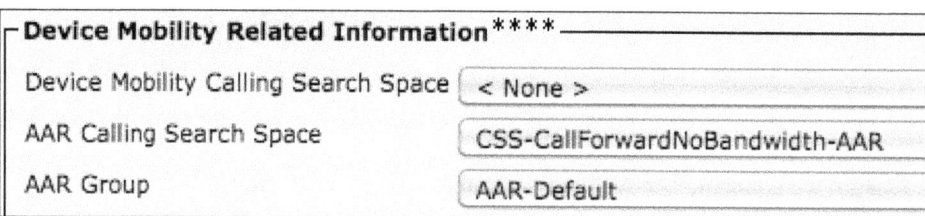

20. Click **Save**.
21. Finally, configure the AAR settings under the directory number line settings (**Call Routing | Directory Number**).
22. Locate the directory number for which we are applying AAR settings, and open the configuration page.

23. Specify the **AAR Destination Mask** (typically the full DID, that is, **Direct Inward dialing**) and the **AAR Group** under the section titled **AAR Settings**.
24. Alternatively, to send AAR calls to voice mail, check the **Voice Mail** check box. The **AAR Group** and **AAR Destination Mask** settings are unnecessary in this case.

	Voice Mail	AAR Destination Mask	AAR Group
AAR	☐ or	4155556969	AAR-Default
	☑ Retain this destination in the call forwarding history		

25. Click **Save**.

How it works...

When Unified Communications Manager denies a call due to insufficient bandwidth, AAR settings take effect. After the call is denied, the dial prefix from the AAR group is prefixed to the AAR Destination Mask number. Automated Alternate Routing will then take this new number and try to match a route pattern available to it through the calling search space created. The call is then routed normally.

There's more...

Implementing Automated Alternate Routing in an environment with a traditional dial plan can be quite complex, depending on how the platform is configured. The design notes for Automated Alternate Routing are:

AAR Groups

AAR Groups define the dialing relationship between groups, allowing us to configure specific dial prefixes that may be required to route the call properly to the PSTN via the local gateway.

When utilizing an E.164 compatible dial plan, generally only one AAR Group is required as demonstrated in the *How to do it...* section of this recipe. This greatly simplifies configuration and is expandable to an infinite number of sites.

For systems that use a more traditional dial plan, an AAR Group is generally required for each site. This is necessary to ensure that the number is formatted correctly before it is handed off to the gateway to be routed to the PSTN.

AAR Destination Mask

The AAR Destination Mask is the full DID as reachable from the PSTN.

Partitions

Depending on the environment, additional partitions may be required to support AAR, typically where an E.164 compatible dial plan is not being utilized.

The sole purpose of an AAR partition is to define the route patterns, which can be used to route the call outside to the PSTN.

Calling search spaces

As with partitions, the number of calling search spaces required depends greatly on the dial plan, this will generally coincide with the number of partitions required for AAR.

Route patterns

When using logical call routing with an E.164 compatible dial plan, no additional route patterns are typically required. Calls will match the \+! pattern and be routed normally out of the local gateway.

If the dial plan is not E.164 compatible, the number of new route patterns required depends heavily on the gateway. In the case where the called and the calling party transformations are not available, the route patterns must format the call to be accepted by the gateway. Depending on how the Off-Net route patterns are configured, additional route patterns may not be required. Specifically, when each site has site-specific route patterns with a site-specific partition, the site-specific partition can be added to the calling search space.

3
Media Resources and Music On Hold

In this chapter, we will cover the following necessary aspects of configuring media resources to support conferencing, transcoding, and Music On Hold:

- Configuring software conference bridges
- Configuring IOS conference bridges
- Configuring transcoders
- Configuring media termination points
- Configuring media resource groups
- Configuring media resource group lists
- Implementing unicast Music On Hold
- Configuring multicast Music On Hold
- Adding custom media files for Music On Hold

Introduction

In this chapter we will focus on various media related aspects of a Unified Communications Manager platform, and how to configure them.

Media Resources and Music On Hold

Configuring software conference bridges

Cisco's Unified Communications Manager supports software-based conference bridges with a few limitations. Most notably, software conference bridges only support the G.711 (a-law and u-law) and G.722, and have limitations as to how many conferences they support. It is important to remember that software conference bridges are very processor intensive and may affect call processing.

How to do it...

To configure a software conference bridge, perform the following:

1. First, we must start the **Cisco IP Voice Media Streaming App** through the **Cisco Unified Serviceability** page (https://192.168.1.5:8443/ccmservice/).

2. Activate the **Cisco IP Voice Media Streaming App** by navigating to **Tools | Service Activation**.

3. Check the box next to the **Cisco IP Voice Media Streaming App**, and click on **Save**:

CM Services	
Service Name	Activation Status
☑ Cisco CallManager	Activated
☑ Cisco Tftp	Activated
☐ Cisco Messaging Interface	Deactivated
☐ Cisco Unified Mobile Voice Access Service	Deactivated
☑ Cisco IP Voice Media Streaming App	Activated
☑ Cisco CTIManager	Activated

4. Once the application shows **Activated,** return to the Unified CM Administration page.

5. Next, verify that the conference bridge is registered (**Media Resources | Conference Bridge**).

6. Click on **Find** to show the available conference bridges.

7. Locate the software conference bridge prebuilt when Unified Communications Manager was installed. This typically starts with CFB_:

	Conference Bridge Name ▲	Description	Device Pool	Status
☐	CFB_2	CFB_SFOCUCMPUB01	DP-SFO	Registered with 192.168.1.5

How it works...

Software conference bridges are prebuilt by the system after installation of a Unified Communications Manager publisher or subscriber. The software conference bridge can only be used after enabling the **Cisco IP Voice Media Streaming App** through the **Unified Serviceability** page.

> To utilize the conference bridge, it must first be added to a media resource group that is contained in a media resource group list configured on the device. The specifics of how to configure this are detailed in this chapter.

There's more...

By default, the Cisco IP Voice Media Streaming App enables not only software conference bridges, but also annunciators and media termination points. Depending on the environment and how this service is used, it may be prudent to disable the unnecessary services to free up the server for more processing of calls.

Cisco IP Voice Media Streaming App Service parameters

To disable any unnecessary services, perform the following:

1. Navigate to the **Service Parameters** page (**System | Service Parameters**).
2. Select the server responsible for the IP Voice Media Streaming App from the **Server** drop-down.
3. Select the **Cisco IP Voice Media Streaming App** from the **Service** drop-down.
4. Disable any unused services by setting the **Run Flag** to **False**. Doing so will free up the system to process additional calls by the remaining services.
5. Increase the **Call Count** parameter if necessary.

> The more calls the system is configured to accept, the higher the processor impact will be.

Design considerations for software conference bridges

Software conference bridges are resource intensive. It is recommended that if software conference bridges will be largely used, a dedicated server also be used so that call processing isn't affected.

In such a case, it is recommended that the annunciator and MTP services are disabled via the service parameters.

Configuring IOS conference bridges

Hardware-based conference bridges are generally recommended over software conference bridges, as they support a larger range of codecs and free up server hardware for other tasks.

 IOS is Cisco's Internet Operating System, the technology that powers their routers and switches.

How to do it...

To configure an IOS conference bridge, perform the following:

1. Navigate to the **Conference Bridge** page (**Media Resources | Conference Bridge**).
2. Click on **Add New** to add a new conference bridge.
3. For the **Conference Bridge Type*** select **Cisco IOS Enhanced Conference Bridge.**
4. Specify the **Conference Bridge Name**. This is the name configured on the IOS device.
5. Select an appropriate **Device Pool** and **Device Security Mode**.
6. Set a **Location** if desired:

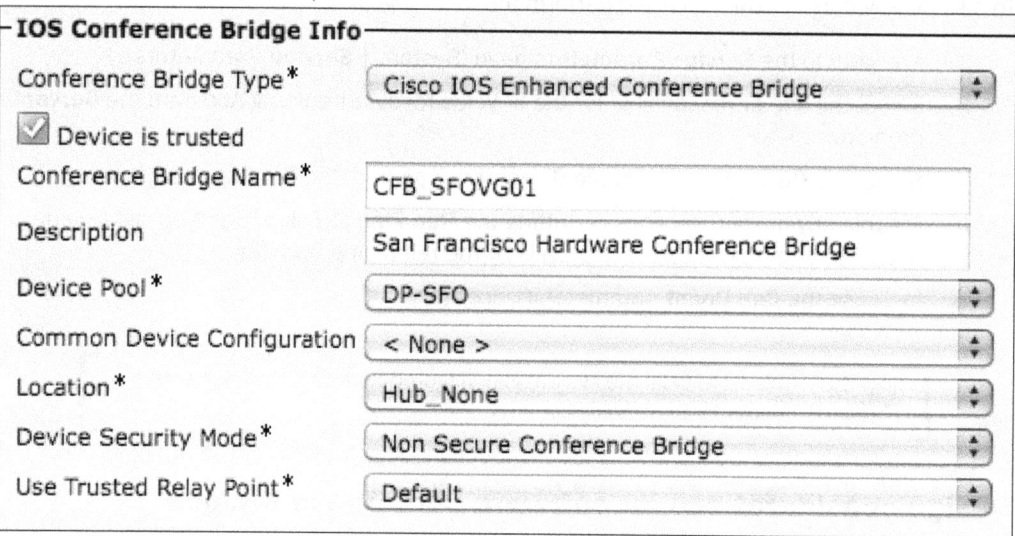

7. Click on **Save**.

8. Once the conference bridge has been configured on both the IOS device and on Unified Communications Manager, the conference bridge should show as registered.

>  For an example configuration for an IOS device refer to Cisco's *CallManager and IOS Gateway DSP Farm Configuration Example* (http://www.cisco.com/en/US/products/sw/voicesw/ps556/products_configuration_example09186a0080334294.shtml)

How it works...

Cisco IOS conference bridges use the **Skinny Client Control Protocol** (**SCCP**) to interface with Unified Communications Manager. When the IOS device receives a conference request from the Unified Communications Manager, the maximum conference resources per conference are pre-allocated. That means if a conference bridge is configured for a maximum of eight participants, eight slots will be reserved regardless of how many participants are in the conference.

Configuring transcoders

Transcoders are often necessary for third-party software appliances such as voice mail systems and IVRs. Additionally, when using a low bandwidth codec such as G.729, transcoding will be necessary.

How to do it...

To configure transcoders using IOS devices, perform the following:

1. Navigate to the **Transcoder** page (**Media Resources | Transcoder**).
2. Click on **Add New** to add a new transcoder.
3. Select a **Transcoder Type**. This selection is determined by the hardware in use.
4. Specify the **Device Name**. This is the name as configured on the IOS device.

5. Select an appropriate **Device Pool**:

   IOS Transcoder Info

Transcoder Type*	Cisco IOS Enhanced Media Termination Point
Description	
Device Name*	XCD_SFOVG01
Device Pool*	DP-SFO
Common Device Configuration	< None >
Special Load Information	
☐ Trusted Relay Point	

   (Save)

6. Click on **Save**.

Once the transcoder is configured on both the IOS device and the Unified Communications Manager, it will show as registered.

For an example configuration for an IOS device see Cisco's *Enhanced Transcoding and Conferencing for IOS Voice Gateways in a CallMananger Network using DSP Resources Configuration Example* (http://www.cisco.com/en/US/products/sw/voicesw/ps556/products_configuration_example09186a008084fe1f.shtml).

How it works...

Like conference bridges, transcoders use the Skinny Client Control Protocol to communicate with Unified Communications Manager. Transcoders are utilized based on region settings.

Configuring media termination points

Media termination points (MTPs) describes a type of device that is generally used when two end points cannot speak a common protocol. For example, a Media Termination Point can be used to transcode G.711 u-law to a-law and vice versa. Media Termination Point devices are commonly required for DTMF conversion with third party fax servers.

Getting ready

This recipe assumes the Cisco IP Voice Media Streaming App service has been enabled as described in the *Software Conference Bridge* recipe of this chapter.

How to do it...

To configure a hardware Media Termination Point, perform the following:

1. Navigate to the **Media Termination Point** page (**Media Resources | Media Termination Point**).
2. Click on **Add New** to add a new Media Termination Point.
3. There is only one option for **Media Termination Point Type,** that is, **Cisco IOS Enhanced Software Media Termination Point**.
4. Specify the **Media Termination Point Name**. This is the name as configured on the IOS device.
5. Select an appropriate **Device Pool**:

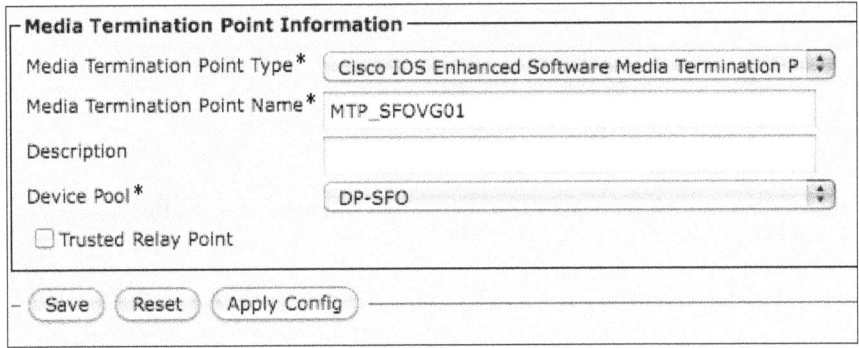

6. Click on **Save**.

How it works...

Media termination points are utilized as needed and instructed by the Unified Communications Manager. They must be configured as part of a media resource group to be utilized.

There's more...

In addition to hardware media termination points, the Unified Communications Manager software provides support for software media termination points. These are automatically created when the system is installed. They are active when the Cisco IP Voice Media Streaming App service is activated.

Configuring media resource groups

Throughout the recipes in this chapter, we've mentioned the need for media resource groups. In this recipe, we will explain how to configure them and discuss how they are used.

Getting ready

This recipe assumes media resources have been previously configured as detailed in the previous recipes.

How to do it...

To configure a media resource group, perform the following:

1. First, navigate to the configuration page for media resource groups (**Media Resources | Media Resource Group**).
2. Click on **Add New** to create a new media resource group.
3. Specify a **Name** for this group.
4. Select the appropriate media resources from the **Available Media Resources** list, using the down arrow:

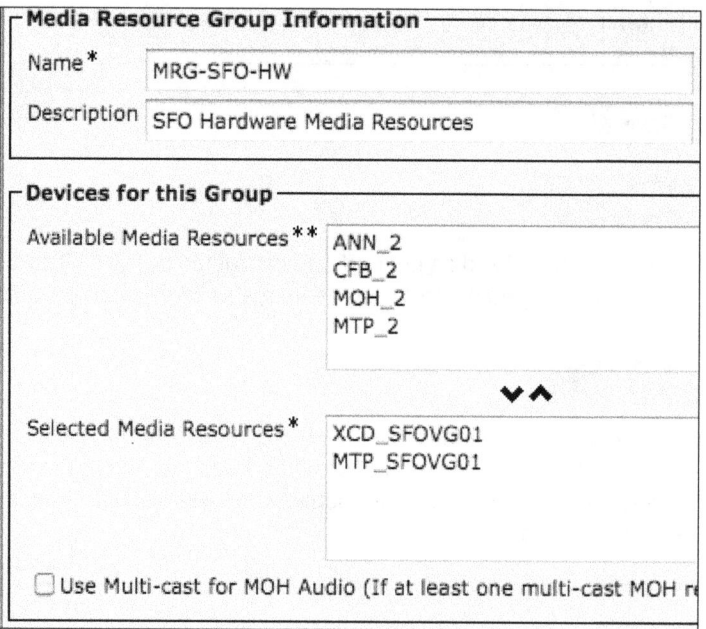

5. Click on **Save**.

How it works...

Media resource groups specify a set of media resource devices, such as transcoders and conference bridges. This group is part of a media resource group list.

It is good practice to separate hardware-based media resources from software-based. The reason relates to media resource lists and the order of the resources within them. This will be described in more detail in the next recipe.

Configuring media resource group lists

As the name may imply, media resource group lists are an ordered list of media resource groups which themselves are a listing of media resources. Media resource group lists define the order (and therefore, priority) of media resources to be used by a device.

Getting ready

This recipe assumes all necessary media resource groups have been created as detailed in the previous recipe.

How to do it...

To configure media resource group lists, perform the following:

1. Navigate to the configuration page for media resource group lists (**Media Resources | Media Resource Group List**).
2. Click on **Add New** to add a new media resource group list.
3. Specify a meaningful **Name**.
4. From the **Available Media Resource Groups** list, select the appropriate media resource groups.

Media Resources and Music On Hold

 Order is important here. Hardware resources in general should be before software resources.

Media Resource Group List Information
Name* MRGL-SFO

Media Resource Groups for this List
Available Media Resource Groups

Selected Media Resource Groups
MRG-SFO-HW
MRG-SFO-PUB

Save

5. Click on **Save**.

How it works...

Media resource group lists specify, in order, a group of devices available for various media related tasks such as transcoding and conferencing. These lists must be applied to a device to be used.

How we decide to group media resources is an important consideration. We generally do not mix hardware with software media resources, such as software media termination points and conference bridges. The reason is entirely related to performance and the potential impact on call processing.

Software-based media resources have a considerable processing impact, whereas hardware-based resources are specifically designed to perform media-related tasks, such as transcoding and conferencing, and can do so efficiently. For this reason, software resources should only be used as a last resort when hardware isn't available.

There's more...

In order for a device to utilize media resources, it must be assigned a media resource group list.

Applying media resource group lists to devices

Now that we have created the necessary media resource group lists, we will apply them to our devices so that they may take advantage of the media resources.

To apply media resources to an end point, such as a phone, perform the following:

1. Navigate to the end points configuration page (**Device | Phone**).
2. Locate the end point to which the media resource group list will be applied.
3. Specify the **Media Resource Group List** under the **Device Information** section:

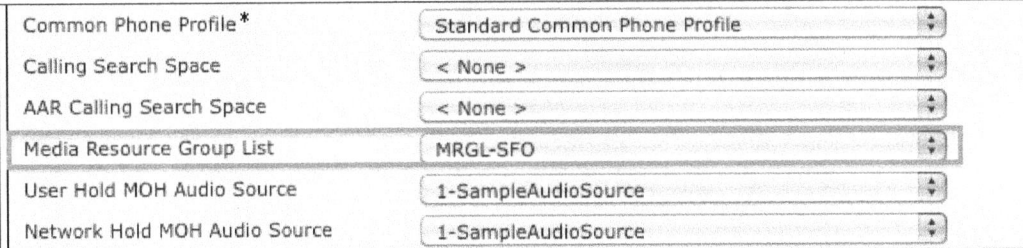

4. Click on **Save**.
5. Next, click on **Apply Config**.
6. On the pop up window, click on **OK**.

Implementing unicast Music On Hold

Music On Hold can be of two types, unicast or multicast. Unicast Music On Hold offers a quick and easy way to get Music On Hold up and running quickly, but at a cost of bandwidth.

Getting ready

This recipe assumes all the necessary media resource groups and media resource group lists have been created.

How to do it...

To configure unicast Music On Hold, perform the following:

1. First, find the system created Music On Hold device and verify that it is registered. (**Media Resources | Music On Hold Server**).

    If the Music On Hold server doesn't show as registered, then the Cisco IP Voice Media Streaming App has not been enabled.

2. Next, configure the appropriate **Device Pool** for the **Music On Hold Server**.
3. If necessary, specify a **Location**.
4. If required, change the **Maximum Half Duplex Streams** and **Maximum Multi-Cast Connections**:

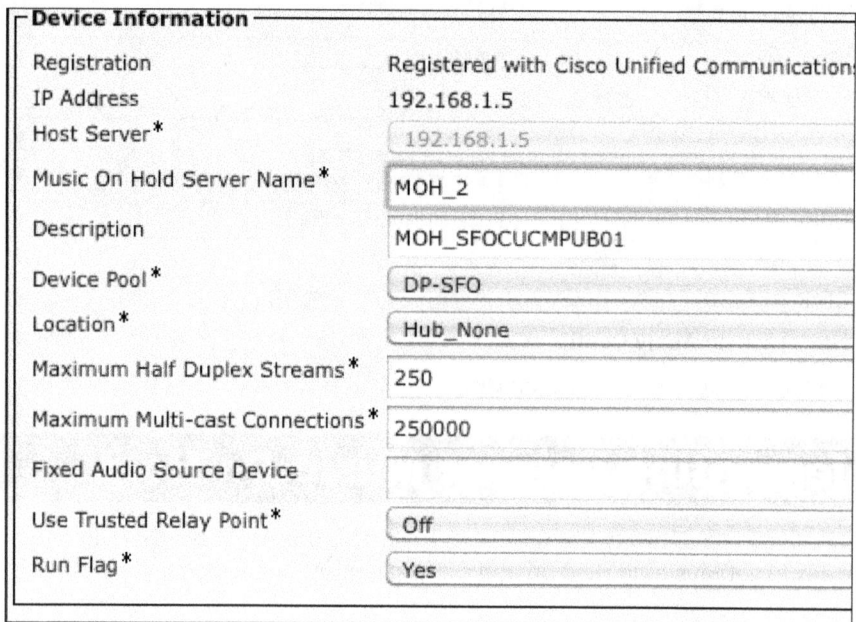

5. Click on **Save**.

6. Next, add the Music On Hold server to the appropriate media resource groups (**Media Resources | Media Resource Group**).

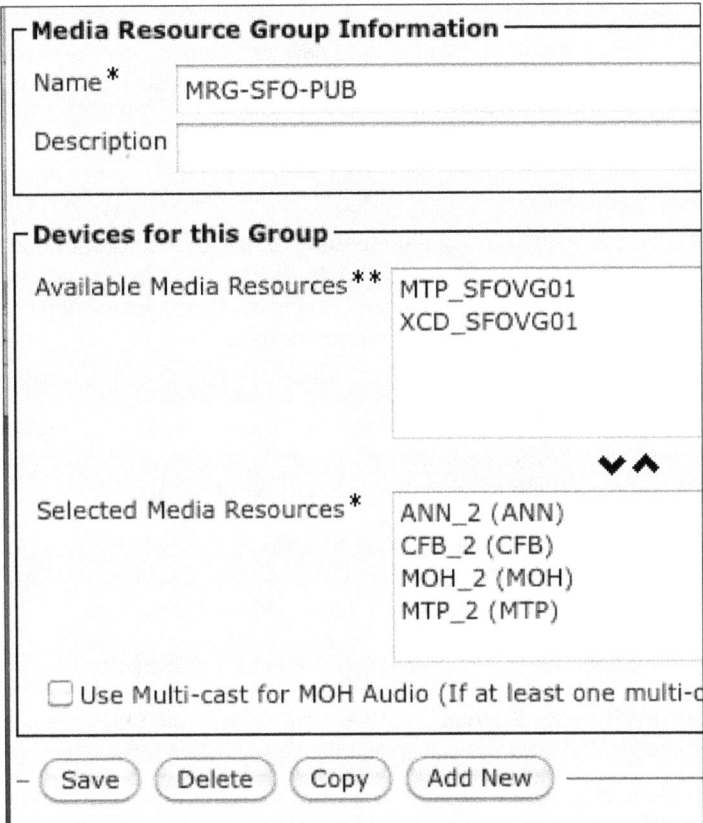

7. With the media resource group list applied, we are nearly ready to test.
8. On our devices we must set the following fields:
   - **Media Resource Group List**
   - **User Hold MOH Audio Source**
   - **Network Hold MOH Audio Source**

 The least obvious of these fields are the two audio sources. If we do not specify these, no audio will be heard when a caller is placed on hold. Instead they may hear beeps depending on how the system parameters are configured.

9. Click on **Save**.

10. Next, click on **Apply Config**.
11. On the pop up window, click on **OK**.

 After the device downloads its new configuration file, we can test placing a call on hold and the generic hold music will be heard.

How it works...

In this particular example we use the built-in features of the Unified Communications Manager to serve unicast Music On Hold to end points. While unicast MOH is simple and quick to configure, it does come at a bandwidth and processing cost, as each device on hold that is hearing music will require a separate voice stream for data.

Because each device on hold has its own stream for Music On Hold, the Music On Hold service may run out of available resources to handle new requests for Music On Hold. In this situation, where the Music On Hold server becomes fully utilized, multicast Music On Hold may prove to be a better solution to serve a large number of clients.

If multicast Music On Hold is not an option, due to hardware or network requirements, adding an additional dedicated Music On Hold server to the media resource groups and lists can provide better coverage and high availability of Music On Hold resources.

In this recipe we mentioned two types of Music On Hold audio sources:

- **User Hold MOH Audio Source:** The User Hold MOH Audio Source is used when another IP phone places the call on hold using the *Hold* softkey.
- **Network Hold MOH Audio Source:** The Network Hold MOH Audio Source is used when a call is placed on hold as a result of:
    - Call transfer
    - Call park
    - Conference setup

There's more...

In some cases it may be necessary to utilize both unicast and multicast Music On Hold. This may be due to devices that do not support multicast Music On Hold, such as wireless Cisco IP Phones.

Unicast and multicast in the same cluster

To support a configuration that requires both unicast and multicast Music On Hold, we have two options, that are explained next.

Chapter 3

Separate Music On Hold servers

If multiple servers are available for Music On Hold, we can configure one for unicast and one for multicast (**Media Resources | Music On Hold Server**).

Single Music On Hold server

If only a single Music On Hold server is available and both unicast and multicast Music On Hold are required, simply add the Music On Hold resource to two media resource groups, one with **Use Multi-cast for MOH Audio** checked and another without.

Regardless of which model we choose, at least two media resource groups will be required: one for unicast and one for multicast Music On Hold. After the appropriate media resource groups and list have been configured, they must be configured to the appropriate devices. Depending on how the environment is built, it may be easier to apply MRGL settings to Device Pools, or in bulk using the Bulk Administration Tool.

Codec selection

Codec selection can be configured in the IP Voice Streaming Media App service parameter (**System | Service Parameters**).

Under the **Clusterwide Parameters** section, select the desired codecs from the **Supported MOH Codecs** list; by default only **711 mu-law** is selected. Multiple codecs may be selected for Music On Hold; however, region settings will determine the actual codec to be used:

Clusterwide Parameters (Parameters that apply to all servers)	
Supported MOH Codecs *	711 mulaw 711 alaw 729 Annex A
MOH Fixed Audio Quality level *	Medium Quality
IP DSCP to Cisco Unified Communications Manager *	CS3(precedence 3) DSCP (011000)
Multicast MOH IP DSCP *	EF DSCP (101110)
MTP DTMF Duration *	100
MTP DTMF Power (volume) *	9
There are hidden parameters in this group. Click on Advanced button to see hidden parameters.	

Configuring multicast Music On Hold

Compared to unicast Music On Hold, multicast Music On Hold streams a single data stream, providing Music On Hold to any device which requests and supports it.

Getting ready

This recipe assumes that all the necessary Media Resource Groups and Media Resource Group Lists have been created.

This recipe also assumes the appropriate IOS devices have been configured for multicasting.

How to do it...

To configure multicast Music On Hold, perform the following:

1. First, configure a server for multicast Music On Hold (**Media Resources | Music On Hold Servers**).
2. Select the Music On Hold server to be configured.
3. Under the section **Multi-cast Audio Source Information**, check the box titled **Enable Multi-cast Audio Sources on this MOH Server**.
4. For the **Increment Multi-cast on** field, select **IP Address**:

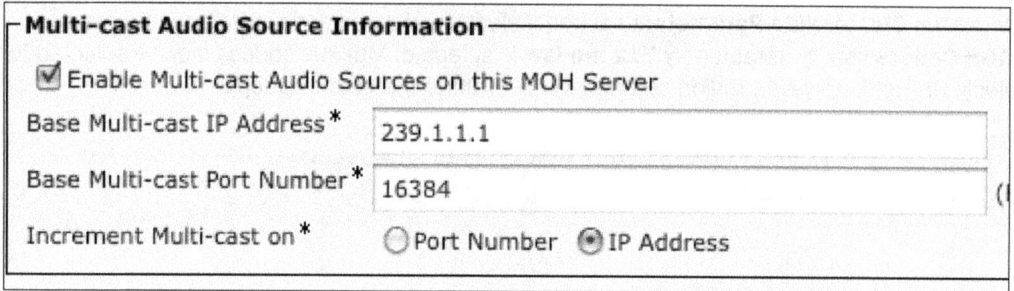

5. Click on **Save**.
6. Create a new Media Resource Group as described in this chapter. When done, check the box **Use Multi-cast for MOH Audio**.

> You may see **[Multicast]** appended to the Music On Hold server's name, this only indicates it is available for streaming multicast Music On Hold, and will still function for unicast Music On Hold.

7. Click on **Save**.
8. Add the newly created multicast media resource group to a media resource group list, as described earlier in this chapter.
9. Click on **Save**.

10. Finally, enable the Music On Hold Audio Source for multicast streaming by clicking on **Allow Multi-casting** (**Media Resources | Music On Hold Audio Source**):

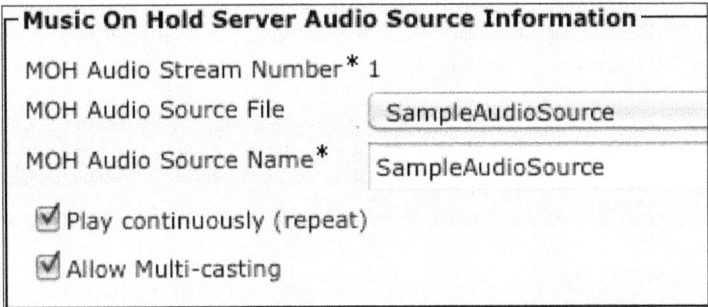

 Apply the newly created multicast media resource group list to the appropriate devices. Ensure the audio source selected is capable of multicasting.

How it works...

By configuring the Music On Hold Server to allow multicasting, and configuring media resources to use the multicast Music On Hold server, devices with the selected media resource group list will stream the audio source capable of multicasting.

When enabling multicasting on a Music On Hold Server, an IP Address will be prepopulated. If we need to use another IP address for any reason, the range of valid multicast IP addresses is 224.0.1.0 to 239.255.255.255. However, Cisco recommends using the 239.1.1.1 to 239.255.255.255 range to avoid using a public multicast address.

Music On Hold audio source selection process

When determining which audio source to use, Unified Communications Manager uses the settings in the following order:

1. Directory number
2. Device
3. Common device configuration
4. Cluster-wide defaults

When a caller is placed on hold, Unified Communications Manager will first try to use the audio source specified by the directory number, if any.

If none are available, CUCM will try the Device Audio Source settings, so on and so forth with common device configuration settings and cluster-wide defaults.

Media Resources and Music On Hold

See also

For additional information on Music On Hold and media resources, consult the Solution Reference Network Design for Cisco Unified Communications Manager (http://www.cisco.com/en/US/docs/voice_ip_comm/cucm/srnd/8x/uc8x.html).

Adding custom media files for Music On Hold

To add a custom Music On Hold audio source, the source file must be in PCM/WAV format.

How to do it...

To add a new Music On Hold audio source, perform the following:

1. Add a new Music On Hold Audio Source (**Media Resources | Music On Hold Audio Source**).
2. If the music file is not already uploaded, click on the **Upload File** button:

3. When the new window opens, browse to the audio file then click on **Upload File**.
4. After the file is uploaded, it will be available under the **MOH Audio Stream Source File** list.
5. Select an available **MOH Audio Stream Number**.
6. Select the newly uploaded media file under **MOH Audio Source File**.
7. Depending on the media type, it may be appropriate to play the file continuously. If this is the case, check the box **Play continuously**.
8. If this media file is to be used with multicast streams check **Allow Multi-casting**.
9. Click on **Save**.

This new audio source may now be applied to devices and directory numbers.

> To avoid any unnecessary legal ramifications, avoid using media files you are not licensed to use.

4
Tracing and Troubleshooting Tools

In this chapter, we will cover some basic tools used in troubleshooting, specifically the Real-Time Monitoring Tool.

- Configuring user permissions for the Real-Time Monitoring Tool
- Collecting traces using the Query Wizard
- Configuring the e-mail server for the Real-Time Monitoring Tool.
- Creating custom alerts in the Real-Time Monitoring Tool
- Configuring custom alert actions
- Capturing packets
- Analyzing the Dial Plan with the Dialed Number Analyzer

Introduction

Troubleshooting is a vast subject that could be covered in its own book; however, due to the scope of this book, this chapter will focus on some common problems and the troubleshooting tools provided by the Unified Communications Manager platform.

Configuring user permissions for the Real-Time Monitoring Tool

The Real-Time Monitoring Tool (RTMT) provides a graphical user interface to many facets of the system, and provides various tools such as trace and log collecting, custom alerts, and performance monitoring.

Tracing and Troubleshooting Tools

To use the Real-Time Monitoring Tool, an end user must be assigned to a user group that is allowed to use this tool. For this recipe, we will use the Standard CCM Super Users user group for our user. Roles associated with the Real-Time Monitoring Tool are discussed later in this recipe.

How to do it...

To grant access to the Real-Time Monitoring Tool to end users, perform the following:

1. First, navigate to the end users configuration page (**User Management | End User**).
2. Ensure the user has the proper user group specified; if not, add it. In this case, we add **Standard CCM Super Users**.

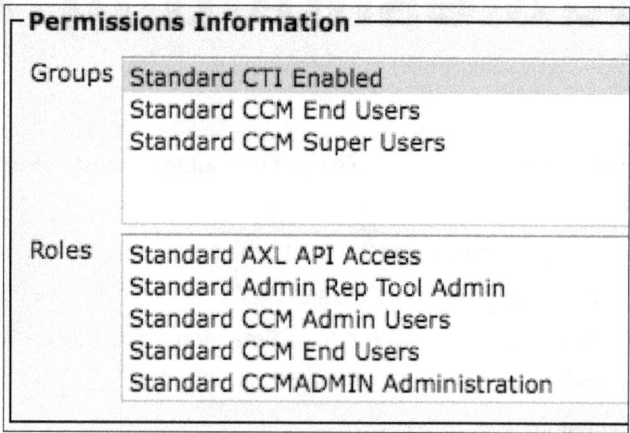

3. Click **Save**.

How it works...

By default, the Standard CCM Super Users user group has permissions to use the Real-Time monitoring Tool; by assigning this group to our admin users, we grant them permissions to use the Real-Time Monitoring Tool.

Custom user group for the Real-Time Monitoring Tool

Sometimes we may want to grant access to facilities of the Real-Time Monitoring Tool to non admin users. To do so, we have some Roles at our disposal.

- **Standard RealtimeAndTraceCollection**: View and configure the Real-Time Monitoring Tool, including collecting traces.

- **Standard SERVICEABILITY**: Allows the assigned user to view and configure the following in the Real-Time Monitoring Tool:
    - Alert Configuration
    - Profile Configuration
    - Trace Collection
- **Standard SERVICEABILITY Administration**: Allows the assigned user to view and configure all windows in the RTMT.
- **Standard SERVICEABILITY Read Only**: Allows the assigned user to view configuration in the RTMT.

There's more...

Sometimes, we may want to create a general purpose user account for accessing the Real-Time Monitoring Tool; to this end, we will create an application user (**User Management | Application User**).

1. First, create the new application user by clicking **Add New**.
2. Specify the **User ID**; for this recipe we will use rtmtuser.
3. Specify the **Password** and **Confirm Password**.
4. Click **Save**.
5. After the page reloads, click **Add to User Group** in the section **Permissions Information**.
6. A new window will open, allowing us to search the available user groups. If none are present, click **Find** to populate the list.
7. Add the **Standard RealtimeAndTraceCollection** user group to the application user by first checking the box next to the user group. Click **Add Selected**.

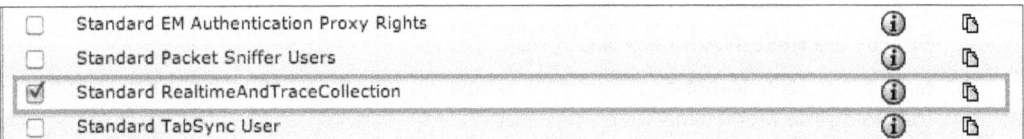

8. Click **Save**.

Tracing and Troubleshooting Tools

9. The **Permissions Information** section will appear as shown in the following screenshot:

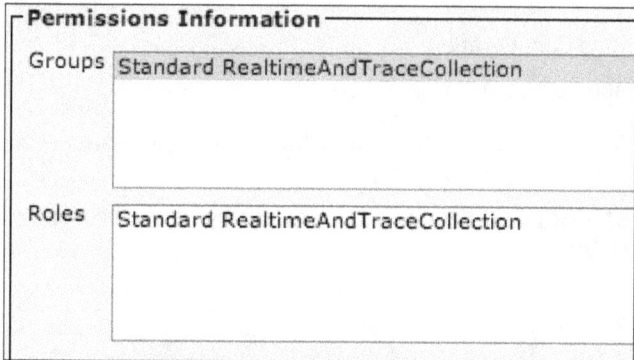

Collecting traces using the Query Wizard

The Real-Time Monitoring Tool provided by CUCM has many features and facilities; for the purpose of this recipe, we will cover using the Query Wizard to generate trace files for review.

Getting ready

This recipe assumes the Real-Time Monitoring Tool has already been downloaded from CUCM (**Application** | **Plugins** | **Cisco Unified Real-Time Monitoring Tool – Windows** or **Linux**).

How to do it...

To run the Query Wizard in the Real-Time Monitoring Tool, perform the following:

1. First, log into the Real-Time Monitoring Tool.
2. Specify the **Host IP Address** of CUCM.
3. Specify the **User Name** and associated **Password** for the account permitted to use the Real-Time Monitoring Tool.

Chapter 4

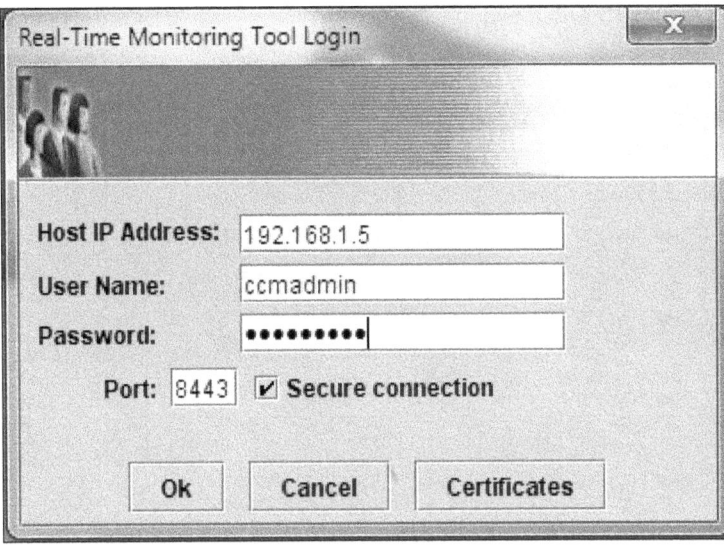

4. Click **Ok** to log in.
5. Next, we may be prompted to select a Configuration List. Select the appropriate **Configuration List** and click **Ok**.
6. Once the Configuration List is loaded, navigate to Trace & Log Central (**Tools | Trace & Log Central**).
7. For this recipe, we will be using the Query Wizard. Double-click it to open the wizard (**Trace & Log Central | Query Wizard**).

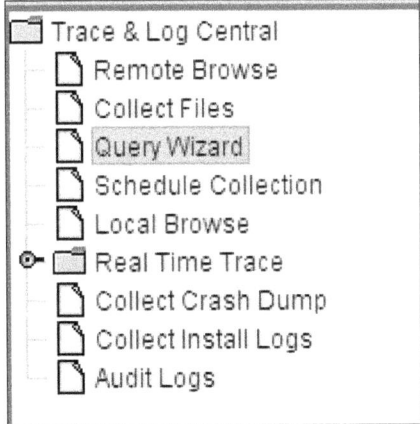

8. Once the Query Wizard window opens, we are prompted to either use a saved query or to customize our own. For this recipe, will create a Custom Query. So, select **Custom Query** and click **Next**.

Tracing and Troubleshooting Tools

9. We are prompted with a window displaying all the Unified Communications Manager services and servers. This screen shows us CCM Services. Select the check boxes for each service for which we are collecting logs.

10. Click **Next**.

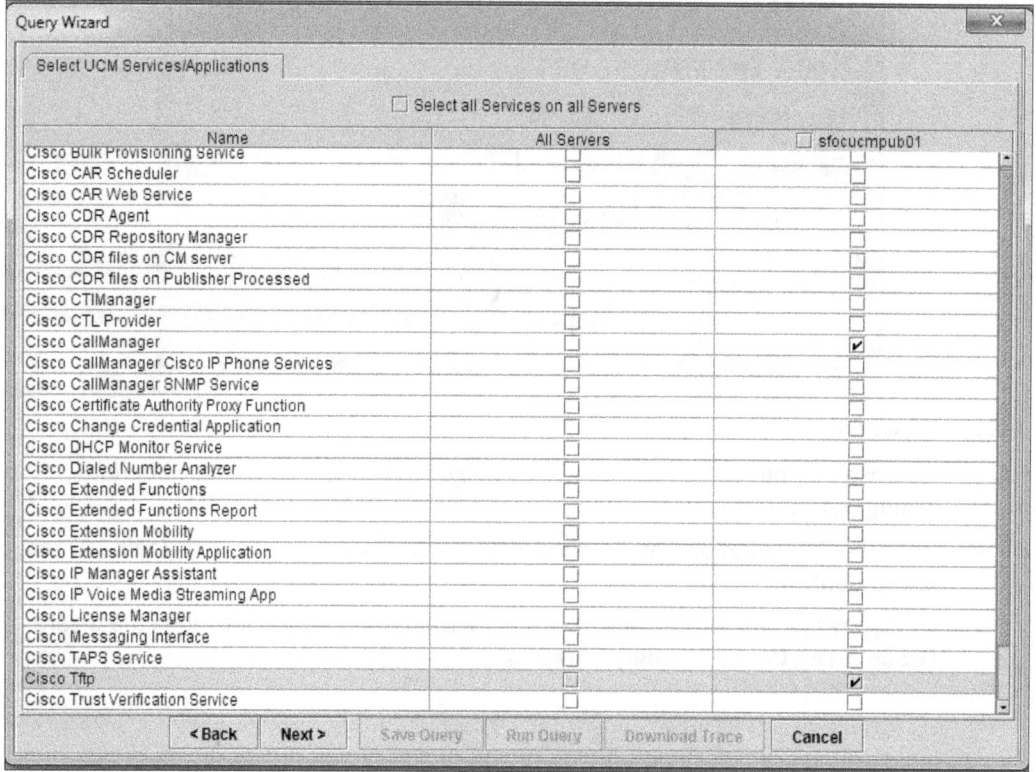

In the previous example, we are collecting logs for the **Cisco CallManager** and **Cisco Tftp** services from sfocucmpub01 (the publisher used in this book).

1. Next, select which system services we wish to collect traces for, much the same as in the previous step.

2. Next, we are given the option to collect traces from a given time period. In this recipe, we collect traces from the last 30 minutes.

Chapter 4

3. Select an appropriate **Query Time Option**.
4. If desired, enter a **Search String**.
5. If necessary, select the appropriate **Impact Level** for generating the trace.

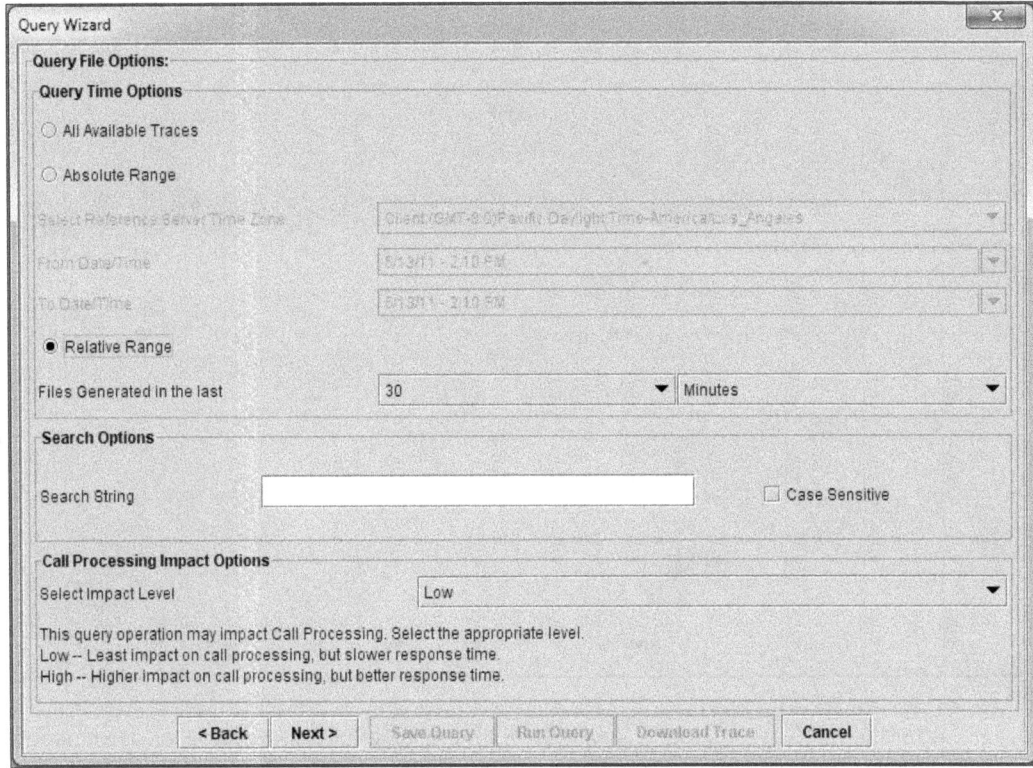

6. Finally, we can select how we want to go about collecting the traces. Select an appropriate download option.

Tracing and Troubleshooting Tools

7. Click **Run Query** or **Download Trace**, depending on the download option chosen.

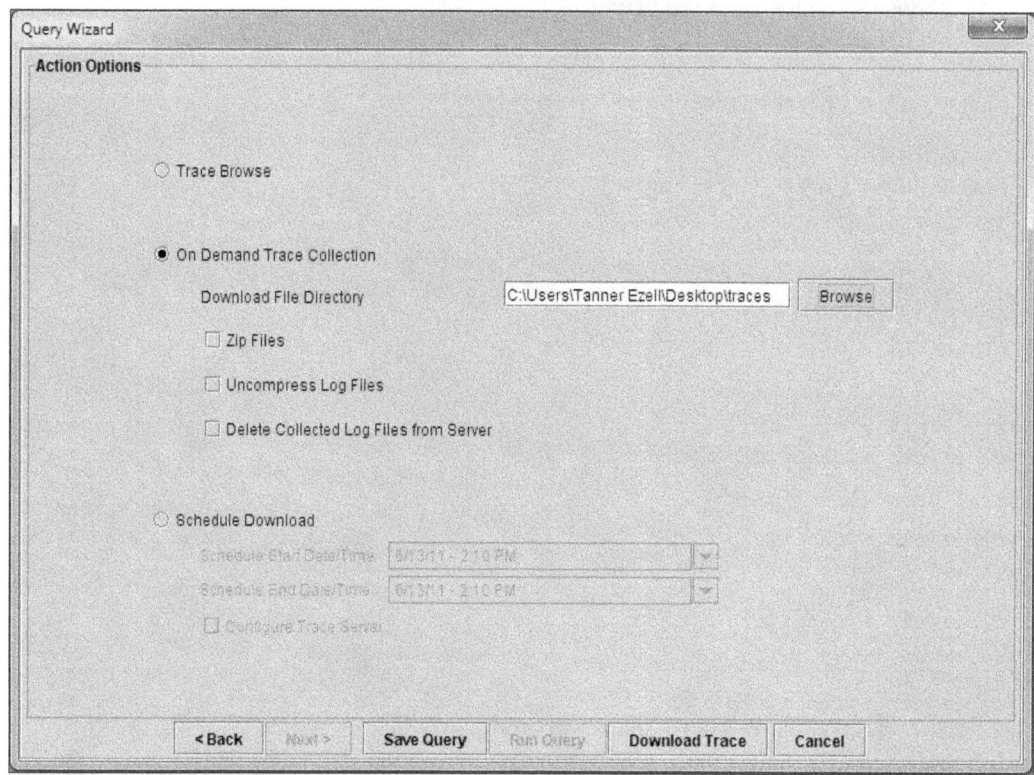

8. After the trace is completed, the files will be available for downloading, or downloaded directly depending on which option was selected.

How it works...

The Real-Time Monitoring Tools work by requesting from the CUCM server trace information; it can also poll the CUCM server up to the second real-time information data gathering.

See also

This recipe barely scratches the surface of the utility of the Real-Time Monitoring Tool; for further reading, see *Cisco Unified Real-Time Monitoring Tool Administration Guide* (http://www.cisco.com/en/US/docs/voice_ip_comm/cucm/service/8_5_1/rtmt/RTMT.html).

Configuring the e-mail server for the Real-Time Monitoring Tool

In order for the Real-Time Monitoring Tool to send e-mail alerts, we must first tell it where our mail server is. This recipe will detail that process.

How to do it...

To configure the e-mail server, perform the following:

1. First, log in to the Real-Time Monitoring Tool.
2. Once logged-in, select from the menu, **System | Tools | Alert | Configure Email Server**.
3. The **Mail Server Configuration** window will open.
4. Specify the e-mail server in the **Mail Server** field.
5. Specify the **Port** of the e-mail server.
6. Specify the **Sender User Id**; this will be the account from which the e-mails are sent.

7. Click **Ok**.

How it works...

In order to use the Alerts e-mail feature, we must first specify an e-mail server from which the Real-Time Monitoring Tool can relay e-mail messages.

Creating custom alerts in the Real-Time Monitoring Tool

One useful feature of the Real-Time Monitoring Tool is the ability for the tool to send e-mails when an alert is triggered. In this recipe, we will set up a simple alert, which sends an e-mail when less than five MTP resources are available.

Getting ready

For e-mail alerts, the e-mail server must be configured as specified in the previous recipe.

How to do it...

To configure a custom alert in the Real-Time Monitoring Tool, perform the following:

1. First, log in to the Real-Time Monitoring Tool.
2. To create a custom alert, we must add a performance counter by first navigating to the performance monitoring page (**System | Performance | Open Performance Monitoring**).
3. From the tree, we must find the value we want to monitor; for this recipe we will add the **ResourceAvailable** counter from **Cisco MTP Device**.
4. To monitor the counter, double-click it. Depending on the counter we may be asked to specify an **Instance**, or **device** to monitor.
5. Once the counter has been added we can configure alerts by first right-clicking the counter and selecting **Set Alert/Properties...**.
6. The **Alert Properties: General** window will open.
7. Specify the **Severity** and **Description** for the Alert.

8. Optionally, uncheck **Enable Alert** to disable the alert.

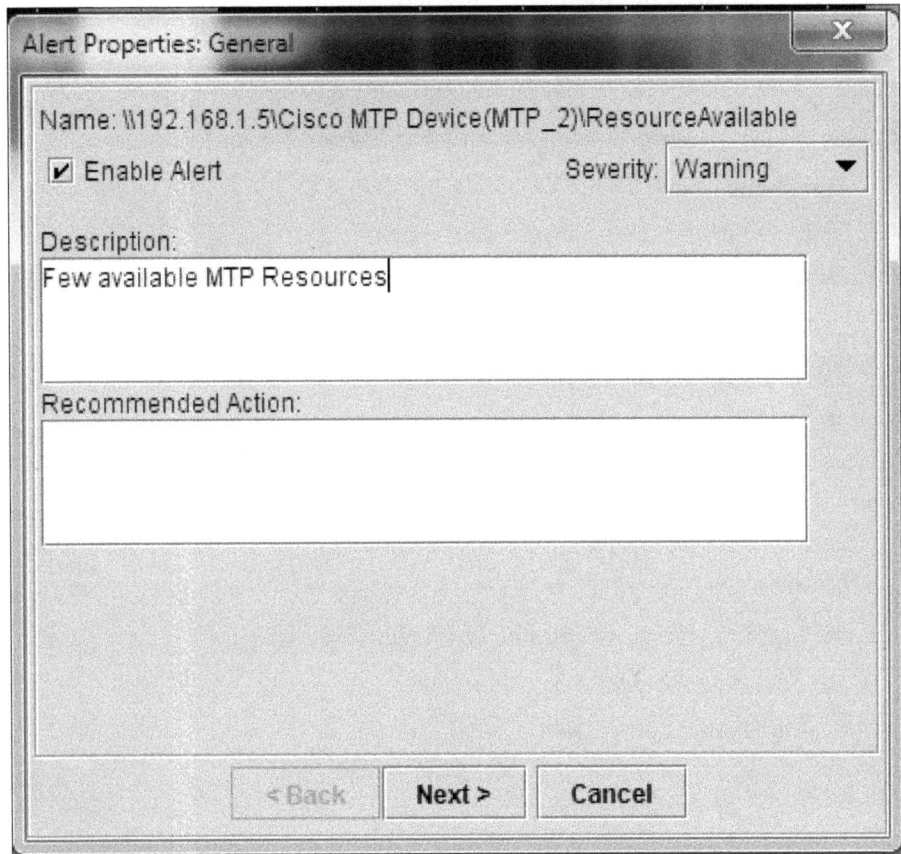

9. Click **Next**.
10. Next, we are greeted by the **Threshold & Duration** window.
11. Specify the threshold **Value.**

12. Specify the **Value Calculated As** as appropriate.
13. If desired, specify a **Duration**; once this duration has elapsed, the alert should be triggered.

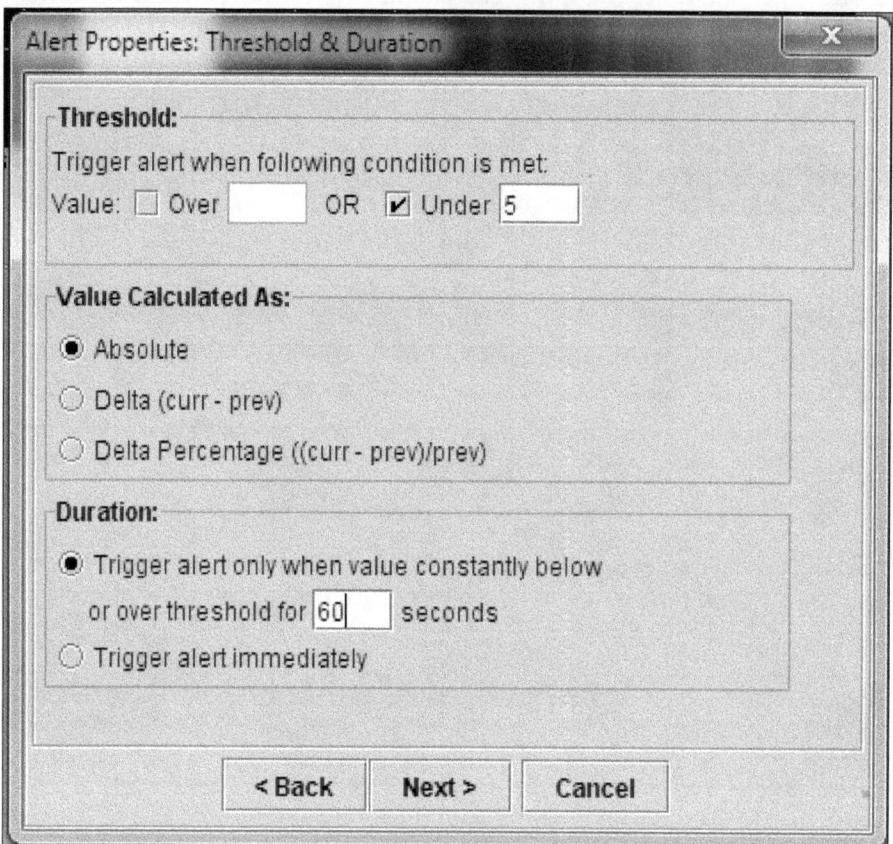

14. Click **Next**.
15. The **Frequency & Schedule** window then opens.
16. Select the **Frequency** for which the alert will generate messages.

17. Select the **Schedule** on which the alert will run.

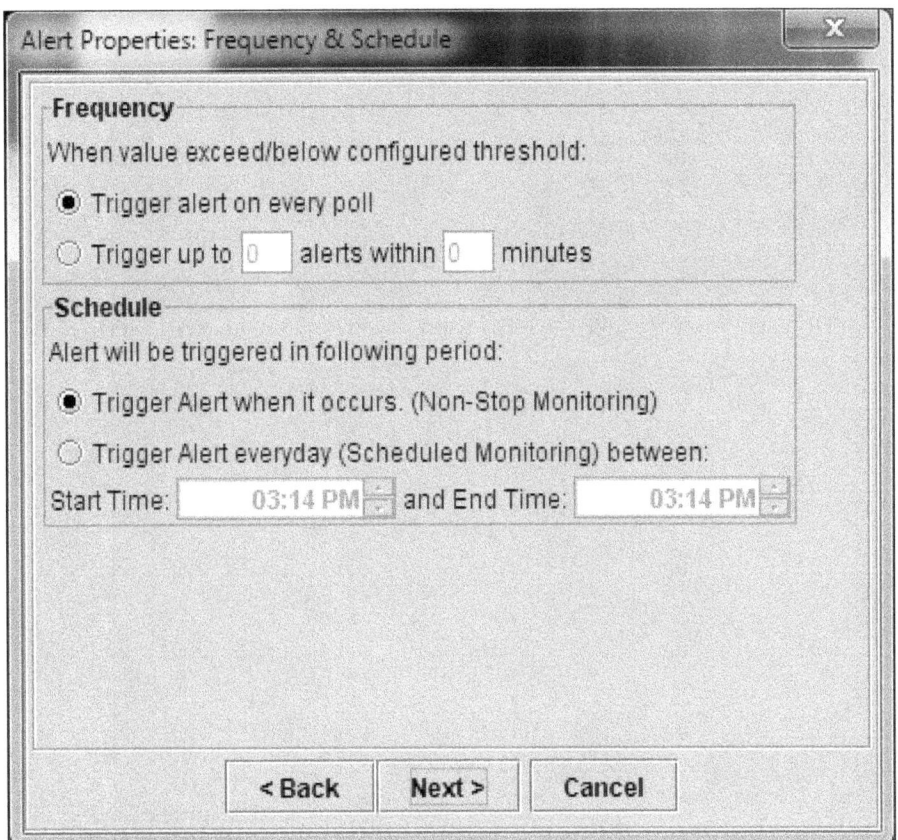

18. Click **Next**.
19. Finally, the **Email Notification** window will appear.
20. If no e-mail alert is desired, uncheck **Enable Email**.
21. Select the **Trigger Alert Action** from the drop-down, or configure a new one. This process is detailed in another recipe.

Tracing and Troubleshooting Tools

22. Specify the **User-defined email text** to be e-mailed upon triggering the alert.

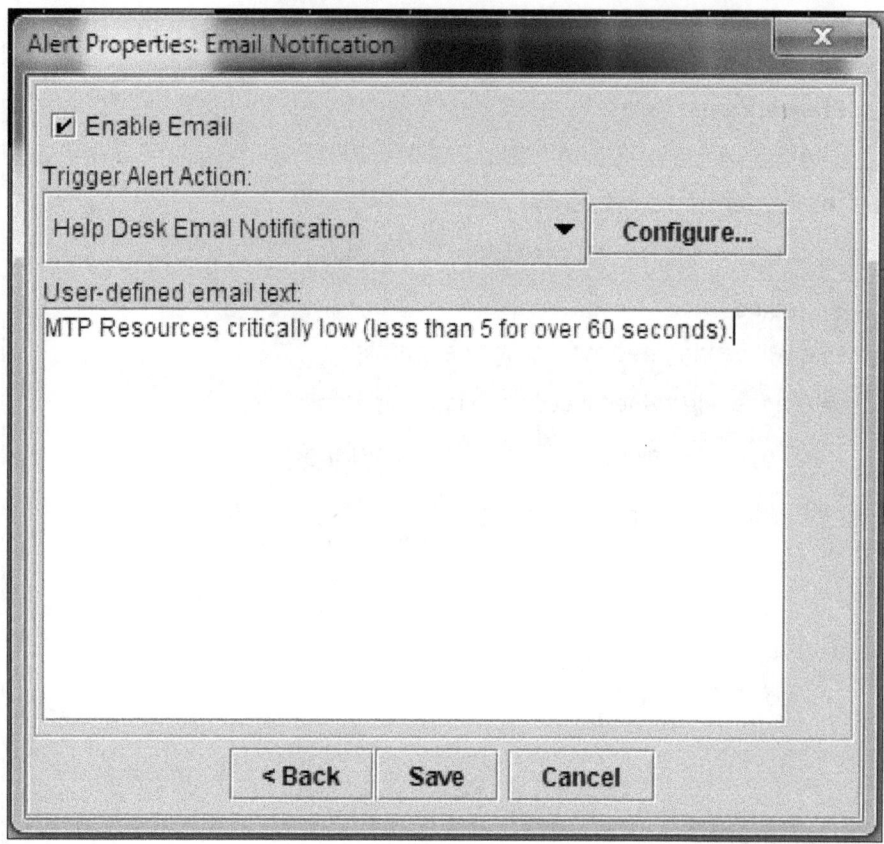

23. Click **Save**.

How it works...

By defining a custom alert and its actions, we can set up notifications for important system events, such as a lack of MTP resources, and generate alerts when they happen. We can further specify that alerts only work at certain times, or for certain nodes in the cluster.

Configuring custom alert actions

As mentioned in the previous recipe, the alert actions from the Trigger Alert Action drop-down specify the list of users who shall receive an alert e-mail.

Getting ready

This recipe continues from the end of the previous recipe.

How to do it...

To configure an alert action, perform the following:

1. Starting from the **Alert Properties: Email Notification** window, next to **Trigger Alert Action** click **Configure**.
2. The **Alert Action** window will open. To add a new alert action, click **Add...**.
3. The **Action Configuration** window will open.
4. Specify a **Name**.
5. Specify a **Description** of the action.
6. Add a recipient by clicking **Add**.
7. When the new window appears, enter an e-mail address in the **Enter email/epage address** field.
8. Click **Ok**.
9. Repeat this process for each recipient.

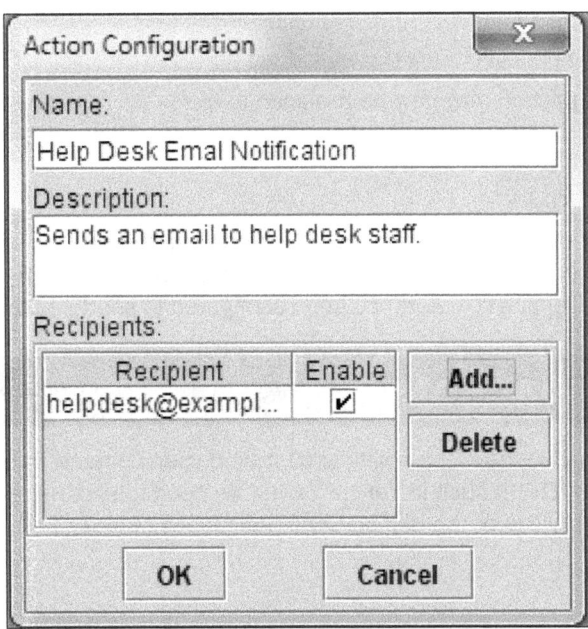

10. Click **Ok**.

11. The **Alert Action** window will now show the new action.

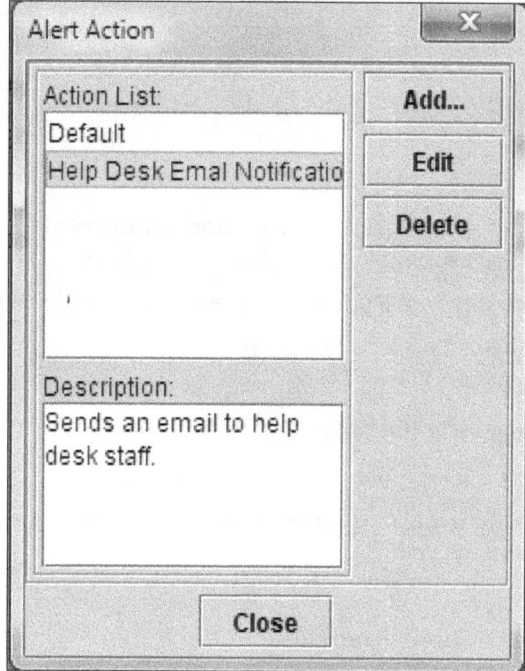

12. Click **Close**
13. The new alert action may now be assigned to alerts.

How it works...

By creating a new action alert, we can create, in effect, distribution lists for alerts. The action alert is then applied to an alert, which, when triggered, will result in each user being sent an e-mail alert; this is assuming the alert has been configured to send e-mail notifications.

Capturing packets

In some cases, we may not have the ability to capture packets directly from the network, such as when using Secure RTP. In such instances, when we need to see the raw data, we can use the packet capturing utilities of the Unified Communications Manager.

How to do it...

To begin capturing packets, perform the following:

1. First log into the command-line interface via secure shell (ssh).
2. Once logged-in, the command that we will utilize is `utils network capture`.

    There are many options that can be used with this command; they can be seen by typing "?" after the command. These options will be explained further in the *How it works...* section of this recipe.

3. For this recipe, we will attempt to capture packets destined for a specific host, 192.168.1.142. We will issue the command `utils network capture eth0 count 10000 size all host ip 192.168.1.142 file cap_1_142`.

    This command will be explained in the *How it works...* section of this recipe.

   ```
   admin:utils network capture eth0 count 10000 size all host ip
      192.168.1.142 file cap_1_142
   Executing command with options:
      size=ALL              count=10000
        interface=eth0
      src=                  dest=                  port=
        ip=192.168.1.142
   ```

4. With the packet capture running, perform any tests or tasks desired for the capture.
5. Once we're ready and have captured what we need, we close the capture by issuing a *Ctrl+C* on the secure shell from the first step.
6. When we are ready to collect the packet captured, we may use one of two methods: the command line or the Real-Time Monitoring Tool. As we're already at the command line, it may be quicker to use the command line, but for many files it may be easier to use the Real-Time Monitoring Tool.
7. We can collect the log via the command line by issuing the command:
   `file get activelog platform/cli/cap_1_142.cap`.

Tracing and Troubleshooting Tools

 You can use wildcards for collecting multiple files

```
admin:file get activelog platform/cli/cap_1_142.cap
Please wait while the system is gathering files info ...done.
Sub-directories were not traversed.
Number of files affected: 1
Total size in Bytes: 24
Total size in Kbytes: 0.0234375
Would you like to proceed [y/n]? y
SFTP server IP: 192.168.106
SFTP server port [22]:
User ID: administrator
Password: **********
Download directory: /captures/
Transfer completed.
```

How it works...

The packet capture mechanism of the Unified Communications Manager works like any capturing utility. In this recipe, we took a capture of the default interface eth0. We specified to capture 10,000 packets; because we are saving this capture to a file, we can specify a size of `all`, saving to the file `cap_1_142.cap`. The options supported by the utility are as follows:

- `page`: Pause output
- `numeric`: Show hosts as dotted IP addresses
- `file fname`: Output the information to a file
- `count num`: A count of the number of packets to capture

 The maximum count to output to the secure shell or terminal is 1000, for a file it is 100,000

- `size bytes`: The number of bytes of the packet to capture

 The maximum number of bytes to output to the secure shell or terminal is 128. For a file it can be any number, or **all**

Chapter 4

- `src addr`: The source address of the packet as a host name or IPV4 address
- `dest addr`: The destination address of the packet as a host name or IPV4 address
- `port num`: The port number of the packet (either `src` or `dest`)
- `host protocol addr`: The **protocol** should be one of the following:
    - `ip`
    - `arp`
    - `rarp`
    - `all`

>  The host address of the packet is a host name or IPv4 address. This option will display all packets to and from that address.
>
> If using the `host` option, do not use `src` or `dest`.

There's more...

In this recipe, we demonstrated using the command-line interface to gather the files. Now we will demonstrate using the Real-Time Monitoring Tool.

The process for collecting packet capture logs is very similar to using the Query Wizard, but, instead of the Query Wizard, we will select Collect Logs.

1. First, log into the Real-Time Monitoring Tool
2. Navigate to **Trace & Log Central** (**Tools | Trace & Log Central**).
3. For this recipe, we will use **Collect Files**; double-click it to open the wizard (**Trace & Log Central | Collect Files**).
4. We will not be selecting any UCM Services or Applications for this recipe, simply click **Next**.

Tracing and Troubleshooting Tools

5. Under the **Select System Services/Applications** tab, select **Packet Capture Logs** near the bottom.

Name	All Servers	sfocucmpub01
Cron Logs	☐	☐
Event Viewer-Application Log	☐	☐
Event Viewer-System Log	☐	☐
Host Resources Agent	☐	☐
IPT Platform CLI Created Reports	☐	☐
IPT Platform CLI Logs	☐	☐
IPT Platform Cert Monitor Logs	☐	☐
IPT Platform CertMgr Logs	☐	☐
IPT Platform Cluster Manager Logs	☐	☐
IPT Platform GUI Logs	☐	☐
IPT Platform IPSecMgmt Logs	☐	☐
IPT Platform RemoteSupport Logs	☐	☐
Install File Signing	☐	☐
Install and Upgrade Logs	☐	☐
MIB2 Agent	☐	☐
Mail Logs	☐	☐
Mgetty Logs	☐	☐
NTP Logs	☐	☐
Netdump Logs	☐	☐
Packet Capture Logs	☐	✔
Prog Logs	☐	☐
SAR Logs	☐	☐
SNMP Master Agent	☐	☐
Security Logs	☐	☐
Service Manager	☐	☐
Spooler Logs	☐	☐
System Application Agent	☐	☐
UDS - User Data Services	☐	☐

[< Back] [Next >] [Finish] [Cancel]

6. Click **Next**

7. Specify the time range and download options as shown in the following screenshot:

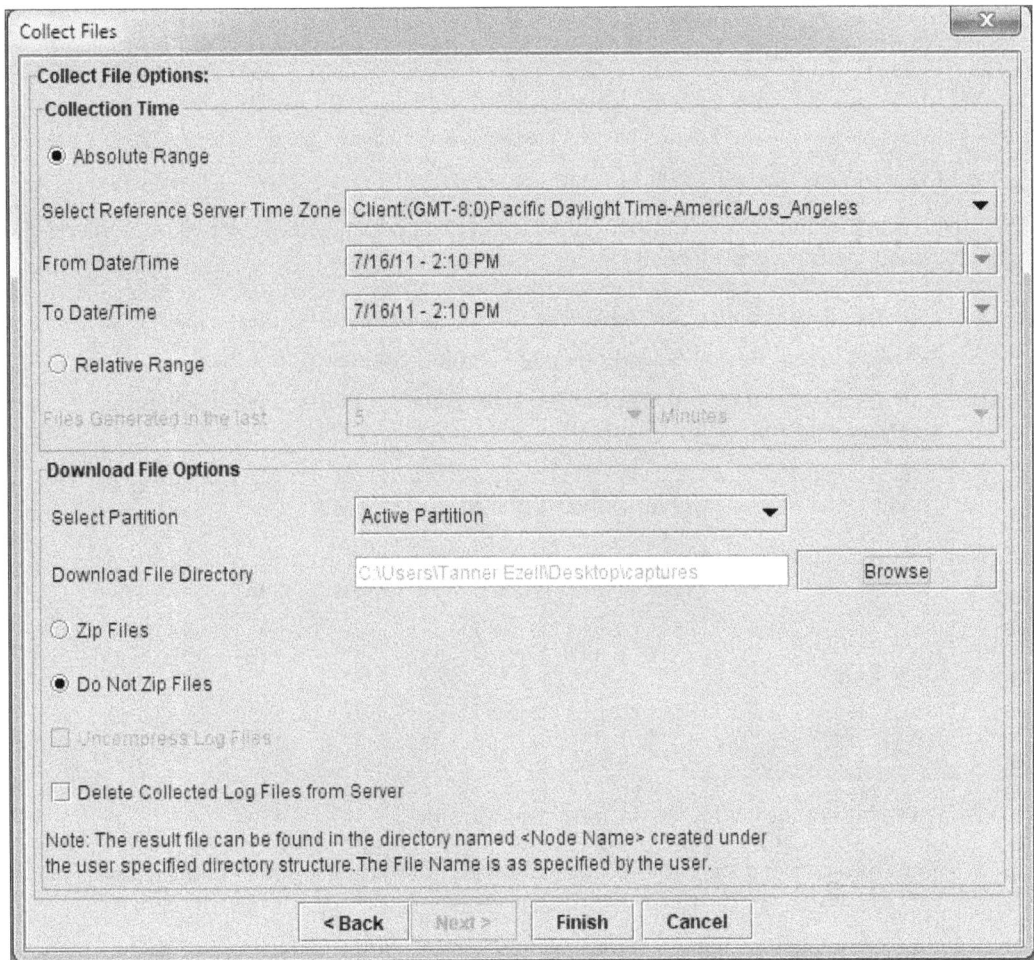

8. Click **Finish**.

The capture files will be downloaded to a point where they can be analyzed with the appropriate software, such as the freely available Wireshark.

Analyzing the Dial Plan with the dialed number analyzer

Call routing with Unified Communications Manager can become quite complex and intricate; when faced with dial plan related problems, the Dialed Number Analyzer can provide insight.

Tracing and Troubleshooting Tools

The Dialed Number Analyzer is a complex and involved tool, this recipe will try only to introduce its use. To learn more about this powerful tool, I recommend reading the *Cisco Unified Communications Manager Dialed Number Analyzer Guide* (http://www.cisco.com/en/US/docs/voice_ip_comm/cucm/dna/8_0_1/dnaguide.pdf) for more comprehensive coverage.

Getting ready...

This recipe requires the Dialed Number Analyzer services be activated; if it has not already been activated, perform the following:

1. First log into the Unified Serviceability page (https://cucm:8443/ccmservice).
2. Navigate to the Service Activations page (**Tools | Service Activation**).
3. Activate the **Cisco Dialed Number Analyzer Server** and **Cisco Dialed Number Analyzer** services.

4. Click **Save**

How to do it...

To use the Dialed Number Analyzer, perform the following:

1. First, navigate and log into the Dialed Number Analyzer (https://cucm/dna).

   > The credentials used would be the same as those used to log into Unified Serviceability.

2. There are many analysis options available to us; perform the desired analysis by selecting the option from the **Analysis** menu. A common option is the Phone option, which is what we will use for this recipe (**Analysis | Phone**).

3. In this recipe, we are given the option to search for the device to use as a template for analysis. Search for an appropriate device name and click **Find**.

4. Once we locate the device, click the hyperlink under **Device Name** (Line).

5. After the page reloads, we are presented with various options and information; first, the status and configuration information for the selected phone is presented.

Registration	Unknown
IP Address	Unknown
Device Name	CIPC-TEZELL
Description	IP Communicator for Tanner Ezell
Owner User ID	None
Device Pool	DP-SFO
Call Classification	OnNet
Calling Search Space	CSS-SFO-Device
AAR Calling Search Space	None
Media Resource Group List	MRGL-SFO
Device Time Zone	America/Los_Angeles

6. This information is used as the template for analysis of the call. Select the line to use as the template for analysis. This can be particularly useful for troubleshooting line level calling search space issues.

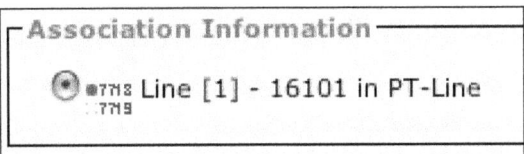

7. Enter the digits as they would be dialed by the user on the device.

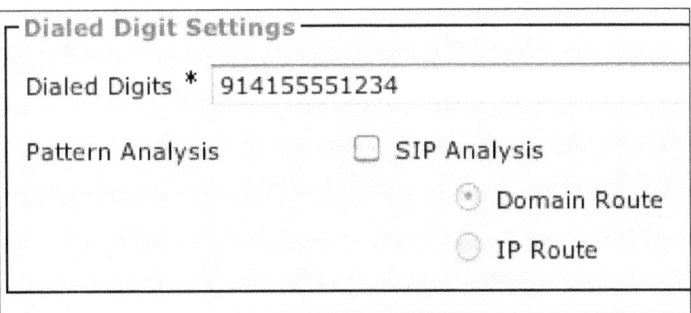

8. Finally, specify **Date and Time Settings**; this is particularly useful for testing the time of routing!

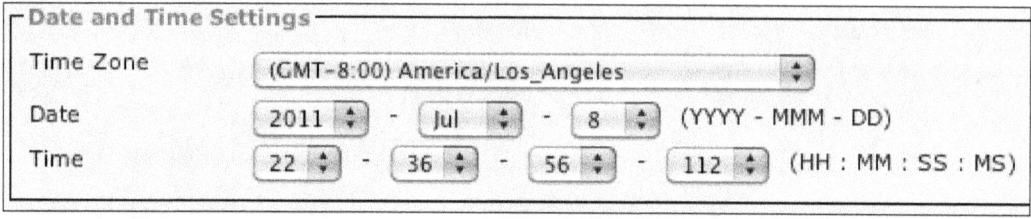

9. Click **Do Analysis.**
10. At this point, a new window will pop up, showing the results of the analysis. Depending on the results of the analysis, you will be presented with a **Results Summary**, such as the following one:

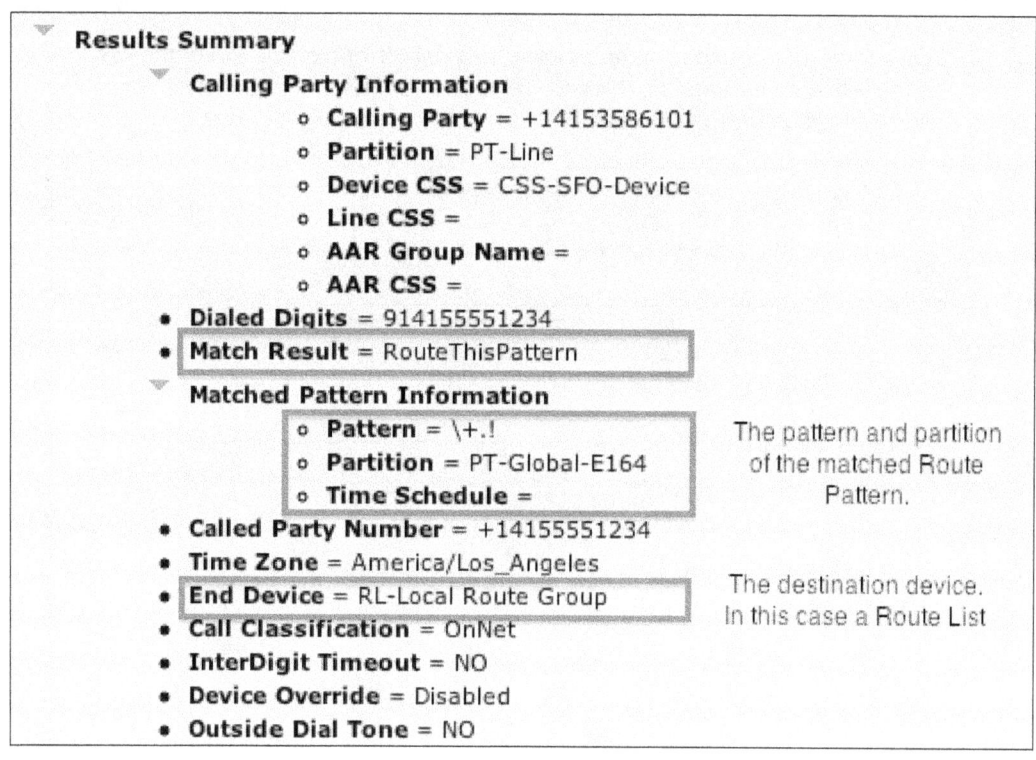

I have highlighted some sections of note from the **Results Summary**. The complete results will be broken down in the *There's more...* section of this recipe.

How it works...

The Dialed Number Analyzer works fairly simply; we provide it with appropriate call routing information such as calling search spaces and line partitions, which the utility then uses to perform analysis. The resulting output shows the call flow and transformations of the call, from the initial dialed digits to the final called number.

There's more...

From the previous example, the breakdown of the analysis is as follows:

```
TranslationPattern :Pattern= 9.1[2-9]XX[2-9]XXXXXX
    o Partition = PT-US-DialPlan
    o Positional Match List = 14155551234
    o Calling Party Number = +14153586101
    o PreTransform Calling Party Number = 16101
    o PreTransform Called Party Number = 914155551234
    Calling Party Transformations
            • External Phone Number Mask = YES
            • Calling Party Mask =
            • Prefix =
            • CallingLineId Presentation = Default
            • CallingName Presentation = Default
            • Calling Party Number = +14153586101
    ConnectedParty Transformations
    Called Party Transformations
            • Called Party Mask =
            • Discard Digits Instruction = PreDot
            • Prefix = +
            • Called Number = +14155551234
```

Firstly, we are presented with a translation pattern that matches the dialed digits from the analysis. Remember how call routing works; the partition that contains this translation pattern is included in the Calling Search Space for the device.

The import bit to note is the final **Called Party Transformations | Called Number**; this number is used to continue call routing.

Translation patterns have their own calling search spaces. After the dialed number has been modified, call routing will resume using the calling search space of the translation pattern and NOT of the originating device.

Route Pattern :Pattern= \+.!
- **Positional Match List** = 14155551234
- **DialPlan** =
- **Route Filter**
  - **Filter Name** =
  - **Filter Clause** =
- **Require Forced Authorization Code** = No
- **Authorization Level** = 0
- **Require Client Matter Code** = No
- **Call Classification** =
- **PreTransform Calling Party Number** = +14153586101
- **PreTransform Called Party Number** = +14155551234
- **Calling Party Transformations**
  - **External Phone Number Mask** = NO
  - **Calling Party Mask** =
  - **Prefix** =
  - **CallingLineId Presentation** = Default
  - **CallingName Presentation** = Default
  - **Calling Party Number** = +14153586101
- **ConnectedParty Transformations**
  - **ConnectedLineId Presentation** = Default
  - **ConnectedName Presentation** = Default
- **Called Party Transformations**
  - **Called Party Mask** =
  - **Discard Digits Instruction** = PreDot
  - **Prefix** = +
  - **Called Number** = +14155551234

Chapter 4

In the previous screenshot, we see the Route Pattern **\+.!** is matched. We can see the calling party and called party information that will be sent to the device specified by this route pattern.

- **Route List :Route List Name**= RL-Local Route Group
    - **RouteGroup :RouteGroup Name**= Standard Local Route Group
        - **PreTransform Calling Party Number** = +14153586101
        - **PreTransform Called Party Number** = +14155551234
        - **Calling Party Transformations**
            - **External Phone Number Mask** = Default
            - **Calling Party Mask** =
            - **Prefix** =
            - **Calling Party Number** =
        - **Called Party Transformations**
            - **Called Party Mask** =
            - **Discard Digits Instructions** =
            - **Prefix** =
            - **Called Number** =

Finally, the call is sent to a route list, **RL-Local Route Group**. This route list is the device specified on the route pattern previously matched. If there were to be any modifications before sending the call to its final destination they would be listed here.

The Dialed Number Analyzer is a powerful utility for troubleshooting dial plans; be sure to check out the official guide for more in-depth information.

5
Device and Unified Mobility

In this chapter, we will cover:

- Configuring physical locations
- Configuring device mobility groups
- Configuring device pools for device mobility
- Configuring device mobility info
- Enabling device mobility
- Configuring mid-call feature access codes
- Configuring Session Handoff
- Enabling Intelligent Session Control
- Implementing mobility access lists
- Configuring remote destination profiles
- Configuring remote destinations
- Implementing Mobile Voice Access
- Enabling Enterprise Feature Access
- Adding the Mobility softkey

Device and Unified Mobility

Introduction

In this chapter, we focus on device and unified mobility features and functionality. We will cover configuring device mobility and what it entails for the users. Additionally, we will cover implanting Single Number Reach, an often-requested feature.

Configuring physical locations

Physical locations are a component of device mobility and are one of the factors used when determining if a device is roaming.

Getting ready

Have a list of the locations for each site and create them accordingly.

How to do it...

To configure physical locations, perform the following:

1. Navigate to the physical location configuration page (**System | Physical Location**).
2. Click on **Add New** to create a new physical location.
3. Specify the **Name**.
4. Specify a **Description** if desired:

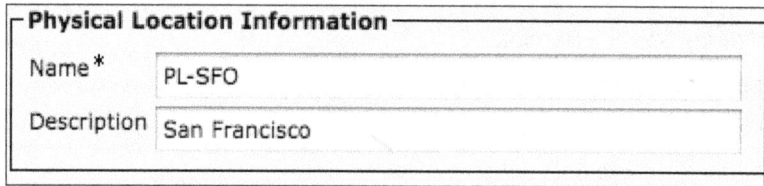

5. Click on **Save**.

Repeat this process for each physical location to be created.

How it works...

Using physical locations, the Unified Communications Manager can determine when a phone is roaming. Physical location affects settings such as date/time.

Chapter 5

Configuring device mobility groups

Device mobility groups are another component of device mobility. They identify locations that are geographically separate but share a common dial plan.

Getting ready

Prepare a list of the device mobility groups to be created, typically one for each country.

How to do it...

To configure a device mobility group, perform the following:

1. First navigate to the device mobility group configuration page (**System | Device Mobility | Device Mobility Group**).
2. Click on **Add New** to create a new device mobility group.
3. Specify a **Name**.
4. Specify a **Description** if desired:

Device Mobility Group Information	
Name*	DMG-US
Description	Device Mobility Group for the US

5. Click on **Save**.

How it works...

Depending on the size and configuration of the system, device mobility groups may not be necessary. They are not required for device mobility to function; instead they serve to logically define locations with a common dial plan.

Configure device pools for device mobility

Once all the physical locations and device mobility groups, if any, have been created, they must be applied to their respective device pools so that they may be used for device mobility.

Device and Unified Mobility

Getting ready

This recipe assumes the physical location and device mobility groups have been created.

How to do it...

To update device pools with device mobility specific information, perform the following:

1. First navigate to the device pool configuration page (**System | Device Pool**).
2. Locate the Device Pool to which the settings will be applied.
3. Scroll down to the section titled **Roaming Sensitive Settings**.
4. Specify the **Physical Location**.
5. Specify the **Device Mobility Group**:

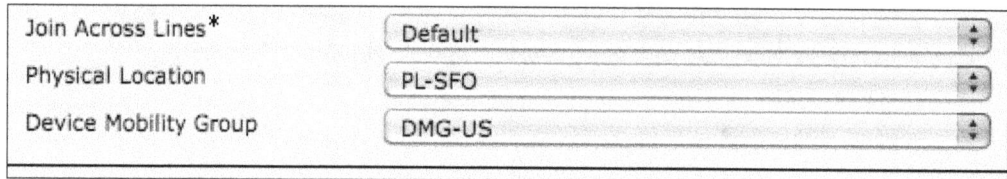

6. Click on **Save**.

Repeat this process for each device mobility enabled device pool.

 Apply Config for the changes to take effect.

How it works...

The Unified Communications Manager uses the device pool information to compare the physical location of the roaming device against the roaming device pool. If they do not match, roaming specific settings will be applied.

Configuring device mobility info

Device mobility info settings specify which subnet belongs to which device pool and is another component of device mobility.

Getting ready

Before creating the device mobility info, it is helpful to have a list of subnets and their masks handy.

How to do it...

To configure subnets for device mobility, perform the following:

1. First navigate to the device mobility info configuration page (**System | Device Mobility | Device Mobility Info**).
2. Click on **Add New** to add a new device mobility info subnet.
3. Specify a **Name**.
4. Specify the **Subnet**.
5. Specify the **Subnet Mask**.
6. Move all the appropriate device pools to the **Selected Device Pools** box:

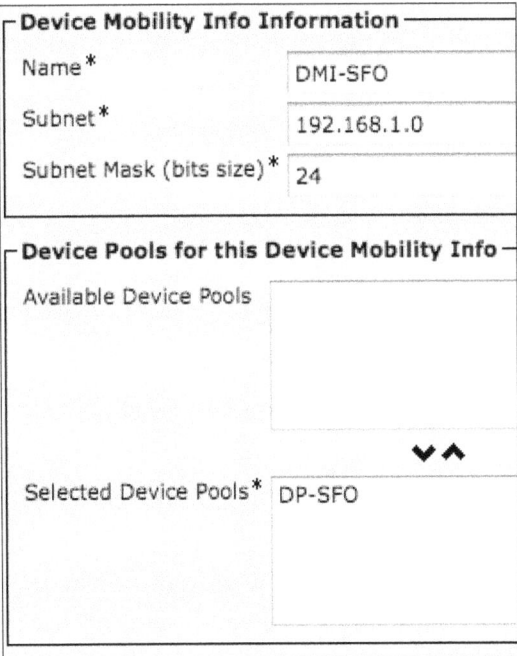

7. Click on **Save**.

How it works...

Device mobility uses the subnet information from device mobility info to find the appropriate device pool to assign the device. If the device pool is different from that configured on the device, roaming settings will be applied.

Enabling device mobility

Device mobility allows the Unified Communications Manager to determine when a phone device is roaming outside its home location, allowing the device to make certain configuration changes to mitigate call routing issues.

There are two ways of enabling device mobility. We will take a look at them in detail.

How to do it...

A service parameter can be used to enable device mobility server wide. This may be achieved by performing the following:

1. First navigate to the service parameters page (**System | Service Parameters**).
2. Select the appropriate server from the **Server** drop-down.
3. Select the **Cisco CallManager** as the **Service**.
4. Scroll down to the section titled **Clusterwide Parameters (Device – Phone)**.
5. From the **Device Mobility Mode** drop-down select **On**:

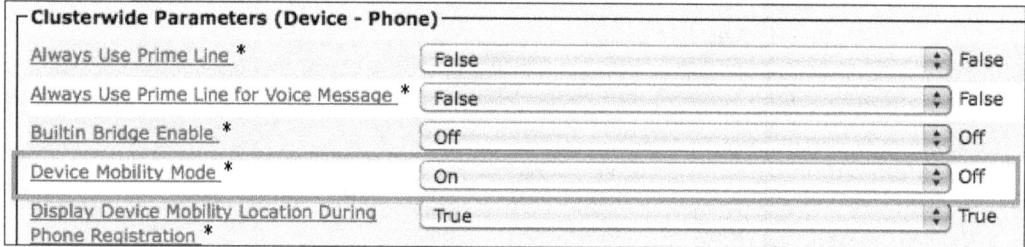

6. Click on **Save**.

Device mobility can be enabled on a per device basis via the phones configuration page; this is achieved by performing the following:

1. First navigate to the phone configuration page (**Device | Phone**).
2. Locate the device on which we are enabling device mobility.

Chapter 5

3. Under the section **Device Information**, find the **Device Mobility Mode** drop-down and select **On**:

Privacy*	Default
Device Mobility Mode*	On
Owner User ID	< None >

4. Click on **Save**.

 Apply Config for the changes to take effect.

How it works...

Device mobility allows the Unified Communications Manager to determine when a phone device is roaming outside its home location. This is determined by the IP subnet, which the phone acquires through DHCP.

When the Unified Communications Manager determines a phone is roaming and its device mobility mode is set to **On**, it instructs the phone to download a new configuration that overwrites the following fields with fields more appropriate to the location:

- **Date/Time Group**
- **Region**
- **Location**
- **SRST Reference**
- **Physical Location**
- **Device Mobility Group**
- **Media Resource Group List**

When roaming between geographic location with dissimilar dial plans, the roaming user can keep his dial plans and the phone will pick up new configuration information for the following fields:

- **Device Calling Search Space**
- **AAR Calling Search Space**
- **AAR Group**

Device and Unified Mobility

Configuring mid-call feature access codes

Mid-call features allow you to hold, transfer, and conference calls by using DTMF digit codes entered on the phone. In this recipe, we will show how to customize those codes and briefly explain how to use them.

Getting ready

If we are not going to use the predefined codes, it is helpful to have these documented and provided as part of end user training material.

How to do it...

To customize the DTMF mid-call feature codes, perform the following:

1. First navigate to the service parameters page (**System | Service Parameters**).
2. Select the appropriate server from the **Server** drop-down.
3. Select the **Cisco CallManager** as the **Service**.
4. Scroll down near the bottom to the section titled **Clusterwide Parameters (System – Mobility)**.
5. Change the **Enterprise Feature Access Codes** as desired:

Clusterwide Parameters (System - Mobility)	
Enterprise Feature Access Code for Hold *	*81
Enterprise Feature Access Code for Exclusive Hold *	*82
Enterprise Feature Access Code for Resume *	*83
Enterprise Feature Access Code for Transfer *	*84
Enterprise Feature Access Code for Conference *	*85
Enterprise Feature Access Code for Session Handoff *	*69

6. Click on **Save**.

[ Feature Access Codes must be unique numbers.]

How it works...

The mid-call features are invoked on the remote end by entering the DTMF patterns as specified in the service parameters. When the remote phone enters the pattern, the Unified Communications Manager will invoke the appropriate feature such as hold, transfer, and so on. The user will then perform the appropriate feature actions, such as resuming a call.

The features for hold and resume work rather simply. The user hits the code to hold, and once again to resume. For Session Handoff, the user hits the code and the desk phone will begin to ring. Once answered, the call will disconnect from the remote device. For transfer and conference, it is best to refer to the documentation as the procedure is a bit more involved.

Not all phones support feature buttons, notably analog devices. Analog devices can instead use custom codes configurable in service parameters.

Configuring Session Handoff

The Session Handoff feature allows users to move a call between desk phone, soft phone, and mobile phones all the while allowing the user to continue the conversation until the other end is picked up.

Configuring Session Handoff requires configuration of two service parameters detailed as follows.

How to do it...

To configure Session Handoff, perform the following:

1. First navigate to the service parameters page (**System | Service Parameters**).
2. Select the appropriate server from the **Server** drop-down.
3. Select **Cisco CallManager** as the **Service**.
4. Scroll down to the section titled **Clusterwide Parameters (Device – General)**.
5. Change the **Session Handoff Alerting Timer**.
6. Finally, scroll down near the bottom to the section titled **Clusterwide Parameters (System – Mobility)**.
7. Configure **Enterprise Feature Access Code for Session Handoff**.
8. Click on **Save**.

Device and Unified Mobility

How it works...

The Feature Access Code specifies the code that needs to be entered to hand a call off to the desk phone. The Session Handoff Alerting Timer specifies how long the phone will ring before waiting to be answered. It is important to note that this value must be greater than the value of the Forward No Answer Timer and Auto Answer Timer parameters. If not, the call does not get forwarded or auto-answered.

Enabling Intelligent Session Control

Intelligent Session Control anchors the call so that when DTMF commands are received, the Unified Communications Manager may perform call control functions such as hold, transfer, and so on.

How to do it...

To enable Intelligent Session Control features, perform the following:

1. First navigate to the service parameters page (**System | Service Parameters**).
2. Select the appropriate server from the **Server** drop-down.
3. Select **Cisco CallManager** as the **Service**.
4. Scroll down to the section titled **Clusterwide Parameters (Feature -- Reroute Remote Destination Calls to Enterprise Number)**.
5. Change **Reroute Remote Destination Calls to Enterprise Number** to **True**:

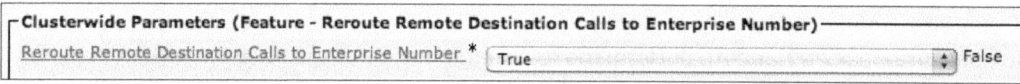

6. Go to the section titled **Clusterwide Parameters (System - Mobility)**.
7. Change **Matching Caller ID with Remote Destination** to **Partial Match**.
8. Change **Number of Digits for Caller ID Partial Match** as necessary:

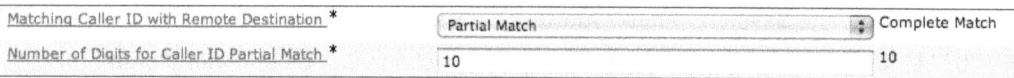

9. Click on **Save**.

How it works...

By setting **Matching Caller ID with Remote Destination** to **Partial Match,** we inform the UCM how many digits to match. If they match a remote destination for the user, the call will be routed to that number.

Be aware that some settings are ignored when the call is rerouted, such as Do Not Disturb, Time-of-day filtering, and Access List.

For E.164 deployments, Partial Match may not be necessary as the number programmed can be programmed in E.164 format, which is strictly dial-able. For these deployments, Complete Match is recommended.

There's more...

Many line settings are ignored when a call is rerouted. To honor the Call Forward All settings of the line, we must change the service parameter **Ignore Call Forward All on Enterprise DN** to **False**. Doing so will prevent calls to be rerouted to the remote destinations if the line has Call Forward All settings configured.

Implementing mobility access lists

As the name may imply, mobility access lists allow us to filter which calls are allowed to be presented to a user configured for mobility.

Getting ready

This recipe assumes previous mobility related configuration has been completed.

How to do it...

To create a new mobility access list, perform the following:

1. First navigate to the access list configuration page (**Call Routing | Class of Control | Access List**).
2. Click on **Add New** to add a new access list.
3. Specify a **Name**.
4. Specify a **Description** if desired.
5. Specify the **Owner**. These rules will apply to the selected user only.

Device and Unified Mobility

6. Specify **Allowed** or **Blocked** as appropriate:

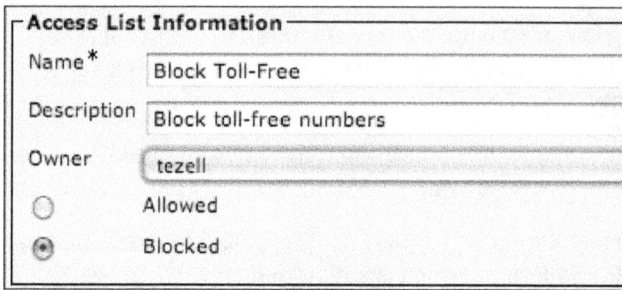

7. Click on **Save**.
8. After the page refreshes, we are presented with the option to add filters.
9. Click on **Add Member**.
10. Select a **Filter Mask** from the drop-down menu.
11. If necessary, specify a **DN Mask**:

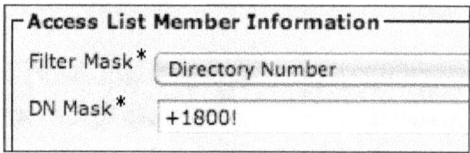

12. Click on **Save**.

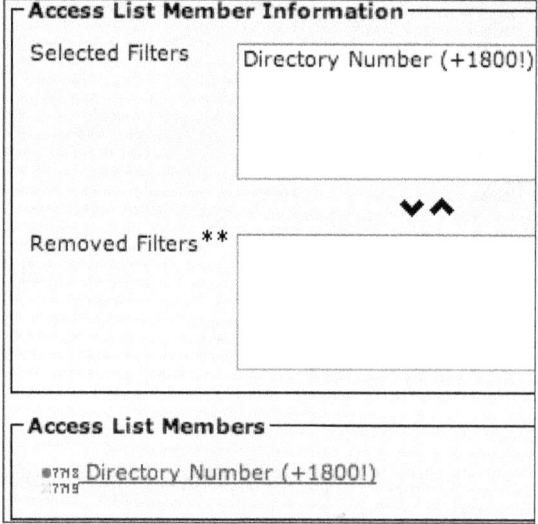

Repeat this process for each required filter.

Chapter 5

How it works...

As a call destined for a mobility configured user hits the system, Unified Communications Manager will check the caller ID against any configured access lists. If the number matches any of the filters, which may be Directory Number, Not Available or Private, they function as follows:

- **Directory Number**: This will attempt to match the DN Mask to the caller ID.
- **Not Available**: Caller ID information is not received.
- **Private**: A number that may be blocked or allowed. Does not present Caller ID information.

With these settings and configurations it is possible to filter out which callers will be rerouted to a mobility user.

 Don't repeat work unnecessarily! Copy common access lists instead of recreating them manually to save time.

Configuring remote destination profiles

Remote destination profiles specify the call routing information to be used. Of particular note here is the rerouting calling search space field.

Getting ready

This recipe assumes the end user already exists in the system.

How to do it...

To create a remote destination profile, perform the following:

1. First navigate to the remote destination profile page (**Device | Device Settings | Remote Destination Profile**).
2. Click on **Add New** to create a new remote destination profile.
3. Specify the **Name**.
4. Specify a **Description** if desired.
5. Select a user from the **User ID** drop-down.
6. Select a **Device Pool**.
7. Select a **Calling Search Space**.

Device and Unified Mobility

8. Select a **Rerouting Calling Search Space**.
9. Select a **Calling Party Transformation Calling Search Space**.
10. If using Calling Party Transformation Patterns, uncheck **Use Device Pool Calling Party Transformation CSS**:

Remote Destination Profile Information	
Name*	RDP-TEZELL
Description	Remote Destination Profile for Tanner Ezell
User ID*	tezell
Device Pool*	DP-SFO
Calling Search Space	CSS-SFO-Device
User Hold Audio Source	< None >
Network Hold MOH Audio Source	< None >
Privacy*	Default
Rerouting Calling Search Space	CSS-SFO-Device
Calling Party Transformation CSS	CSS-SFO-Inbound-ANI
☐ Use Device Pool Calling Party Transformation CSS	
User Locale	< None >
☐ Ignore Presentation Indicators (internal calls only)	

11. Click on **Save**.
12. After the page refreshes, configure a line directory number for the profile. This number must match the directory number and partition for the user.
13. Click on **Save**.

Repeat this process for each directory number associated to the user.

How it works...

The remote destination profile specifies important call routing settings, such as the Rerouting Calling Search Space. The profile also specifies on which extensions and partitions we will allow mobility calls to occur. As will be seen in the next recipe, remote destinations are associated to a directory number.

The **Rerouting Calling Search Space** field is important here. The number that is specified as the remote destination for a user must match a pattern in a partition that is accessible to this calling search space. The call will otherwise be denied. For most cases it is acceptable to use the general calling search space as depicted in the previous screenshot.

Configuring remote destinations

As the name suggests, remote destinations pertain to where we want to route calls for mobility users; commonly, this is a mobile number.

Getting ready

This recipe assumes the remote destination profile has already been created.

How to do it...

To configure a remote destination, perform the following:

1. First, navigate to the remote destination page (**Device | Remote Destination**).
2. Click on **Add New** to add a new remote destination.
3. Specify a **Name** to identify this remote destination.
4. Specify a **Destination Number**.
5. Adjust the **Answer Too Soon Timer** if necessary.
6. Adjust the **Answer Too Late Timer** if necessary.
7. Adjust the **Delay Before Ringing Timer** if necessary.
8. Select the **Remote Destination Profile**.
9. Check **Mobile Phone**.

10. Check **Enable Mobile Connect**:

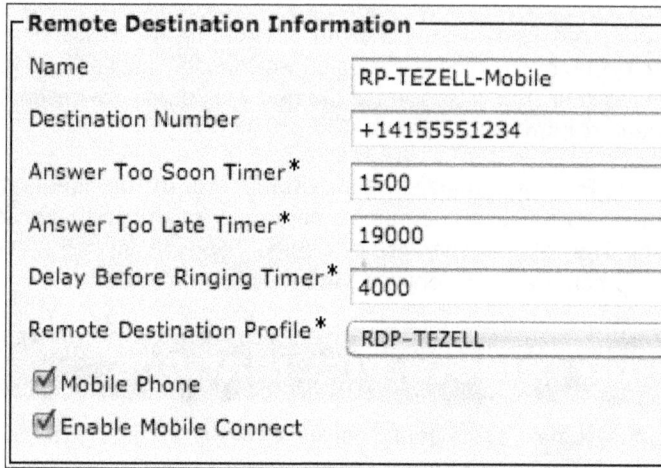

11. Program the schedule as desired, during which this remote destination will be active. This is accomplished by selecting the day(s) and specifying the office hours. Alternatively we may check **All Day** to enable it for the entire day. Don't forget to specify a **Time Zone**:

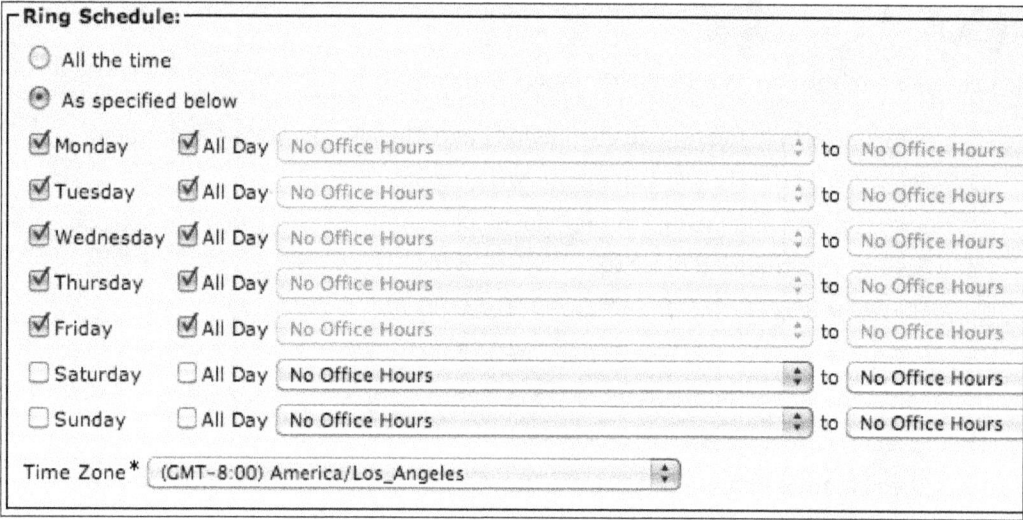

12. If an access list is desired, it may be applied by selecting one of the three options under the section **When receiving a call during the above ring schedule**:

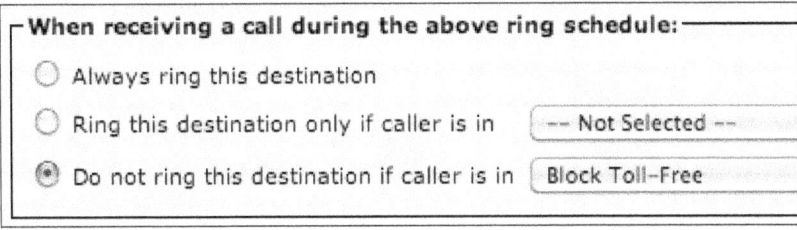

13. Click on **Save**.
14. After the page reloads, the lines from the remote destination profile will show.
15. Check **Line Association** for each line with which we desire this remote destination to be associated:

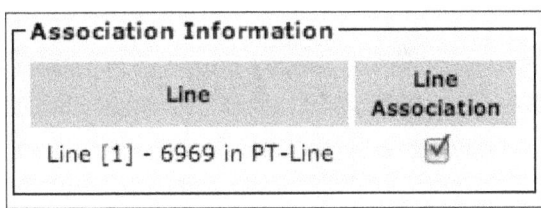

16. Click on **Save**.

How it works...

The remote destination specifies a destination number, a schedule, and an access list to follow. Each remote destination is associated with one or more directory numbers. These directory numbers, along with call routing information, are configured in remote destination profiles.

When a caller rings a number associated with a remote destination, once the timers have been met (and assuming the call is permitted through the schedule and any access lists) the call will be routed to the destination number. This number must be formatted so it may reach its destination. For example, if a 9 is required to reach the outside, the 9 must be placed in front of the number. In effect, the user must be able to dial the number as it would be dialed from a phone with similar call routing settings.

Device and Unified Mobility

There's more...

There are quite a few timers and check boxes for remote destinations. For reference, I have included a brief description of each as follows:

- **Answer Too Soon Timer**: The minimum time in milliseconds required by a caller to ring the destination before it is answered
- **Answer Too Late Timer**: The maximum time in milliseconds Unified Communication Manager will ring the destination number
- **Delay Before Ringing Timer**: The delay before routing the call to the remote destination
- **Mobile Phone**: If **Send Call to Mobile Phone** is specified, this remote destination will be used as the destination
- **Enable Mobile Connect**: Allows an incoming call to ring the remote destination and desk phone at the same time

Implementing Mobile Voice Access

Mobile Voice Access is a technology that allows users to dial numbers as if they were dialing from their desk phone.

Getting ready

This recipe assumes an H323 or SIP gateway is already configured on the system.

Before we can use Mobile Voice Access, it must first be enabled via Service Parameters (**System | Service Parameters**).

Enable Enterprise Feature Access and **Enable Mobile Voice Access** must be set to **True**. We must also set the **Mobile Voice Access Number** as appropriate:

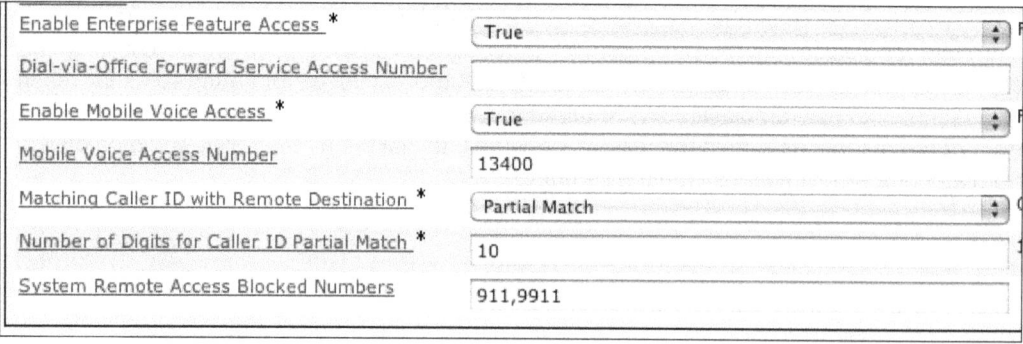

Chapter 5

How to do it...

There are various components for making Mobile Voice Access work; we will go through them one by one:

1. First we must configure the Mobile Voice Access directory number (**Media Resources | Mobile Voice Access**).
2. Click on **Add New**.
3. Specify the **Mobile Voice Access Directory Number**.

   >  This must be the same as the **Mobile Voice Access Number** as configured in the Service Parameters!

4. Specify the **Mobile Voice Access Partition**.
5. Under **Mobile Voice Access Localization,** select the desired locales:

   Mobile Voice Access Information
   Mobile Voice Access Directory Number* 13400
   Mobile Voice Access Partition PT-System

   Mobile Voice Access Localization
   Available Locales
   Selected Locales* English United States

6. Click on **Save**.

Next we can configure the gateway:

1. Load the Voice XML script to the gateway by issuing the following commands:
    ```
    application service CCM
    http://192.168.1.5:8080/ccmivr/pages/IVRMainpage.vxml
    ```

     If the IOS version is prior to 12.3(13), the command should be **call application voice Unified CCM**

2. Configure an H323 dial-peer for the Mobile Voice Access script:
    ```
    dial-peer voice 200 voip
    service CCM
    incoming-called number 13400
    destination-pattern 13400
    session target ipv4:192.168.1.5
    codec g711ulaw
    dtmf-relay h245-alphanumeric
    novad
    ```

3. Alternatively, when using an SIP gateway for Mobile Voice Access, configure the dial-peer. Sample configuration for SIP gateway VoIP dial-peer is as follows:
    ```
    dial-peer voice 200voip
    service CCM
    destination-pattern 13400
    rtp payload-type nse 99
    session protocol sipv2
    session target ipv4:192.168.1.5
    incoming called-number .T
    dtmf-relay rtp-nte
    codec g711ulaw
    ```

     If the IOS version is prior to 12.3(13), the command should be application CCM and not service CCM.

     When a call is placed from an internal extension, the system presents only the internal extension as the caller ID. If an H.323 or SIP gateway is used we can use translation patterns to address this issue.

4. If desired, enable hairpinning on the gateway:

   ```
   voice service voip
   allow-connections h323 to h323
   allow-connections sip to sip
   ```

How it works...

Mobile Voice Access uses a Voice XML script on a gateway. When the gateway receives a call on the Mobile Voice Access directory number, it references the service we created on the gateway called CCM. The script communicates with the Unified Communications Manager to identify users and authenticate if necessary, along with various other services.

When Mobile Voice Access is called, the system will prompt the user for the phone number and PIN, if any of the following are true:

- The number from which the user is calling is not one of the remote destinations for the user
- The user or the carrier for the user blocks caller ID (Unknown Number)
- The number does not get matched by the Unified Communications Manager
- Hairpinning is configured for Mobile Voice Access

> When Mobile Voice Access is configured to use hairpinning, users do not get identified automatically by their caller ID. Instead, users must manually enter their remote destination number prior to entering their PIN number.

> While using hairpinning, be advised that the telecom provider may charge additional fees for the service or block it outright.

See also

The Solution Reference Network Design guide for Unified Communications provides a great deal of valuable information relating to Mobile Voice Access and Unified Mobility. To get a more in-depth knowledge of how this feature works I recommend reading the relevant sections (http://www.cisco.com/en/US/docs/voice_ip_comm/cucm/srnd/8x/mobilapp.html).

Device and Unified Mobility

Enabling Enterprise Feature Access

Enterprise Feature Access relies on matching the caller ID to a remote destination profile, unlike Mobile Voice Access, which will allow the user to authenticate to make a call.

Getting ready

This recipe assumes the gateway dial-peers have been configured as per the previous recipe as well as the service parameters **Enable Enterprise Feature Access** and **Enable Mobile Voice Access** have been set to **True**.

How to do it...

To enable Enterprise Feature Access, perform the following:

1. First, navigate to the Enterprise Feature Access Number configuration page (**Call Routing | Mobility | Enterprise Feature Access Number Configuration**).
2. Click on **Add New**.
3. Specify the **Number** that will activate the service.
4. Specify the **Route Partition**. If desired, we can make this the default number:

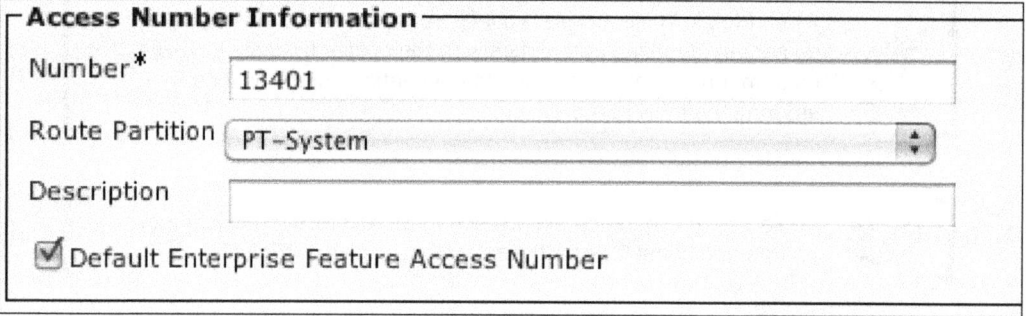

5. Click on **Save**.

How it works...

Enterprise Feature Access relies on much the same configuration as Mobile Voice Access, and is fundamentally the same. In this recipe we simply specify the number used to activate this service.

Chapter 5

Adding the Mobility softkey

To use the Mobility feature we must have access to the *Mobility* softkey, which may not be part of the user's softkey template.

How to do it...

To add the *Mobility* softkey, perform the following:

1. First navigate to the softkey template configuration page (**Device | Device Settings | Softkey Template**).
2. Create a new template or modify an existing user-created template.
3. Select **Configure Softkey Layout** from **Related Links** and click on **Go**.
4. From the **Select a call state to configure** drop-down, select **On Hook**.
5. Move the *Mobility* softkey from the left to the right, and place it in the desired order.

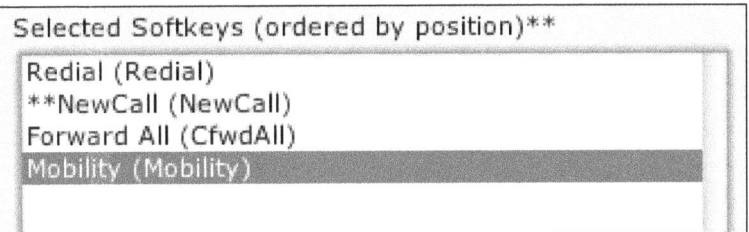

6. Click on **Save**.
7. Repeat steps 4 to 6 for the connected call state as shown in the following screenshot:

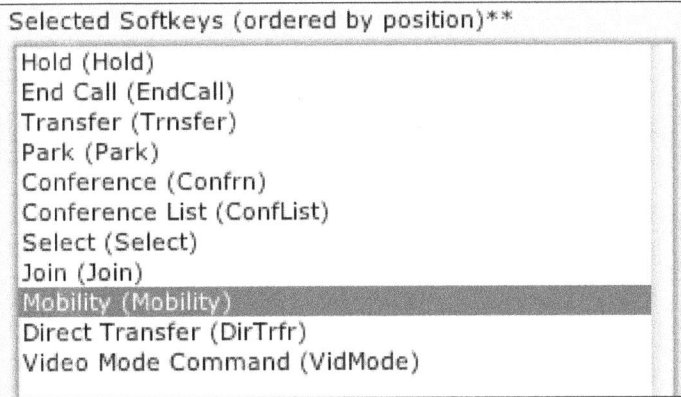

8. Reset the affected devices for the changes to take effect.

123

Device and Unified Mobility

How it works...

Quite simply, in order to use Mobility, the user must have a softkey template configured with the *Mobility* softkey. This allows a user to answer a call on either a desk phone or cell phone and seamlessly transfer the call between each device with the click of the softkey.

6
User Management

In this chapter, we will cover:

- Enabling LDAP synchronization
- Configuring an LDAP Directory
- Enabling LDAP authentication
- Configuring custom LDAP filters
- Configuring credential policies
- Configuring default credential policies
- Assigning credential policies
- Configuring user roles
- Configuring user groups
- Assigning user groups to end users

Introduction

Users are our primary customers. We want to provide the best, the most seamless experience for them. At the same time, we want to try and limit the amount of work required to get users on the system. To that end we can sync directly with Active Directory or any LDAP server.

Once we have our users on the system, we often need to provide some of them with higher levels of access to the system as compared to the others. We will attempt to address these problems in this chapter.

User Management

Enabling LDAP synchronization

End user synchronization with active directory is a very effective way of importing end users, as well as information from their accounts such as their telephone information, location, and so on into the system.

How to do it...

To enable synchronization with active directory, perform the following:

1. First navigate to the LDAP System page (**System | LDAP | LDAP System**).
2. Check the box titled **Enable Synchronization from LDAP Server**.
3. From the **LDAP Server Type** drop-down, select the appropriate type for the environment.
4. From the **LDAP Attribute for User ID** drop-down, choose the appropriate attribute that will import as the end user ID:

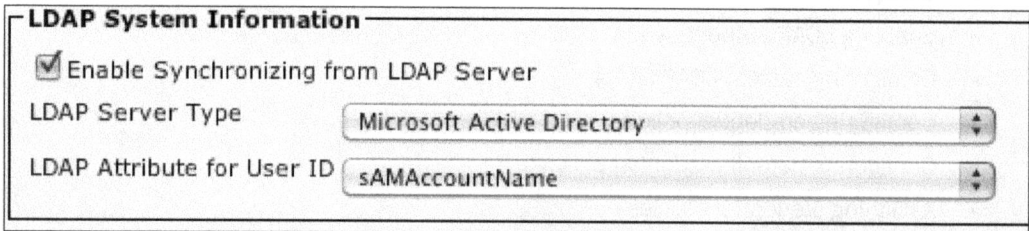

5. Click on **Save**.

How it works...

The checkbox must be set to enable LDAP synchronization on the Unified Communications Manager. Without this, users will not be synchronized with the system.

Configuring an LDAP Directory

The LDAP Directory specifies where the Unified Communications Manager will pull user information from. We may use filters for greater granularity in what is imported.

Getting ready

This recipe assumes LDAP synchronization has been enabled.

How to do it...

To add a new LDAP Directory to synchronize with, perform the following:

1. First navigate to the LDAP Directory page (**System | LDAP | LDAP Directory**).
2. Click on **Add New.**
3. Specify a **LDAP Configuration Name**.
4. Specify the **LDAP Manager Distinguished Name**.

 This active directory user must have access rights to the LDAP Directory.

5. Specify the **LDAP Password** for the user.
6. Specify the **LDAP User Search Base**.

 This can be quite complex depending on the organization. Consult the person who manages the corporate active directory to ensure the search base will meet our needs.

7. If a filter is desired, select one from the **LDAP Custom Filter** drop-down:

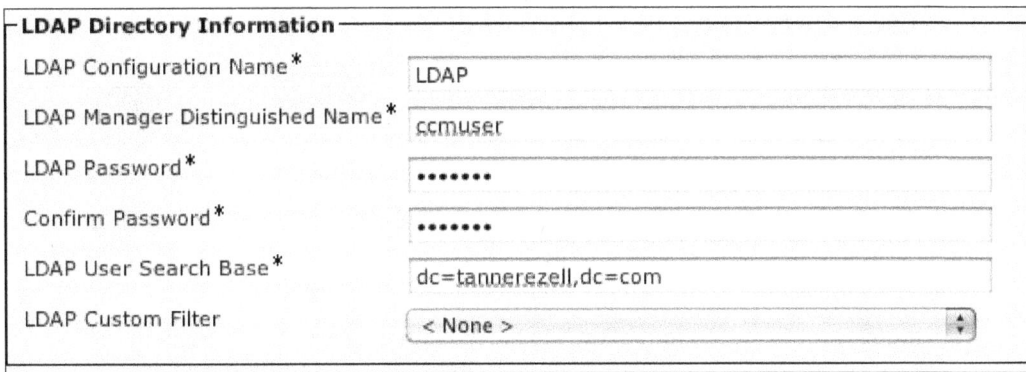

 The `ccmuser` here is an active directory user with permissions to read in the Organizational Unit specified by the LDAP User Search Base field. It is important to note this is not a user on the UCM itself.

8. Configure the schedule for LDAP synchronization under the **LDAP Directory Synchronization Schedule** section.
9. To synchronize only once, check **Perform Sync Just Once**.

User Management

10. Specify the interval desired for resynchronization. The next synchronization period will be calculated for us automatically:

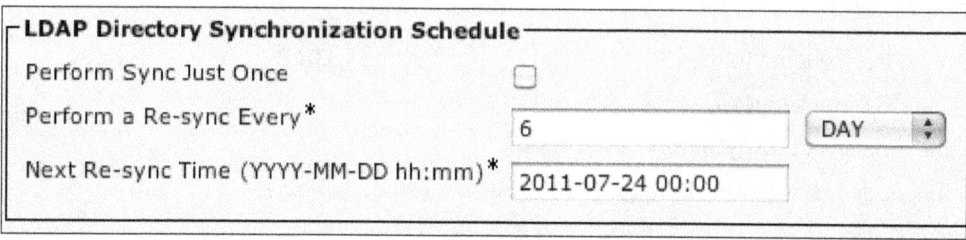

11. Under the section **User Fields to Be Synchronized,** change any fields as appropriate for the environment.
12. Specify the **Host Name or IP Address for Server**.
13. Specify the **LDAP Port**.

 Domain controllers typically use port 389.
Global catalog servers typically use port 3268.

14. Check **Use SSL** if desired.

    For additional servers click on **Add Another Redundant LDAP Server** and repeat steps 12 to 14:

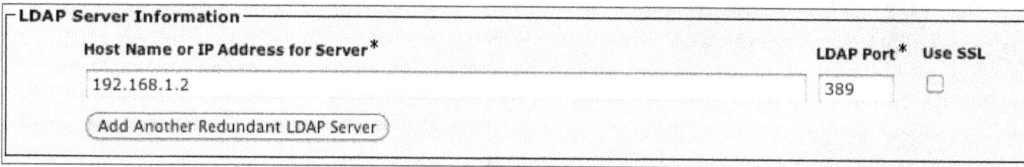

15. Click on **Save**.

    Assuming the correct information has been entered, users should begin to be synchronized. This can be confirmed by checking the **End User** section.
    (**User Management | End User**)

How it works...

The user specified under **LDAP Manager Distinguished Name** in step 4 is used by the Unified Communications Manager to query information from the LDAP Server based on the LDAP User Search Base provided. Additionally, if a filter is supplied, the user imported must meet the filter criteria before being added to the database.

Users will be synchronized depending on the schedule specified. The Unified Communications Manager will only reflect users that are added or removed after synchronization.

The search base is particularly important and can be quite complex in some circumstances. It is recommended that the search base is provided by someone familiar with the corporate active directory.

Enabling LDAP authentication

While not necessary, LDAP authentication does provide a more seamless user experience and can allow users to use their active directory passwords when logging into the administration or user interfaces.

Getting ready

This recipe assumes LDAP synchronization is already enabled, configured, and end users have been imported.

How to do it...

To configure LDAP authentication perform the following:

1. First, navigate to the LDAP authentication page (**System | LDAP | LDAP Authentication**).
2. Check **Use LDAP Authentication for End Users**.
3. Specify the **LDAP Manager Distinguished Name**.

>  This active directory user must have access rights to the LDAP Directory.

4. Specify the **LDAP Password for the user**.
5. Specify the **LDAP User Search Base**.

User Management

6. Under **LDAP Server Information** configure the LDAP Servers to authenticate against.
7. Specify the **Host Name or IP Address for Server.**
8. Specify the **LDAP Port**.

> Domain controllers typically use port 389.
> Global catalog servers typically use port 3268.

9. Check **Use SSL** if desired.
10. For additional servers, click **Add Another Redundant LDAP Server** and repeat steps 7 to 9:

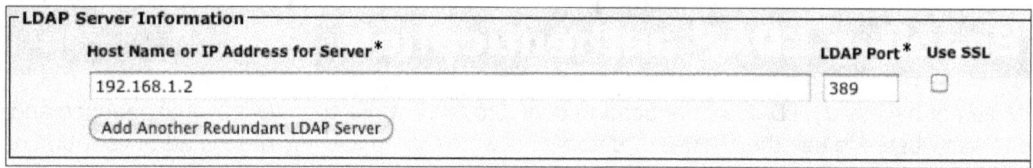

11. Click on **Save**.
12. Assuming no errors are encountered, it should now be possible to authenticate against the LDAP server.

How it works...

As with end user synchronization, the Unified Communications Manager will send authentication requests to the specified LDAP servers using the account specified under **LDAP Manager Distinguished Name**.

> The Unified Communications Manager itself does not store active directory passwords used when authenticating against LDAP. Instead it passes the password to the AD server for authentication.

Configuring custom LDAP filters

LDAP filters allow us to precisely define which user accounts we want imported into the Unified Communications Managers database.

How to do it...

To add a new LDAP filter, perform the following:

1. Navigate to the **LDAP Custom Filter** page (**System | LDAP | LDAP Custom Filter**).
2. Click on **Add New**.
3. Specify a meaningful **Filter Name**.
4. Specify the **Filter**. For this recipe I will use the filter (&(objectclass=user) (!(objectclass=Computer))(ipPhone=*)):

```
LDAP Custom Filter Information
Filter Name*   Users with ipPhone ONLY
Filter*        (&(objectclass=user)(!(objectclass=Computer))(ipPhon
```

5. Click on **Save**.

How it works...

When applied to an LDAP Directory, the filter will be used as the criteria for which user objects will be imported into the Unified Communication Managers database.

Here is a quick breakdown of the filter used in the recipe:

- **objectclass=user**: This specifies that the object must be of the User class
- **!(objectclass=Computer)**: This eliminates Computer objects from being imported.
- **ipPhone=***: Here we require the ipPhone field to have any value

User Management

There's more...

Don't forget to apply the filter to the appropriate LDAP Directory:

LDAP Custom Filter	Users with ipPhone ONLY

Configuring credential policies

By default, there is already a credential policy used by UCM. This should not be confused with the Default Credential Policies covered in the next recipe.

Credential policies allow us to specify granular settings such as lockout duration and number of failed login attempts.

How to do it...

To configure a credential policy, perform the following:

1. First navigate to the **Credential Policy** configuration page (**User Management | Credential Policy**).
2. Click on **Add New** to create a new credential policy.
3. Specify the **Display Name**.
4. Change any of the following fields as desired or required by corporate policies:
    - **Failed Logon**
    - **Reset Failed Logon Attempts Every (minutes)**
    - **Lockout Duration (minutes)**
    - **Minimum Duration Between Credential Changes**
    - **Credential Expires After (days)**
    - **Minimum Credential Length**
    - **Stored Number of Previous Credentials**
    - **Inactive Days Allowed**
    - **Expiry Warning Days**

5. Additionally, check any of the following boxes that apply:
   - **No Limit for Failed Logons**
   - **Administrator Must Unlock**
   - **Never Expires**
   - **Check for Trivial Passwords**

Credential Policy Information		
Display Name*	CP-SFO	
Failed Logon*	3	☐ No Limit for Failed Logons
Reset Failed Logon Attempts Every (minutes)*	30	
Lockout Duration (minutes)*	0	☑ Administrator Must Unlock
Minimum Duration Between Credential Changes (minutes)*	0	
Credential Expires After (days)*	180	☐ Never Expires
Minimum Credential Length*	8	
Stored Number of Previous Credentials*	12	
Inactive Days Allowed*	120	
Expiry Warning Days*	90	
☑ Check for Trivial Passwords		

6. Click on **Save**.

   Repeat steps 2 to 6 for each credential policy required.

   Don't forget, we can modify the default credential policy if desired.

Credential Policy Information		
Display Name*	Default Credential Policy	
Failed Logon*	4	☐ No Limit for Failed Logons
Reset Failed Logon Attempts Every (minutes)*	30	
Lockout Duration (minutes)*	30	☐ Administrator Must Unlock
Minimum Duration Between Credential Changes (minutes)*	0	
Credential Expires After (days)*	90	☐ Never Expires
Minimum Credential Length*	1	
Stored Number of Previous Credentials*	0	
Inactive Days Allowed*	0	
Expiry Warning Days*	0	
☑ Check for Trivial Passwords		

User Management

How it works...

Credential policies are applied to specific end users, enforcing upon those users the specific rules set out by the policy. While most rules are self-explanatory, a brief description of each is included for reference.

- **Failed Logon/No Limit for Failed Logons**: The number of allowed failed logon attempts. When this threshold is reached the system locks the account.
- **Reset Failed Logon Attempts Every**: The number of minutes before the counter is reset for failed logon attempts. After the counter resets, the user can try logging in again.
- **Lockout Duration/Administrator Must Unlock**: The number of minutes an account remains locked when the number of failed logon attempts exceeds the specified threshold.
- **Minimum Duration Between Credential Changes**: The number of minutes that are required before a user can change credentials again.
- **Credential Expires After/Never Expires**: The number of days before a credential will expire.
- **Minimum Credential Length**: The minimum length for user credentials (password or PIN).
- **Stored Number of Previous Credentials**: The number of previous user credentials to store. This setting prevents a user from configuring a recently used credential that is saved in the user list.
- **Inactive Days Allowed**: The number of days that a password can remain inactive before the account gets locked.
- **Expiry Warning Days**: The number of days to start warning notifications before a user password expires.

If you enable **Check for Trivial Passwords,** the following criteria are used to determine if a password or pin is deemed trivial.

Firstly, passwords can contain any alphanumeric ASCII character and all ASCII special characters. The password complexity must meet the following criteria:

- Must contain three of the four allowable characteristics, namely uppercase character, lowercase character, number, and symbol
- Must not use a character or number more than three times consecutively
- Must not repeat or include the alias, username, or extension
- Cannot consist of consecutive characters or numbers (for example, passwords such as 654321 or ABCDEFG)

Additionally, PINs can contain digits (0-9) only. A non-trivial PIN meets the following criteria:

- Must not use the same number more than two times consecutively
- Must not repeat or include the user extension or mailbox or the reverse of the user extension or mailbox
- Must contain three different numbers; for example, a PIN such as 121212 is trivial
- Must not match the numeric representation (that is, dial by name) for the first or last name of the user
- Must not contain groups of repeated digits, such as 408408, or patterns that are dialed in a straight line on a keypad, such as 2580, 159, or 753

Configuring default credential policies

Credential policies specify the defaults for passwords and PINs used by both end users and application users.

Getting ready

Although not necessary, if we are going to apply custom policy rules to the default policies, we will need to create them first as described in the previous recipe.

How to do it...

To configure the default PIN and Password for end users, perform the following:

1. First navigate to the **Credential Policy Default** page (**User Management | Credential Policy Default**).
2. There are three options to choose from. We will start with the first, that is, the password for end users.
3. Click on the appropriate link.

Credential Policy Default

Name	Credential User	Credential Type
Default Credential Policy	End User	Password
Default Credential Policy	Application User	Password
Default Credential Policy	End User	PIN

4. If desired, change the default password by entering the password into the **Change Credential** field, and once again in the **Confirm Credentials** field.

5. Specify the **Credential Policy**. The previous recipe describes creating and configuring the credential policies.

6. Select the desired options for this policy. A brief description of each field is provided in the next section:

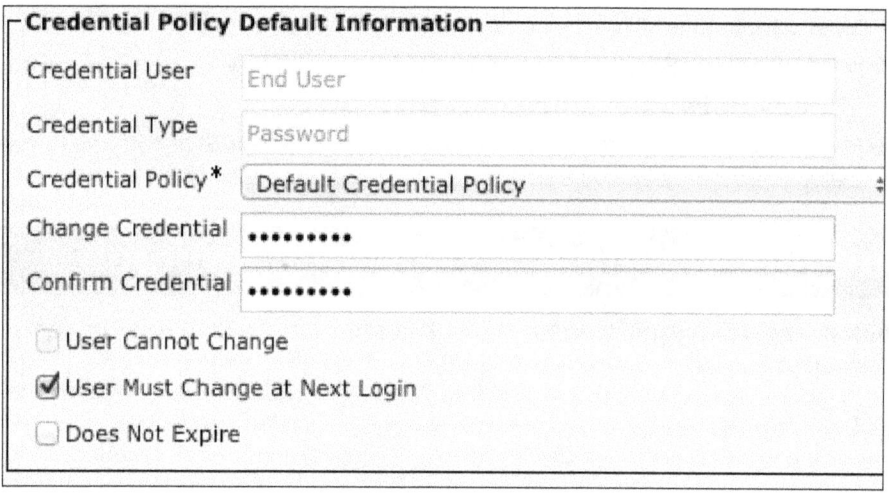

7. Click on **Save**.

Repeat steps 3 to 6 for each policy you wish to modify.

The default credential policy for end user PINs can be set as shown in the following screenshot:

The default credential policy for application users' passwords can be set as shown in the following screenshot:

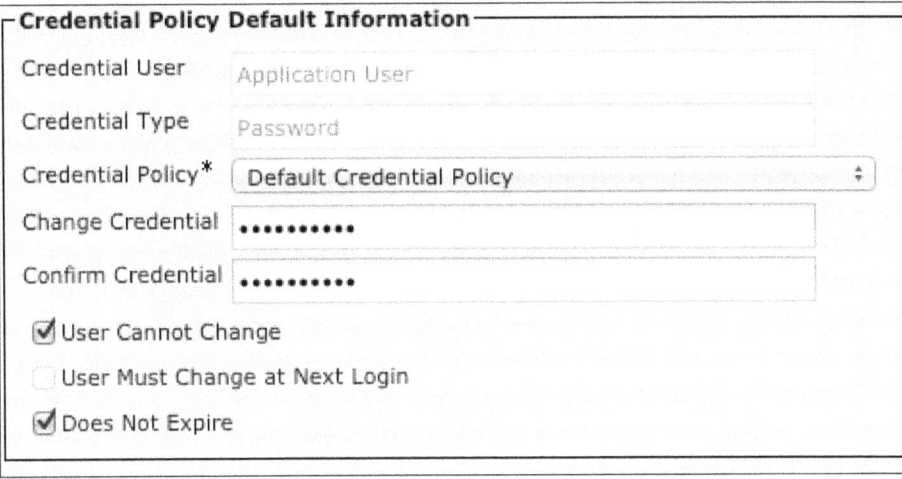

How it works...

The default credential policies set the default behavior for PINs and Passwords, and apply to all users by default.

 The default credential policy for end user passwords does not apply when the system is using LDAP authentication.

By changing the default credential, be it password or pin, any users who have not already changed their password will be required to log in using the new password and/or pin. Users may change their password and pin via the CCMUser web interface (http://192.168.1.5/ccmuser).

 192.168.1.5 is the IP address of the UCM used in the examples. Make sure to supply the appropriate IP to your environment.

While most fields are self-explanatory, a brief description is included for reference:

- **Credential Policy**: The default credential policy for this credential group.
- **Change Credential**: The new default credential for this group.
- **Confirm Credential**: For verification, re-enter the login credential that you entered in the **Change Credential** field.

User Management

- **User Cannot Change**: Checking this box blocks users that are assigned this policy from changing this credential.

You cannot check this checkbox when **User Must Change at Next Login** is checked. The default setting for this checkbox specifies unchecked.

- **User Must Change at Next Login**: Checking this box requires users that are assigned this policy to change this credential at next login. Use this option after you assign a temporary credential.

You cannot check this checkbox when the **User Cannot Change** checkbox is checked. The default setting for this checkbox specifies unchecked.

- **Does Not Expire**: Checking this box blocks the system from prompting the user to change this credential. You can use this option for low-security users or group accounts.

If this checkbox is checked, the user can still change this credential at any time. When this checkbox is unchecked, the expiration setting in the associated credential policy applies.

Assigning credential policies

Now that the credential policies are set up and in place, we can assign them to end users and application users, individually. Remember that whatever credential policy is assigned, the default will be applied as users are imported or created!

Getting ready

This recipe assumes the credential policies have been created as defined in the previous recipes.

Chapter 6

How to do it...

The procedure for assigning the credential policy is the same for both application users and end users. To assign a credential policy to a user, perform the following:

1. First, navigate to the end user or application user's configuration page (**User Management | End User** or **User Management | Application User**).
2. Find the user we will be modifying.
3. At the user's page we are presented with two **Edit Credential** buttons next to the **Password** and **PIN** fields. Click on the button appropriate to the field we are applying the credential rules to:

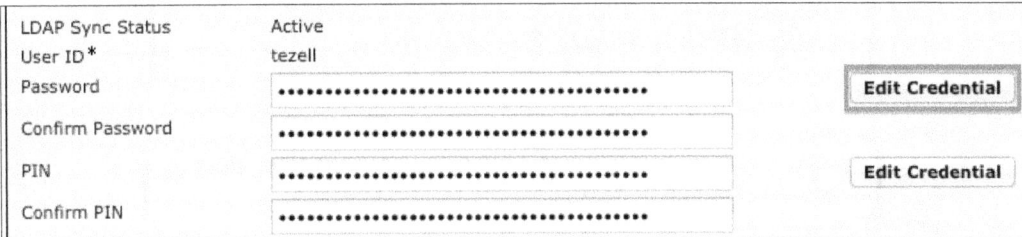

4. Now select the boxes that will apply to this user; a brief description of each will be provided in the next section.
5. Specify the **Authentication Rule**. This is the Credential Policy we created in an earlier recipe.

6. Click on **Save**.

User Management

How it works...

By setting the authentication rule to the user, the rules as specified by the Credential Policy will be enforced for the user.

While most fields are self-explanatory, the following is a brief description of each:

- **Locked By Administrator**: Checking this box locks the account and blocks user access.
- **User Cannot Change**: Checking this box blocks this user from changing the credential.

Use this option for group accounts.

You cannot check this checkbox when the **User Must Change at Next Login** checkbox is checked.

- **User Must Change at Next Login**: Checking this box requires the user to change the credential at next login.

Use this option after you assign a temporary credential.

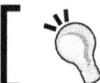
You cannot check this checkbox when the **User Cannot Change** checkbox is checked.

- **Does Not Expire**: Checking this box blocks the system from prompting the user to change the credential.

You can use this option for low-security users or group accounts.

If this checkbox is checked, the user can still change this credential at any time. When this checkbox is unchecked, the expiration setting in the associated credential policy applies.

You cannot uncheck this checkbox if the policy setting specifies **Never Expires**.

- **Reset Hack Count**: Checking this box resets the hack count for this user and clears the **Time Locked Due to Failed Login Attempts** field. After the counter resets, the user can try logging in again.

> The hack count increments whenever an authentication fails due to the submission of an incorrect credential.
>
> If the policy specifies **No Limit for Failed Logons**, the hack count always equals 0.

- **Authentication Rule**: The credential policy applicable to this user credential.
- **Time Last Changed**: This field displays the date and time of the most recent change for this user credential.
- **Failed Logon Attempts**: This field displays the number of failed logon attempts since the last successful logon.
- **Time of Last Field Logon Attempt**: This field displays the date and time for the most recent failed logon attempt for this user credential.
- **Time Locked by Administrator**: This field displays the date and time the administrator locked this user account.
- **Time Locked Due to Failed Logon Attempts**: This field displays the date and time the system last locked this user account due to failed logon attempts.

Configuring user roles

Roles define very specific access rights to various functions and features of the Unified Communications Manager. By creating custom roles, we can provide very granular access rights for application to users.

In most cases, it is unnecessary to create additional roles as many of the predefined are usually suitable.

How to do it...

To create a new role, perform the following:

1. First navigate to the roles configuration page (**User Management | Roles**).
2. Click on **Add New** to create a new role.

User Management

3. From the **Application** drop-down, select the appropriate application. Each application has different assignable permissions.

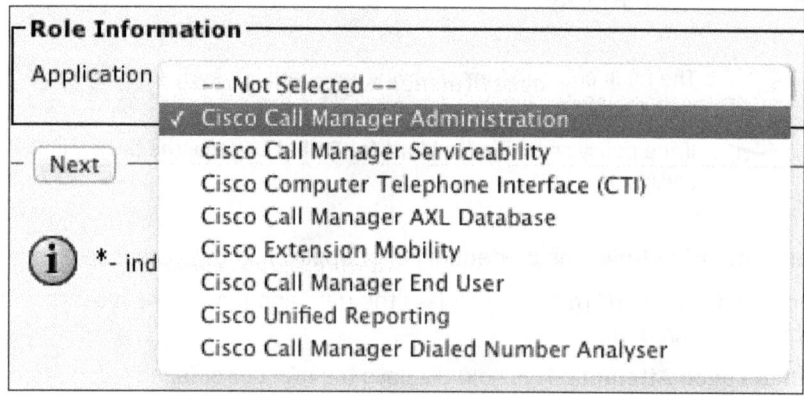

4. Specify a **Name**.
5. If desired, specify a **Description**.
6. Under **Resource Access Information,** select to either allow the ability to **read**, **update**, or both for each resource desired:

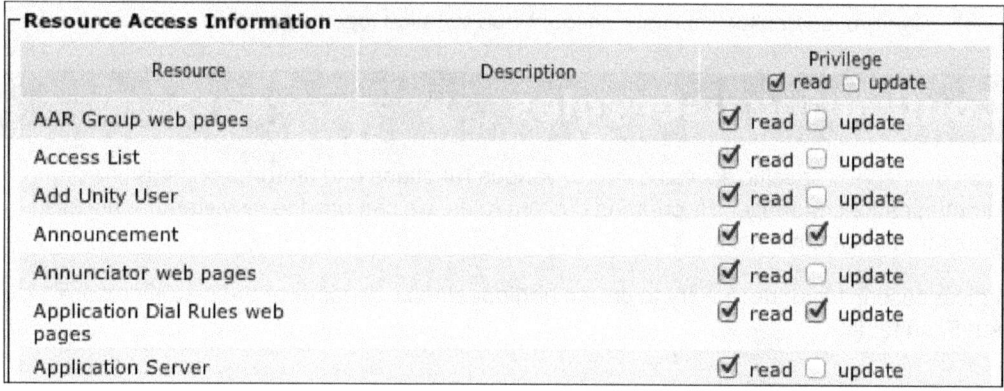

7. Click on **Save**.

How it works...

By specifying the ability to read or update per role we effectively begin to define very granular access rules. To apply a role to a user, we must add it first to a user group.

Chapter 6

Configuring user groups

User groups contain a set of specific roles that are accessible to the users assigned to the group. User groups allow us to specify certain users who may need levels of administrator access, for instance.

How to do it...

To create a new user group, perform the following:

1. First, navigate to the User Group configuration page (**User Management | User Group**).
2. Click on **Add New** to create a new user group.
3. Specify a **Name**:

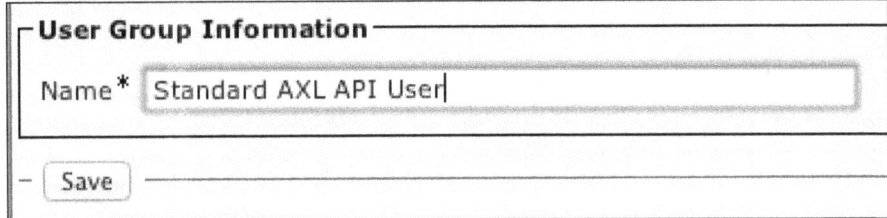

4. Click on **Save**.
5. After the page refreshes, from the **Related Links** drop-down in the upper right corner select **Assign Role to User Group**:

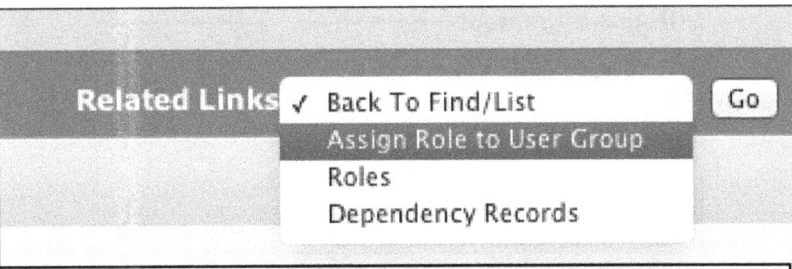

6. Click on **Go.**

User Management

7. Click on **Assign Role to Group**:

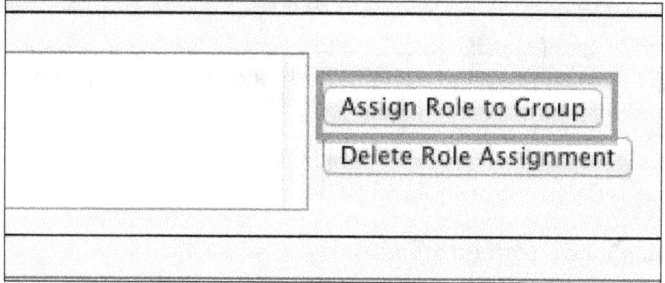

8. Check the box next to each role we are to assign to this **User Group**.

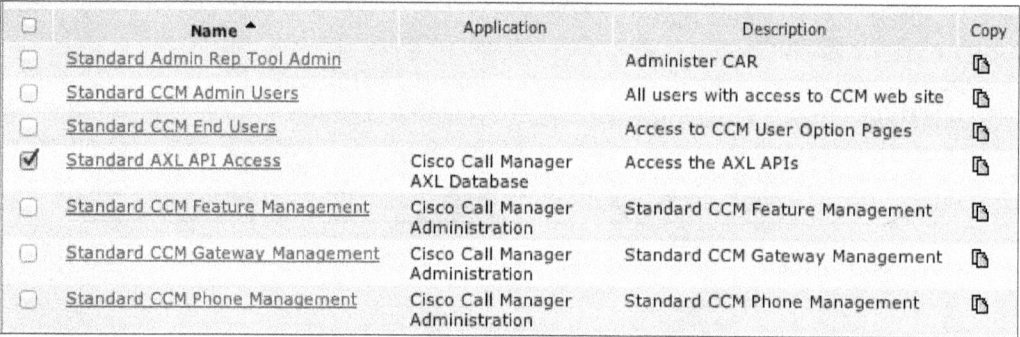

9. Click on **Add Selected**.
10. The selected role(s) will appear in the box titled **Role**:

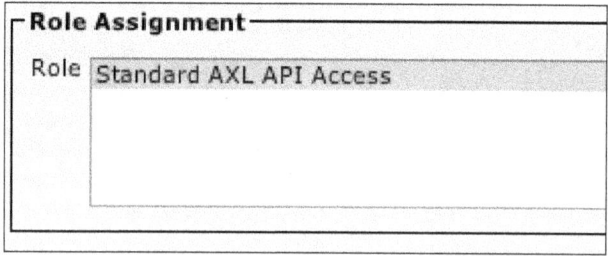

11. Click on **Save**.

The user group may now be assigned to end users and application users. For this particular recipe, I created a standard User Group that I use for assigning AXL permissions.

144

How it works...

By assigning a user group to a user, the roles and permissions of the roles that make up the User Group are enforced for the user they are assigned to.

Assigning user groups to end users

There are various different user groups we commonly assign to users, such as Standard CCM End User for users who need access to the ccmuser page, or Standard CTI Enabled for users using Unified Personal Communicator or WebEx connect.

Getting ready

This recipe assumes the necessary user groups are created and in place.

How to do it...

To assign a user group to an end user, perform the following:

1. First navigate to the End Users configuration page (**User Management | End User**).
2. Locate the end user and navigate through.
3. Scroll to the bottom of the page and click on **Add to User Group**:

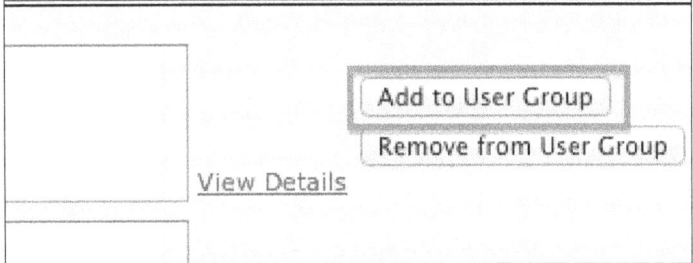

4. We then select the boxes next to each User Group we wish to add:

User Management

5. Click on **Add Selected**.
6. The selected user groups will now appear in the **Groups** box:

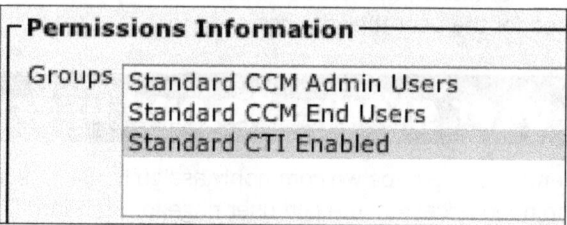

7. Click on **Save**.

 After clicking on **Save**, the **Roles** box will populate with the appropriate roles.

How it works...

Nothing particularly magical here. By assigning the user groups to the end user's account, the roles as specified by those groups will be enforced upon that user.

7
User Features

In this chapter, we will cover:

- Implementing direct transfer to voice mail
- Implementing Meet-Me conferencing
- Implementing call park
- Implementing directed call park
- Configuring the Intercom feature
- Configuring Malicious Call Identification
- Adding a custom ringtone
- Adding a custom background image
- Configuring dual mode for iPhone

Introduction

As discussed in the previous chapter, users are our primary customers. If the end user experience is lacking we will surely be made aware of it. Cisco's Unified Communications Manager provides numerous features and functionalities that benefit the end user and their experience with the telephony system. We will attempt to cover those features in this chapter.

User Features

Implementing direct transfer to voice mail

Users commonly request the ability to transfer calls directly to a user's voice mail box for various reasons. We will configure that feature in this recipe.

Getting ready

Determine the pattern that will be used for transferring a call directly to voicemail. This is generally an 'access code' of sorts followed by a pattern of X's matching the length of our internal extensions.

For example, if we use the asterisk (*) as our access code with a five digit internal dial plan, our pattern would be *XXXXX.

This recipe assumes the implementer is familiar with configuring voice mail pilots.

How to do it...

To implement the direct-to-voice mail functionality, perform the following:

1. First we will need to create a custom voice mail profile. Navigate to the voice mail profiles configuration page (**Advanced Features | Voice Mail | Voice Mail Profiles**).
2. Click on **Add New**.
3. Specify a **Voice Mail Profile Name**.
4. If desired, specify a **Description**.
5. From the **Voice Mail Pilot** drop-down, select the appropriate pilot extension and calling search space.
6. In the **Voice Mail Box Mask** field, the number of Xs entered are equal to the digits in user extensions.

[ If directory numbers are five digits long, we would have the pattern XXXXX.]

Chapter 7

7. Do not check the **Make this the default Voice Mail Profile for the System b**ox:

```
┌─ Voice Mail Profile Information ──────────────────────┐
│                                                        │
│   Voice Mail Profile Name *   Direct2Voicemail         │
│                                                        │
│   Description                 Direct Transfer to Voicemail │
│                                                        │
│   Voice Mail Pilot **         10000/CSS-VM             │
│                                                        │
│   Voice Mail Box Mask         XXXXX                    │
│                                                        │
│   ☐ Make this the default Voice Mail Profile for the System │
└────────────────────────────────────────────────────────┘
```

8. Click on **Save**.

    Next, we must create a CTI route point and assign our desired pattern as the directory number for line one:

9. Navigate to the CTI route points page (**Device | CTI Route Point**).
10. Click **Add New**.
11. Specify a **Device Name**.
12. If desired, specify a **Description**.
13. Specify the **Device Pool**.

> In general we would use the device pool that best corresponds to where the voice mail server is.

14. Specify a **Calling Search Space**.

> The calling search space specified should be able to dial the voice mail pilot extension.

15. Specify the **Location**.
16. If necessary, specify the **Media Resource Group List**.
17. If necessary, specify the **Geolocation**.

18. Uncheck **Use Device Pool Calling Party Transformation CSS**:

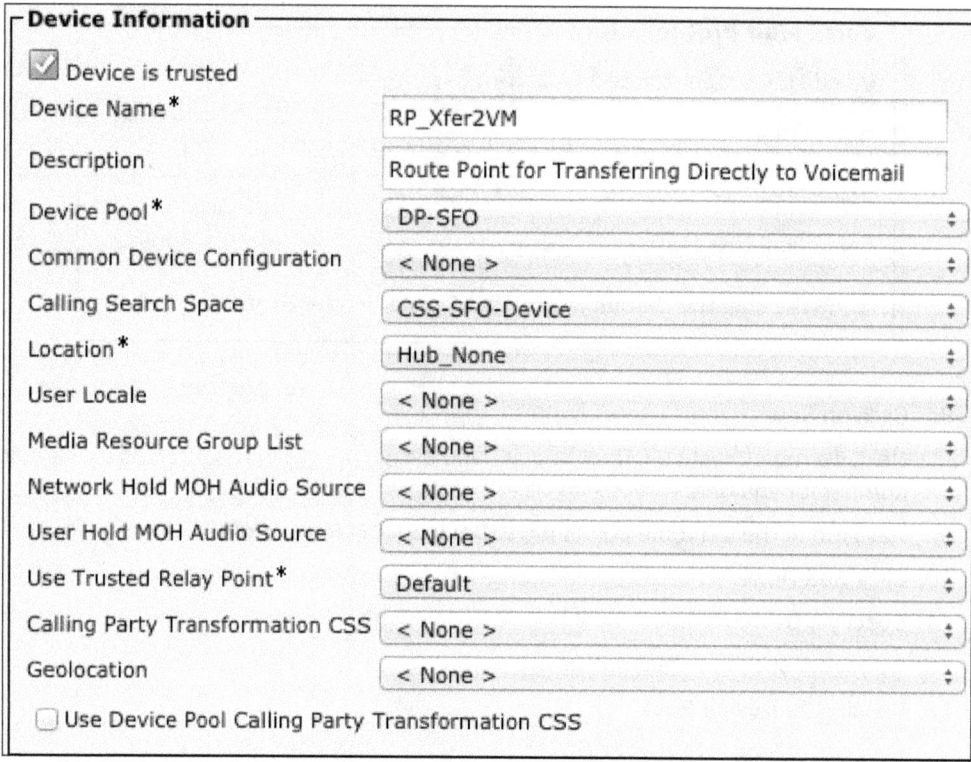

19. Click on **Save**.
20. After the page reloads click **Line [1] – Add a new DN** under the **Association Information** section:

21. For the **Directory Number,** specify the pattern that will be used.
22. Specify the **Route Partition**:

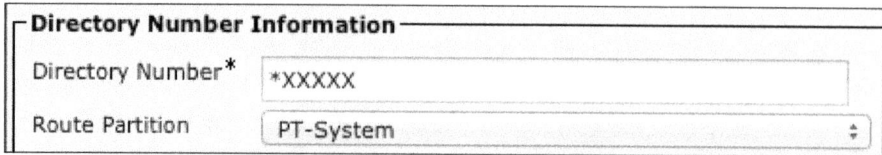

23. Specify the **Voice Mail Profile** we just created in the **Directory Number Settings** section:

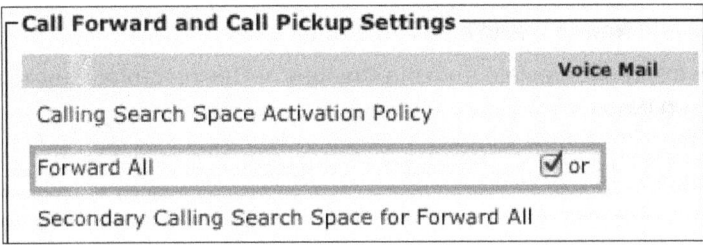

24. Check the **Voice Mail** box next to **Forward All,** under the **Call Forward and Call Pickup Settings** section:

25. Click on **Save**.

How it works...

In this recipe, we had to do two things. First, we created a new voice mail profile specifically for this feature. Secondly, we created a CTI route point with a pattern forwarding all calls to voice mail.

The reason this works is fairly simple. After dialing the direct to voice mail pattern, the forward setting sends all calls to voice mail. The voice mail profile mask will strip off the 'access code' from the DNIS and send the call to voice mail. The DNIS will match the number in the voice mail system and begin playing the greeting for the destination user.

For example, in this recipe we used the pattern *XXXXX with a voice mail profile mask of XXXXX. If we were to dial *12345, the DNIS sent to the voice mail system would be 12345.

Implementing Meet-Me conferencing

Meet-Me conferencing is a simple, built-in way to organize a conference. Its features are extraordinarily limited as a conferencing solution, but work in a pinch.

User Features

How to do it...

To configure Meet-Me conferencing, we must first add the *MeetMe* softkey to the softkey template. To do so, perform the following steps:

> The *MeetMe* softkey is part of the **Standard User** softkey template. The process for adding the softkey is shown next. Skip this part if you are already using the template.

1. Navigate to the **Softkey Template Configuration** page (**Device | Device Settings | Softkey Template**).
2. Click on **Add New** to create a new softkey template.
3. Choose a softkey template from the **Create a softkey template based on** drop-down box:

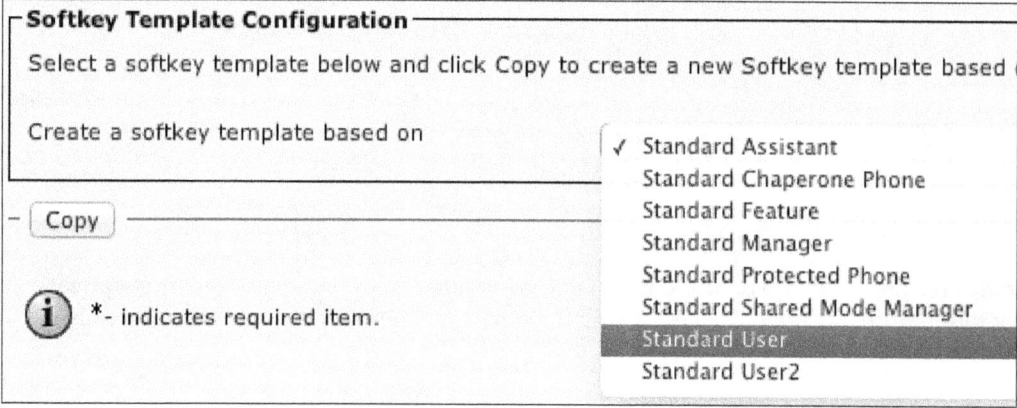

4. Click on **Copy**.
5. From the **Related Links** drop-down box, select **Configure Softkey Layout**:

6. Click on **Go**.
7. Specify a **Name**.
8. Click on **Save**.

9. The *MeetMe* softkey can be used in two call states, namely, **On Hook** and **Off Hook**. Move the key to the **Selected Softkeys** box for each call state desired:

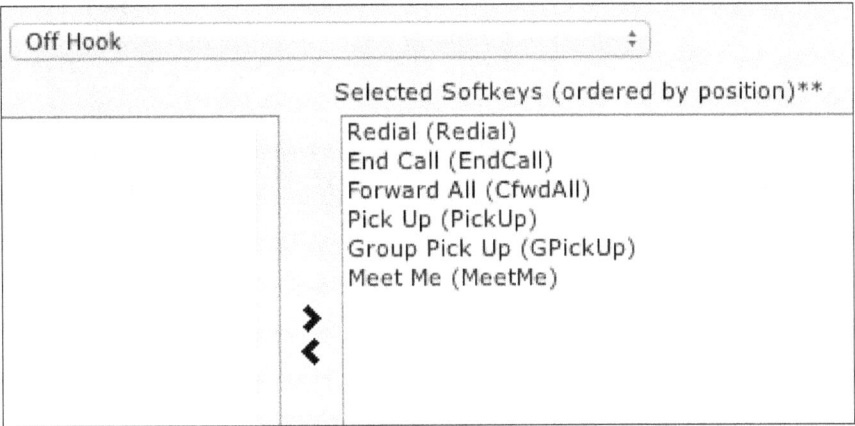

10. Click on **Save**.

The softkey template can now be applied to a phone device.

Now we can configure the Meet-Me conferencing feature.

1. Navigate to the Meet-Me numbers page (**Call Routing | Meet-Me Pattern**).
2. Click on **Add New**.
3. Specify the **Directory Number or Pattern**.
4. If desired, specify the **Description**.
5. Specify the **Partition**.
6. Select the appropriate **Minimum Security Level**:

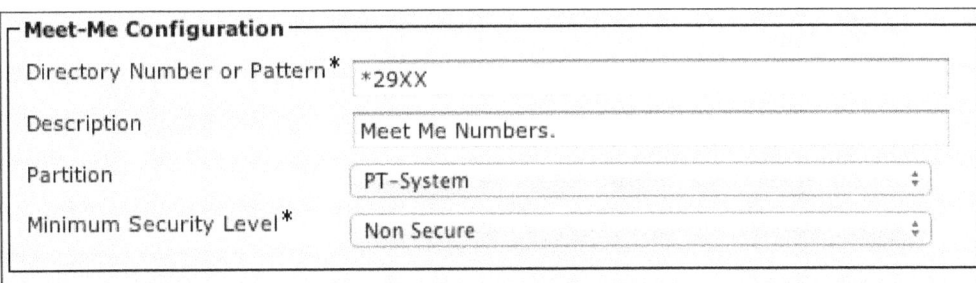

7. Click on **Save**.

User Features

How it works...

Meet-Me conferences are initiated by a host user. This user will take the phone off-hook before pressing the *MeetMe* softkey and dialing the conference number. After a Meet-Me conference has been started, the remaining participants only need to dial the conference number to join in.

Implementing call park

Call park allows us to put a caller on hold without having him connected to a phone device. Additionally call park provides us a number which any user can dial to pick up that call.

Getting ready

Prepare a range or pattern that will be used for the call park directory number or pattern.

How to do it...

To configure call park features, perform the steps given next.

Before we can use the Park feature, we must ensure the softkey is on the softkey template for utilization by the users.

Therefore we will add the Park softkey to the softkey template.

 The *Park* softkey is part of the **Standard User** softkey template. The process for adding the softkey is shown next. Skip this part if you are already using the template.

1. Navigate to the **Softkey Template Configuration** page (**Device | Device Settings | Softkey Template**).
2. Click on **Add New** to create a new Softkey template.
3. Choose a softkey template from the **Create a softkey template based on** drop-down box:

Chapter 7

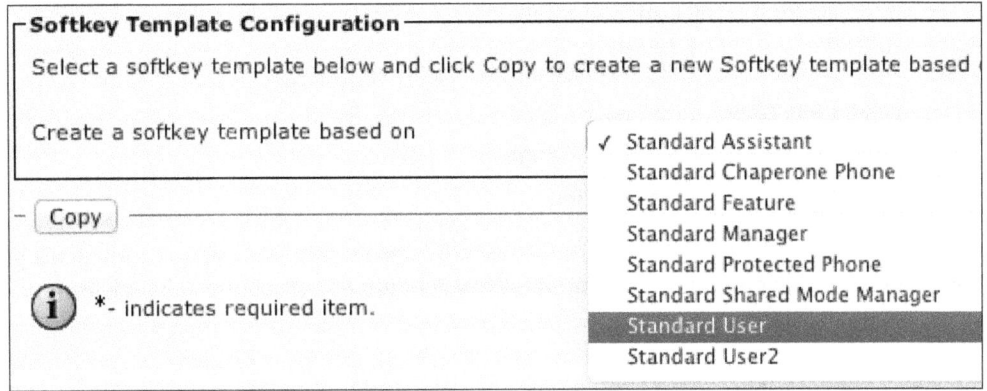

4. Click on **Copy**.
5. Specify a **Name**.
6. Click on **Save**.
7. From the **Related Links** drop-down box, select **Configure Softkey Layout**:

8. Click on **Go**.
9. The **Park** softkey can be used in two call states, namely, **On Hook** and **Off Hook**. Move the key to the **Selected Softkeys** box for each call state desired:

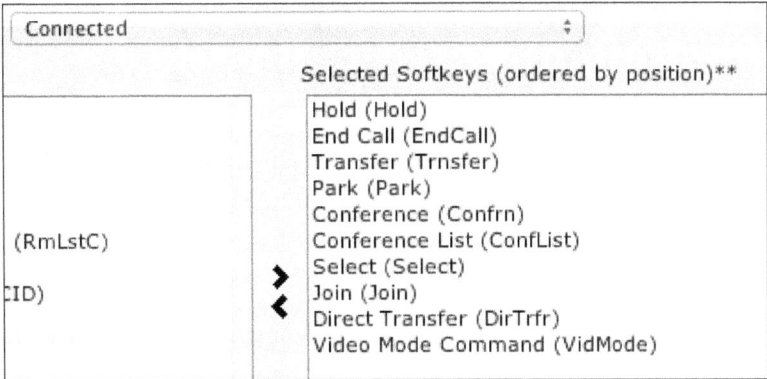

10. Click on **Save**.

User Features

Now we can configure the call park feature itself:

1. Navigate to the **Call Park Configuration** page (**Call Routing | Call Park**).
2. Click on **Add New**.
3. Specify the **Call Park Number/Range**.
4. If desired, specify the **Description**.
5. Specify the **Partition**.
6. Select the **Cisco Unified Communications Manager** to which the call park feature will be registered:

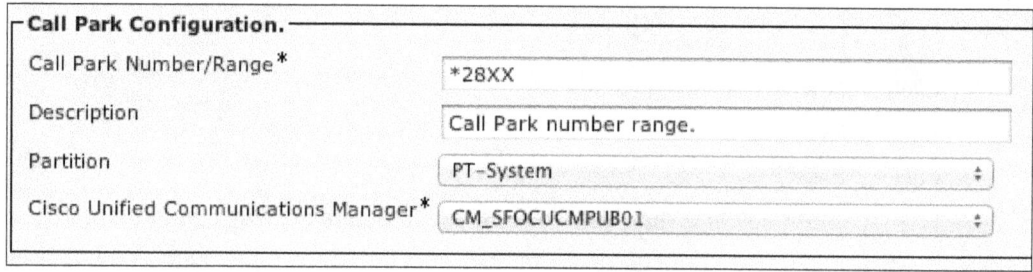

7. Click on **Save**.

How it works...

To activate the call park feature, simply select the **Park** softkey. The phone will display the current number at which the call is parked.

Dialing this number will resume the call from the device that initiated the call to the parked number.

Implementing directed call park

Unlike call park, directed call park places a call at a specific number. Also unlike call park, the directed call park feature can send the parkee (the person being parked) to a specific number, such as a receptionist, if not answered before the call revision timer expires.

Getting ready

Plan out the number or pattern that will be used for the directed call park numbers.

Chapter 7

How to do it...

To configure directed call park, perform the following:

1. First navigate to the Directed Call Park configuration page (**Call Routing | Directed Call Park**).
2. Click on **Add New**.
3. Specify the **Number**. This can also be a pattern.
4. If desired, specify the **Description**.
5. Specify the **Partition**.
6. If desired, specify the **Reversion Number**.
7. Specify the **Reversion Calling Search Space** if using a **Reversion Number**.
8. Specify the **Retrieval Prefix**:

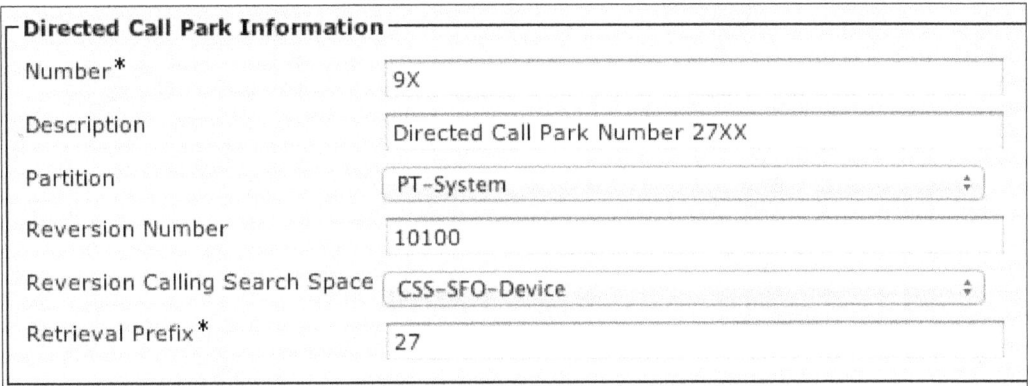

9. Click on **Save**.

How it works...

Directed call park uses the *Transfer* softkey. While it is possible to use the *Park* softkey, it is advisable not to do so.

 If using both Call Park as well as Directed Call Park, ensure that the number ranges do not overlap.

To perform a Directed Call Park, the user must use the Transfer functionality to transfer to the number or pattern specified in step 3.

User Features

To answer the parked call, the user must dial the **Retrieval Prefix** specified in step 8 and then enter the parked number.

Using the recipe as an example, if a user parks a call at the number 99, to retrieve the call, a user must dial 2799.

Unlike Call Park, if the call reversion timer is met, the call will be sent to the **Reversion Number** specified in step 6. This number must be accessible from the **Reversion Calling Search Space**.

Configuring the Intercom feature

Intercom is a popular request among executives and administrative assistants. Intercom allows one-way audio communication between two parties. The Intercom feature will activate even when the receiver is on a call.

Getting ready

Before configuring the Intercom feature, ensure the phone and protocol load will support the feature.

- Cisco 7931 supported with SCCP protocol
- Cisco 7941, 7961, 7970, 7971, and newer support with both SIP and SCCP protocols

How to do it...

To configure an intercom line, perform the following:

1. First navigate to the Intercom Partitions configuration page (**Call Routing | Intercom | Intercom Route Partition**).
2. Click on **Add New**.
3. In the **Name** box, type in the desired partition name and description:

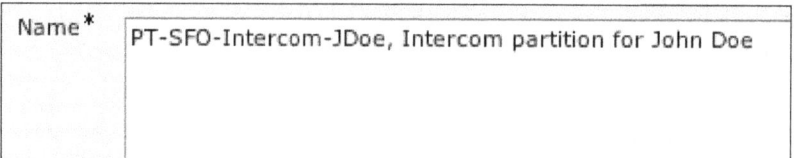

4. Click on **Save**.
5. Next, navigate to the **Intercom Calling Search Space** configuration page (**Call Routing | Intercom | Intercom Calling Search Space**).

[By default, the system will automatically create a Calling Search Space after creating the partition. Skip to step 11 if no additional intercom calling search spaces are desired.]

6. Click on **Add New**.
7. Specify a **Name**.
8. If desired, specify a **Description**.
9. Move the appropriate intercom partitions to the **Selected Intercom Partitions** field:

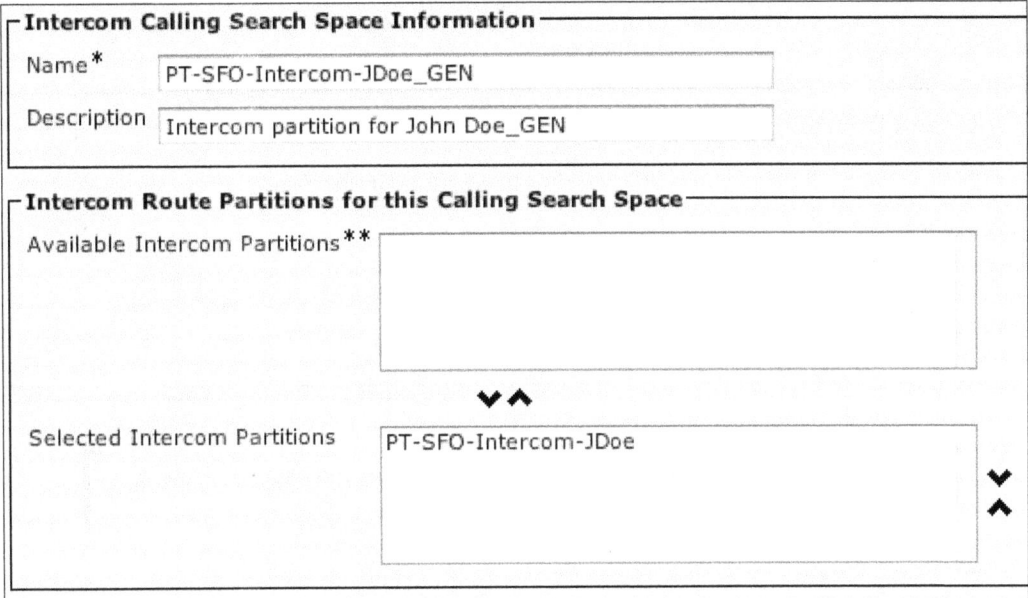

10. Click on **Save**.
11. Next, navigate to the **Intercom Directory Number** configuration page (**Call Routing | Intercom | Intercom Directory Number**).
12. Click on **Add New**.
13. Specify an **Intercom Directory Number** or range.
14. Specify the **Route Partition**.
15. If desired, specify a **Description**.
16. If desired, specify the **Alerting Name** and **ASCII Alerting Name**.
17. Specify the **Calling Search Space**.
18. If desired, specify the **Presence Group**.

19. Select the desired **Auto Answer** settings.
20. Specify the **Default Activated Device** that the receiver of the intercom is using:

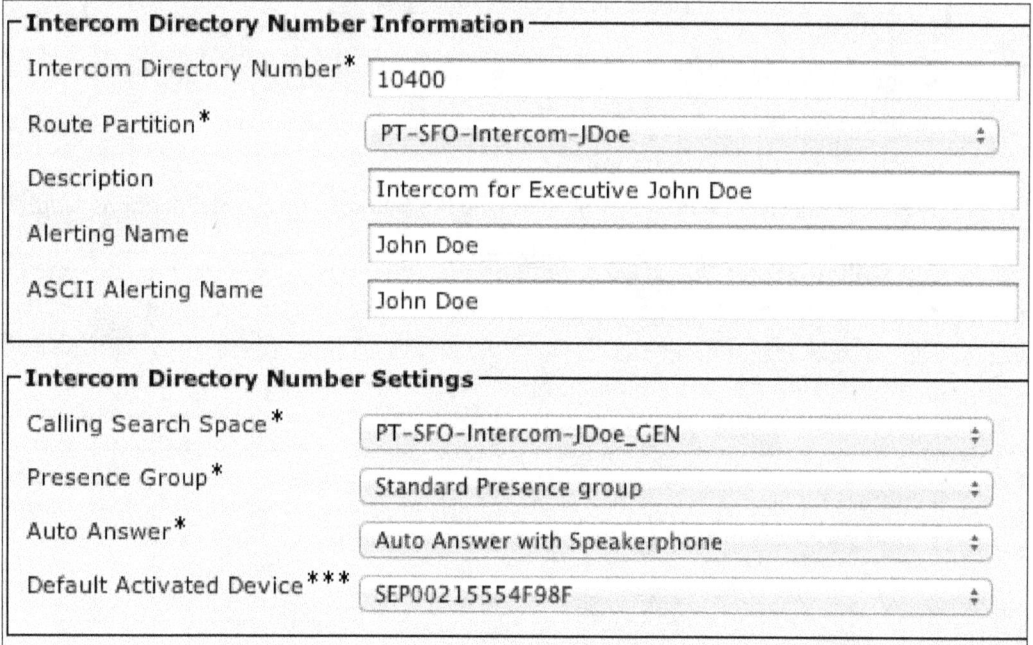

> If we do not set a **Default Activated Device,** the Intercom feature will not work!

21. Click on **Save**.
22. Next we must assign the **Intercom Directory Number** to the user who will initiate the intercom (**Device | Phone**, if using extension mobility, then **Device | Settings | Device Profile**).
23. Scroll down and click on **Intercom [1] - Add a new Intercom**:

24. Specify the **Intercom Directory Number** from step 13.
25. Specify the **Route Partition**.
26. Verify the settings for **Calling Search Space, Presence Group, Auto Answer,** and **Default Activated Device**.
27. Specify the **Display** and **ASCII Display fields**.

28. Specify the **Line Text Label** and **ASCII Line Text Label**.
29. If desired, specify a **Speed Dial**.
30. If desired, specify an **External Phone Number Mask**:

Intercom Directory Number Information

Intercom Directory Number*	10400
Route Partition*	PT-SFO-Intercom-JDoe
Description	Intercom for Executive John Doe
Alerting Name	John Doe
ASCII Alerting Name	John Doe

Intercom Directory Number Settings

Calling Search Space*	PT-SFO-Intercom-JDoe_GEN
Presence Group*	Standard Presence group
Auto Answer*	Auto Answer with Speakerphone
Default Activated Device***	SEP00215554F98F

Line 1 on Device cipc-tezell

Display (Internal Caller ID)	John Doe — Display text as a name instead of a directory number for internal calls. If you spec proper identity of the caller.
ASCII Display (Internal Caller ID)	John Doe
Line Text Label	John Doe
ASCII Line Text Label	John Doe
Speed Dial	
External Phone Number Mask	

31. Select the desired information to be forwarded.

32. Click on **Save**.
33. Finally, ensure the Intercom line is assigned to the phone's visible buttons (if the intercom line appears below "-------- **Unassigned Associated Items** ---------", then it will not be visible to the user) using the **Modify Button Items** button, or by specifying a **Phone Button Template** on the Device configuration page to which the Intercom line is configured.

Modify the button layout by clicking on the **Modify Button Items** button:

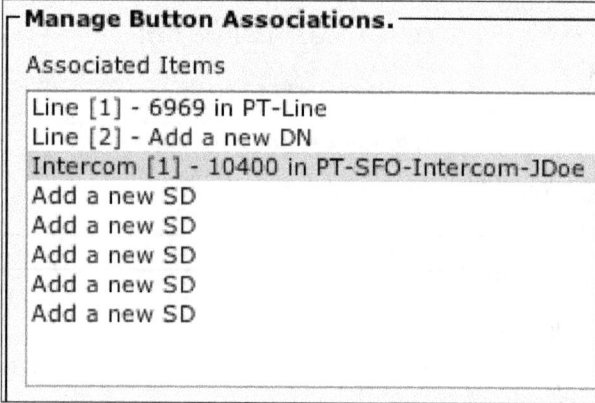

Notice that the intercom line is above the **Unassociated Items** line.

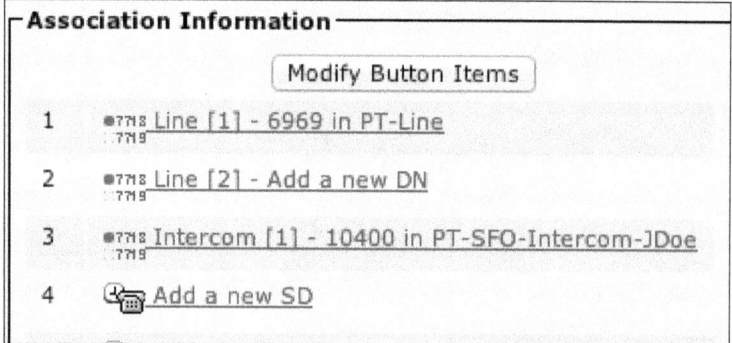

Chapter 7

How it works...

The Intercom feature consists primarily of three components, namely the intercom route partition, the intercom calling search space, and the intercom directory number.

The Route Partition and Calling Search Space behave as any other would. The key to making intercom work is in the Intercom Directory Number. Specifically, the Intercom Directory Number specifies the Default Activated Device, which is the device that will receive the intercom call.

After selecting the appropriate button on the phone to initiate an intercom call, the receiver will begin to hear audio regardless of whether he is on the phone or not. This audio is one way.

Configuring Malicious Call Identification

Malicious Call Identification works by setting a specific flag in the CDR records. These flagged calls can be reported on, attaining whatever information is necessary to take action.

How to do it...

To enable and configure Malicious Call Identification, perform the following:

1. First navigate to the Service Parameters configuration page (**System | Service Parameters**).
2. Select the **Server**.
3. Select the **Cisco CallManager Service**.
4. Under the **System** section (near the top), select **True** for **CDR Enabled Flag**:

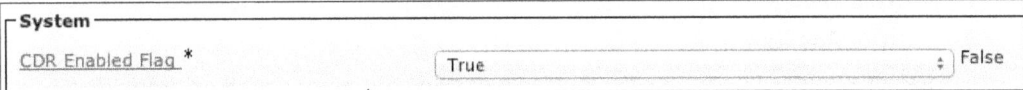

5. Click on **Save**.
6. Next navigate to the **Serviceability** page by clicking on **Cisco Unified Serviceability** from the **Navigation** drop-down:

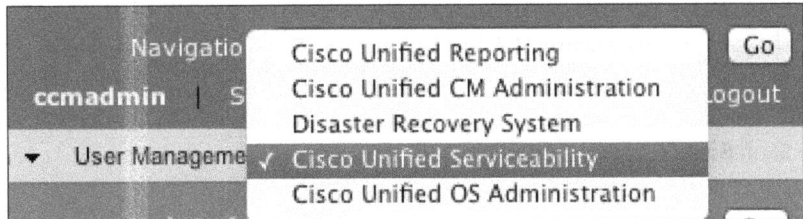

163

User Features

7. Click on **Go**.
8. Navigate to the **Alarm** configuration page (**Alarm | Configuration**).
9. Select the **Server**.
10. From the **Service Group** drop-down select **CM Services**:

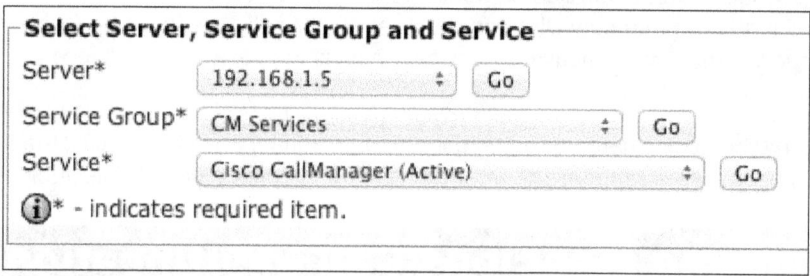

11. From the **Service** drop-down, select **Cisco CallManager**.
12. Click on **Go**.
13. Check **Enable Alarm** under the **Local Syslog** section.
14. Under the same section, select **Informational** from the **Alarm Event Level** drop-down.
15. If using multiple nodes, check **Apply to All Nodes**.
16. Click on **Save**.

Now that the service has been enabled, we can configure a softkey template with the appropriate button and assign it to a device.

1. Navigate back to the Unified CM Administration page.
2. Navigate to the **Softkey Template** configuration page (**Device | Device Settings | Softkey Template**).
3. Click on **Add New**.
4. Select **Standard User** from the **Create a softkey template based on** drop-down.
5. Click on **Copy**.
6. Specify a **Name**.
7. If desired, specify a **Description**.

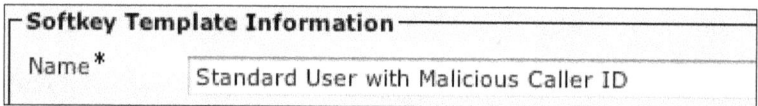

8. Click on **Save**.

9. From the **Related Links** drop-down, select **Configure Softkey Layout**:

10. Click on **Go**.
11. From the **Select a call state to configure** drop-down, select **Connected**.
12. Move the **Toggle Malicious Call Trace (MCID)** to the **Selected Softkeys** field, in the desired position:

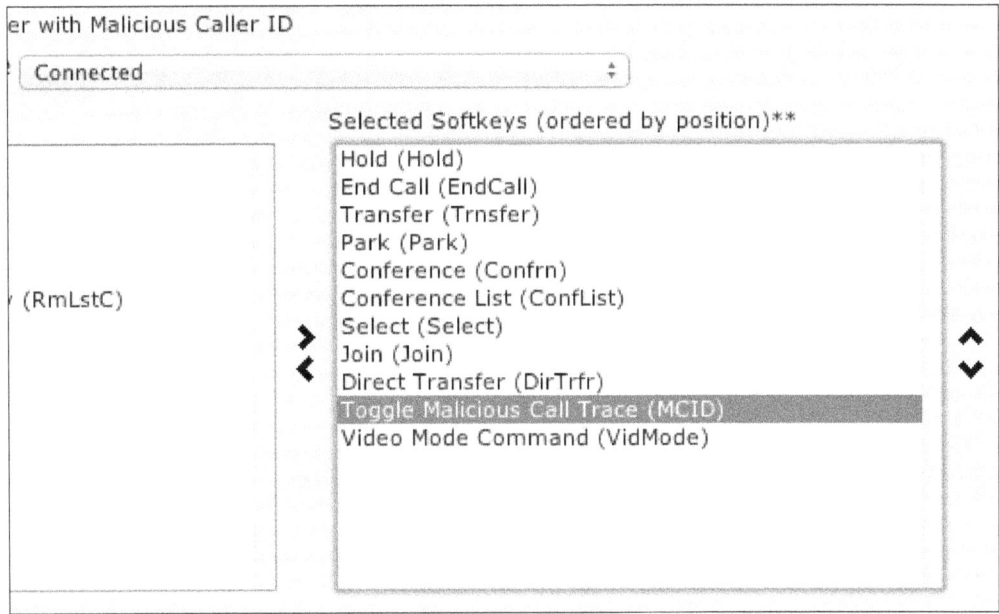

13. Click on **Save**.

At this point we can assign the softkey template we just created to the appropriate devices.

How it works...

After selecting the MCID softkey from the phone, a CDR flag is set for malicious calls. After the button has been selected, we can search the CDR logs for the flag, and determine and provide the information necessary for the authorities to take appropriate action.

User Features

Adding a custom ringtone

The Unified Communications Manager includes quite a few ringtones by default, but sometimes we want to add something with a more personal touch. To do this, we can add custom ringtones.

Getting ready

First, make sure you have a ringtone that conforms to the following:

- Raw PCM (headerless)
- 8000 samples per second
- 8 bits per sample
- uLaw compression
- Maximum ring size should be 16080 samples
- Minimum ring size should be 240 samples

>  The number of samples in the ring must be evenly divisible by 240.

How to do it...

To add a custom ringtone, perform the following for each UCM in the cluster:

1. First we must get the existing `Ringlist.xml` file. This file contains the listing of ringtones.
2. Using your favorite TFTP application, download the `Ringlist.xml` file from the UCM.

```
Tanner Ezell's MacBook Pro:~ tannerezell$ tftp
tftp> connect
(to) 192.168.1.5
tftp> get
(files) Ringlist.xml
Received 2657 bytes in 0.1 seconds
tftp> quit
Tanner Ezell's MacBook Pro:~ tannerezell$
```

3. Modify the `Ringlist.xml` file by adding the appropriate fields. In this example we use the `custom1.raw` file, and give the name `My Custom Ringtone`:

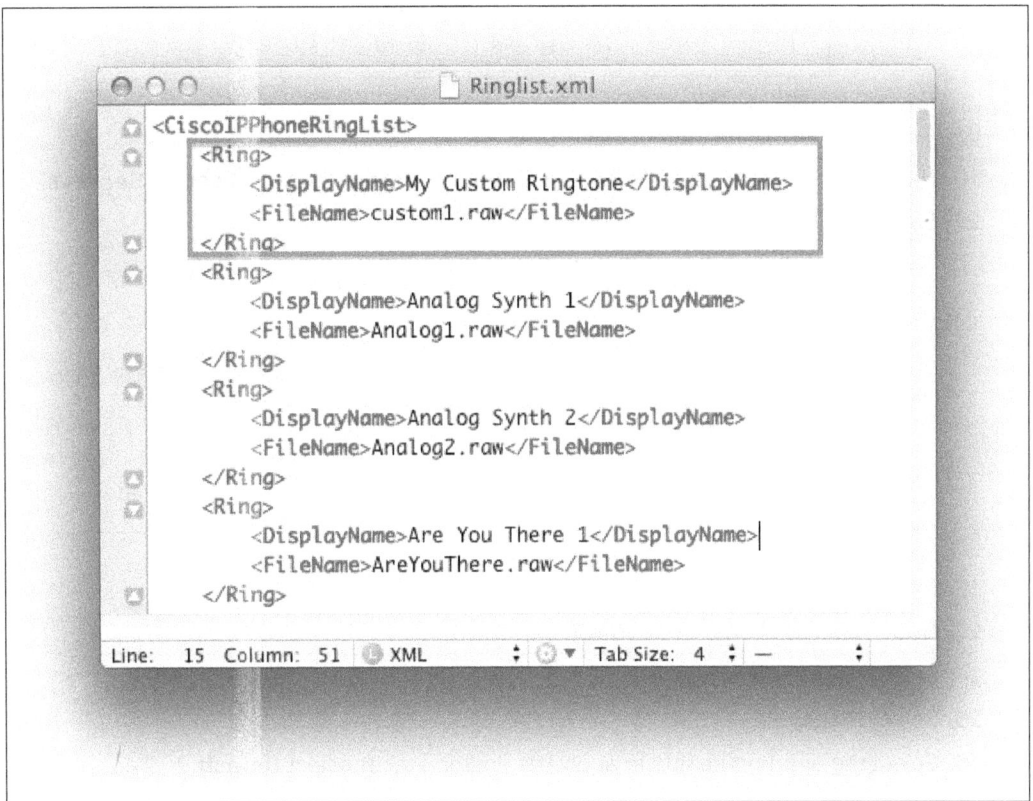

4. After the `Ringlist.xml` file has been modified, we need to upload it and the custom ringtone to the UCM via the OS Administration Page (http://192.168.1.5/ccmplatform).
5. Navigate to the TFTP file management page (**Software Upgrades | TFTP File Management**).
6. Click on **Upload File**.
7. Select the `Ringlist.xml` file and click on **Upload File**:

User Features

8. Select the custom ringtone file and click on **Upload File**:

9. Next, navigate to the Serviceability page (http://192.168.1.5/ccmplatform).
10. Navigate to the feature services page (**Tools | Control Center – Feature Services**).
11. Select the TFTP service:

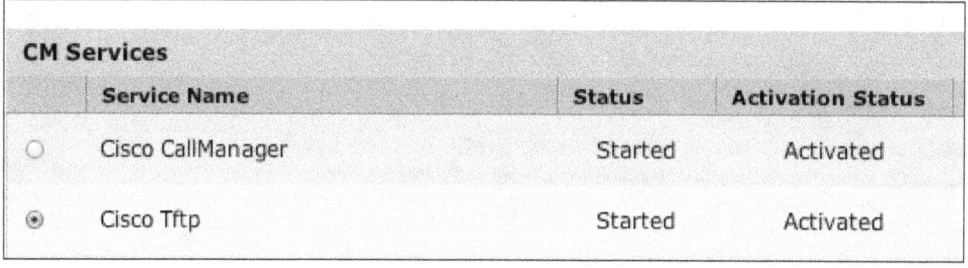

12. Click on **Restart**.
13. Next, from the phone, select **Settings**.
14. Select **User Preferences**.
15. Select **Rings**.
16. Select the appropriate line to apply the ringtone to, or select **Default**.
17. Scroll down to the custom ringtone:

18. Click on **Select**.

The ringtone should now be active!

 If the ringtone does not show up in the **Rings** list, ensure the TFTP service has been restarted.

How it works...

The Ringlist.xml file contains the listing of each ringtone on the system available to devices. By adding a custom entry for our ringtones and restarting the TFTP service, the phones can select the custom ringer.

Adding a custom background image

Much like custom ringtones, custom backgrounds can add personality to an organization or individual's phone.

Getting ready

Ensure the background image and thumbnail is in **Portable Network Graphics** (**PNG**) format. Also ensure the background images dimensions match the requirements for each model:

- For the 7906 or 7911, the image must be 95×34 pixels and 23x8 for the thumbnail
- For the 7941, 7942, 7961, and 7962, the image must be 320×196 pixels and 80x49 for the thumbnail
- For the 7945, 7965, 7970, 7971, and 7975, the image must be 320×212 pixels and 80x53 for the thumbnail

Also ensure the thumbnail is in the correct name format, TN-<filename>.png; for example, if the image name is custom1.png, then the thumbnails name is TN-custom1.png.

How to do it...

To add custom background images, perform the following on each UCM server in the cluster:

1. First we must create the List.xml file.

User Features

2. Using your favorite text editor, edit `List.xml` to add your background image as follows:

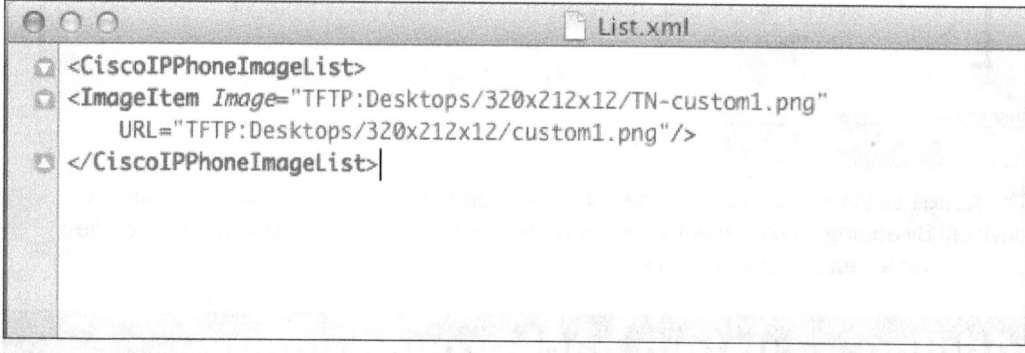

```
<CiscoIPPhoneImageList>
<ImageItem Image="TFTP:Desktops/320x212x12/TN-custom1.png"
    URL="TFTP:Desktops/320x212x12/custom1.png"/>
</CiscoIPPhoneImageList>
```

3. Upload the `List.xml` file to the server via the **OS Administration** page.
4. Navigate to the **TFTP File Management** page (**Software Upgrade | TFTP File Management**).
5. Click on **Upload File**.
6. Select the `List.xml` file and click on **Upload File**, remembering to specify the appropriate directory for each model type:
    - 7906, 7911: /Desktops/95x34x1
    - 7941, 7961: /Desktops/320x196x4
    - 7942, 7962: /Desktops/320x196x4
    - 7945, 7965: /Desktops/320x212x16
    - 7970, 7971, IP Communicator: /Desktops/320x212x12
    - 7975: /Desktops/320x216x16

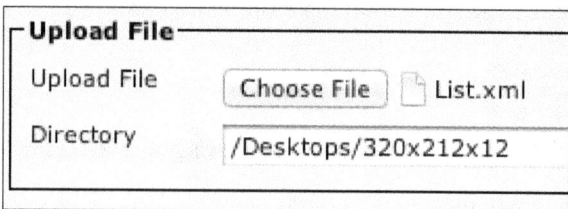

7. Upload the thumbnail and background image in the same way, ensuring the appropriate directory is specified as outlined previously:

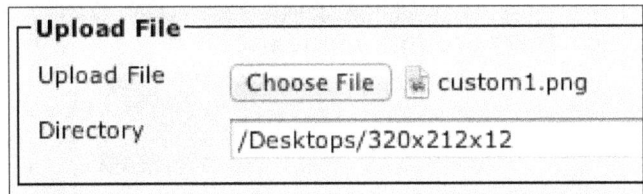

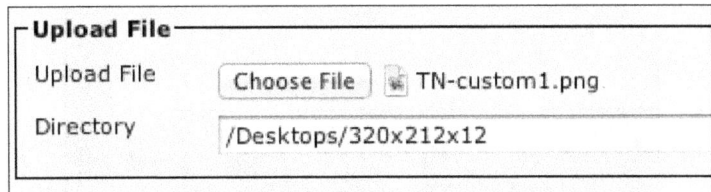

8. Next navigate to the Serviceability page (http://192.168.1.5/ccmservice).
9. Navigate to the Feature Services page (**Tools | Control Center – Feature Services**).
10. Select the **TFTP Service**:

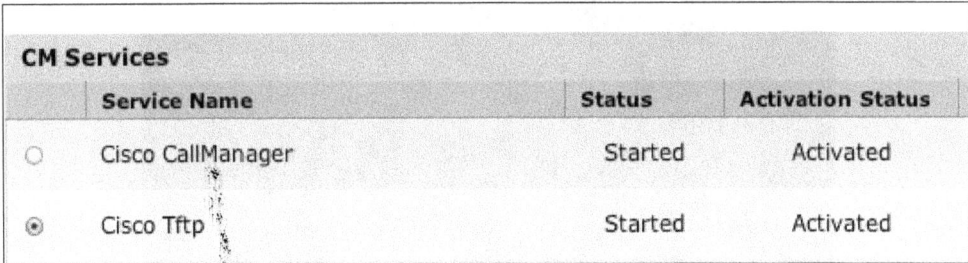

11. Click on **Restart**.
12. Next, from the phone select **Settings**.
13. Select **User Preferences**.
14. Select **Backgrounds**.

User Features

15. Select the custom background image:

16. Click on **Select**.

The background will now be set to the device!

If you're at all curious as to what the previous screenshot shows, it is the Nebula NGC 2024 (`http://en.wikipedia.org/wiki/Flame_Nebula`).

Chapter 7

Configuring dual mode for iPhone

Cisco has graciously released the Cisco Mobile 8.x application for both Android and the iPhone. The instructions here focus on the iPhone specifically, but should apply to Android devices as well.

Getting ready

Before we can set up dual mode for iPhone (or Android), we must first ensure the user exists in the system.

How to do it...

To configure dual mode for iPhone (or Android) perform the following:

1. First navigate to the Phone configuration page (**Device | Phone**).
2. Click on **Add New**.
3. For the **Phone Type**, select **Cisco Dual Mode for iPhone**:

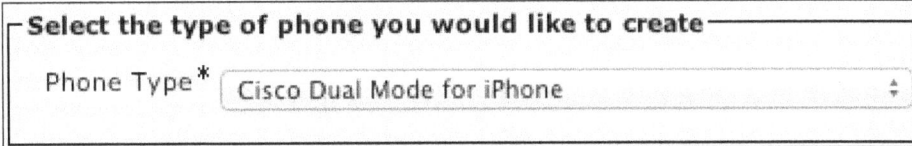

 When configuring dual mode for Android, we may first have to upload the appropriate files, which can be obtained through CCO.

4. Click on **Next**.
5. Specify the **Device Name** in the format `TCT<userid>`.
6. If desired, specify a **Description**.
7. Specify the **Device Pool**.
8. Specify the **Phone Button Template**.

User Features

9. If desired, specify the **Calling Search Space** and **Media Resource Group List**:

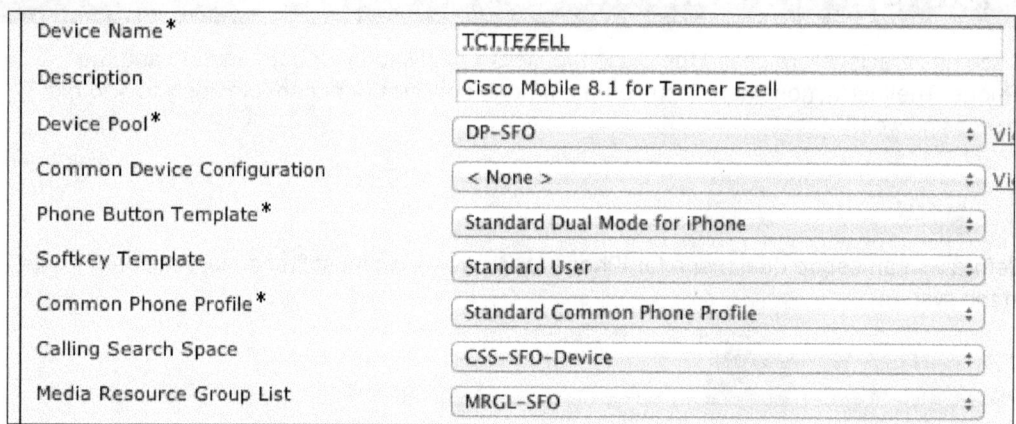

10. Specify a **Location**.
11. Specify the **Owner User ID**.
12. Specify the **Mobility User ID**:

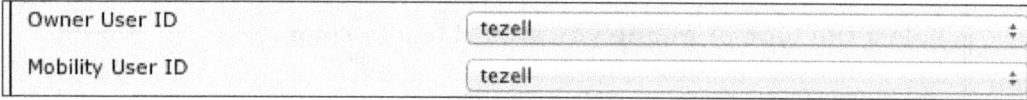

13. Specify the **Device Security Profile**.
14. Specify the **SIP Profile**:

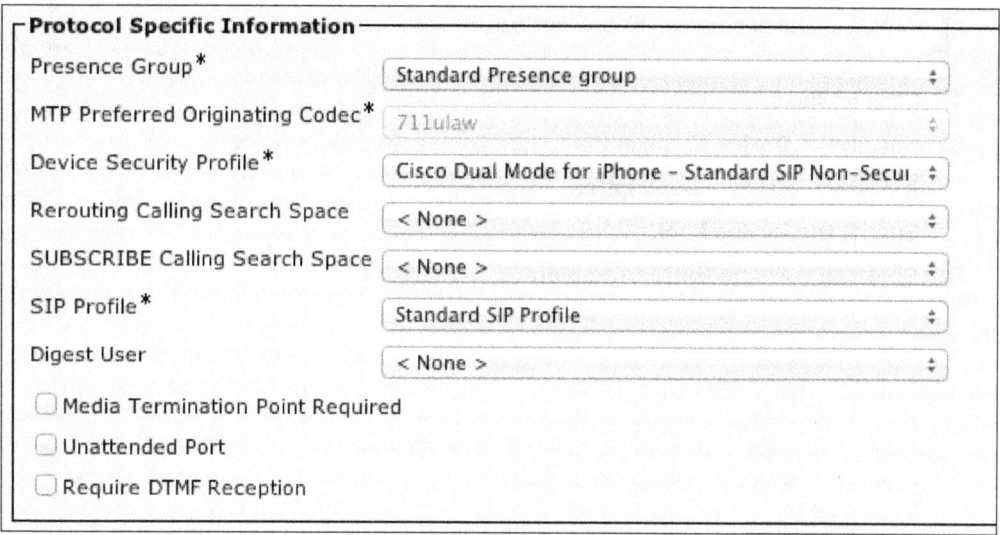

Chapter 7

15. If desired, configure the appropriate settings under the **Product Specific Configuration Layout** section.
16. Click on **Save**.
17. Next, configure Line 1 with the appropriate directory number and line settings:

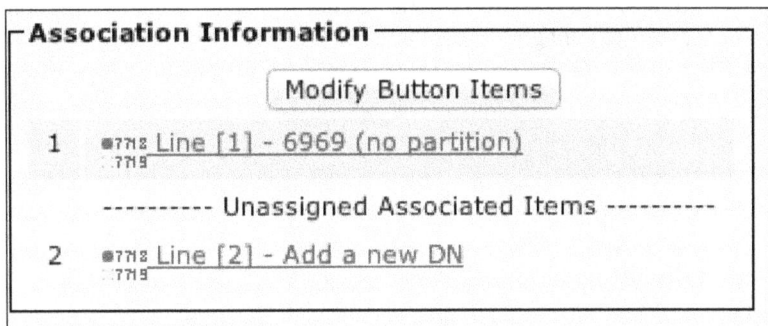

18. Finally, configure the iPhone device by launching Cisco Mobile 8.1 (or newer).

Following the procedure step by step prompts you to enter the appropriate information.

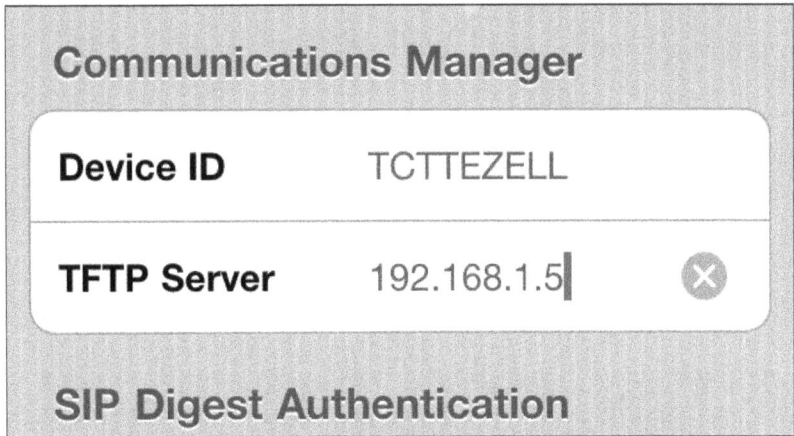

After the device is configured you should get a green phone icon:

User Features

How it works...

Dual mode for iPhone essentially works like any other phone device and is configured as shown.

Configuring the information manually on the device configuration page can reduce the need for users or support staff to configure the device manually.

Advanced Features

In this chapter, we will cover:

- Enabling the Extension Mobility service
- Configuring the Extension Mobility phone service
- Configuring phone devices for Extension Mobility
- Configuring device profiles for Extension Mobility
- Configuring Extension Mobility service parameters
- Enabling the Cross Cluster Extension Mobility services
- Configuring the Cross Cluster Extension Mobility phone service
- Configure users for Cross Cluster Extension Mobility
- Preparing certificates for Cross Cluster Extension Mobility
- Creating a template for Cross Cluster Extension Mobility devices
- Configuring Cross Cluster Extension Mobility parameters
- Configuring intercluster trunks for Cross Cluster Extension Mobility
- Configuring the intercluster service profile for Cross Cluster Extension Mobility
- Configuring monitoring and recording
- Configuring geolocations and filters
- Implementing logical partitioning
- Configuring hotline service parameters
- Configuring a hotline device
- Configuring barge for devices and users
- Configuring privacy for devices and users

Advanced Features

Introduction

This chapter will introduce and explain some of the more advanced topics in the Unified Communications Manager, specifically focusing on extension mobility (including cross cluster), as well as call recording and monitoring.

Additionally, we will introduce geolocations and logical partitioning to ensure our dial plans are in compliance with various local laws regarding Tail End Hop Off (TEHO).

Enabling the Extension Mobility service

Extension Mobility is a feature that allows users to roam between phones, all the while taking their number and specific device settings (such as speed dials and services) with them.

How to do it...

To enable the Extension Mobility service, perform the following:

1. First navigate to the Serviceability page. (`https://cucm/ccmservice`).
2. Navigate to the Service Activation page (**Tools | Service Activation**).
3. Under the **CM Services** section, check the box next to **Cisco Extension Mobility**:

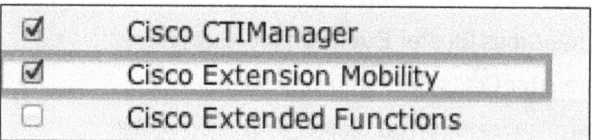

4. Click on **Save**.
5. Next, navigate to the Control Center—Feature Services (**Tools | Control Center—Feature Services**).
6. Under the CM Services section, ensure that the **Cisco Extension Mobility** service is started. If it is not, select the radio button next to the service and click on **Start**.

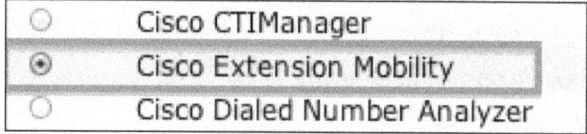

How it works...

The Cisco Extension Mobility service must first be active before end users can use the extension mobility feature.

Configuring the Extension Mobility phone service

Before we can enable Extension Mobility for users, we must first create the service. This service would then be assigned to the appropriate devices and device profiles.

Getting ready

This recipe assumes the Extension Mobility service is already active.

How to do it...

To create the Extension Mobility phone service, perform the following:

1. Navigate to the phone services configuration page (**Device** | **Device Settings** | **Phone Services**).
2. Click on **Add New**.
3. Specify a **Service Name**.
4. Specify the **Service URL**, substitute 192.168.1.5 with the appropriate IP address.

```
http://192.168.1.5:8080/emapp/EMAppServlet?device=
#DEVICENAME#
```

5. Check **Enable**.

Advanced Features

6. If we are to enable this service for all devices, check **Enterprise Subscription**.

```
Service Information
Service Name*          Extension Mobility
ASCII Service Name*    Extension Mobility
Service Description    
Service URL            http://192.168.1.5:8080/emapp/EMAppServlet?device=
Secure-Service URL     
Service Category*      XML Service
Service Type*          Standard IP Phone Service
Service Vendor         
Service Version        
☑ Enable
☐ Enterprise Subscription
```

7. Click on **Save**.

How it works...

Here, we create the IP Phone Service; by doing so, we can then assign this service to our devices and device profiles.

By assigning the service to the appropriate devices and profiles, we give those devices the ability to activate the service.

It's important that we do not to forget to apply the extension mobility service to the device profile, otherwise users will not be able to log out!

Configuring phone devices for Extension Mobility

In order for end users to be able to use the Extension Mobility feature, they must first add the IP Phone Service to their device and device profiles. Additionally, we will have to associate said device profile to the end user's account.

Chapter 8

> This process applies to both Extension Mobility, and Cross Cluster Extension Mobility.

Getting ready

This recipe assumes the Cisco Extension Mobility Service has been activated and the IP Phone Service created.

How to do it...

To configure Extension Mobility, so the end user may use it, perform the following:

First we will configure the device to support Extension Mobility.

1. Navigate to the device on which we will enable Extension Mobility (**Device | Phone**).
2. Under the section **Extension Information,** check **Enable Extension Mobility**.

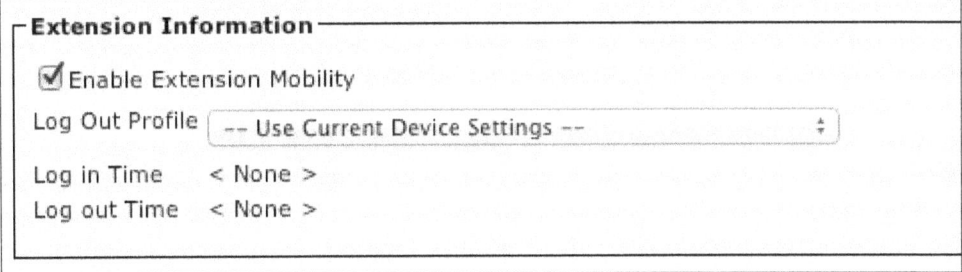

3. Click on **Save**.
4. On the top-right corner, under the **Related Links** drop-down, select **Subscribe/Unsubscribe Services**:

5. Click on **Go**.

Advanced Features

6. Select the appropriate IP Phone Service from the **Select a Service** drop-down.

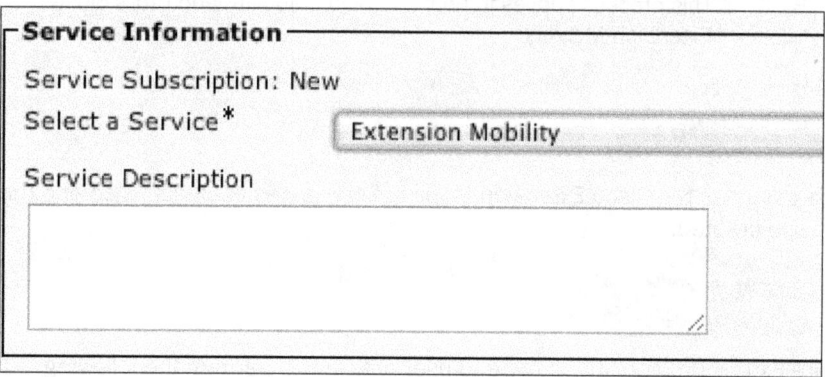

7. Click on **Next**.
8. If desired, change the **Service Name**.

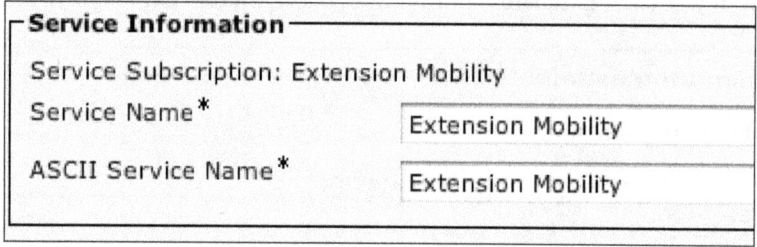

9. Click on **Subscribe**.

The service should now appear under the section **Subscribed Services** as shown in the following screenshot:

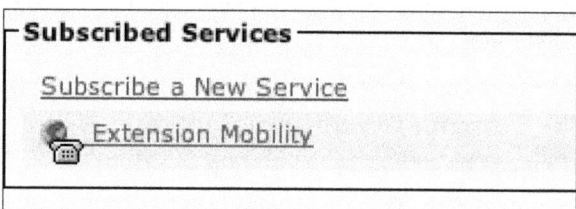

Chapter 8

How it works...

Checking **Enable Extension Mobility** on the device configuration page is one essential step in enabling the feature for the device. We must also subscribe the IP Phone Service to the device so that it will appear under the **Service** button.

 Don't forget to **Apply Config/Reset** the device for the changes to take effect.

Configuring device profiles for Extension Mobility

Enabling Extension Mobility on the phone itself is only part of the process. If we do not subscribe the service to the device profile, the user will be able to log in, but will not able to log out.

 This process applies to both Extension Mobility and Cross Cluster Extension Mobility.

Getting ready

This recipe assumes the Cisco Extension Mobility service has been activated and the IP Phone Service is created.

How to do it...

To configure extension mobility for device profiles, perform the following:

1. Navigate to the **User Device Profile** configuration page. (**Device | Device Settings | Device Profile**).
2. Click on **Add New**.
3. From the **Device Profile Type** drop-down, select the model appropriate to the device the user will log in on.

```
┌─ Select the type of device profile you would like to create ─┐
│                                                              │
│   Device Profile Type*  [ Cisco 7945 ]                       │
│                                                              │
└──────────────────────────────────────────────────────────────┘
```

183

Advanced Features

> In general, the device chosen would match the device typically used by the user. Regardless of the device type chosen here, the user can log in to other devices but will be restricted by the limitations of the physical device.

4. Click on **Next**.
5. From the **Device Protocol** drop-down, select the appropriate protocol used by the device the user will log in on:

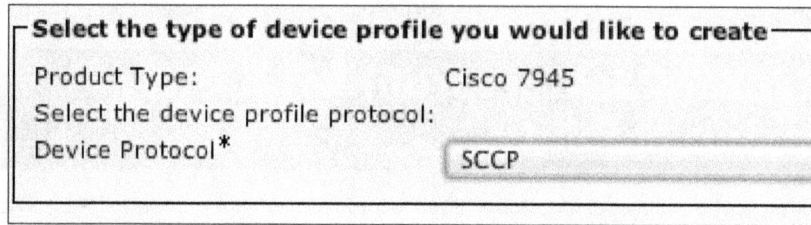

6. Click on **Next**.
7. Specify the **Device Profile Name**.
8. If desired, specify a **Description**.
9. Specify the **Phone Button Template**.
10. Change other settings as necessary, including **Softkey Template**, **Privacy**, and so on:

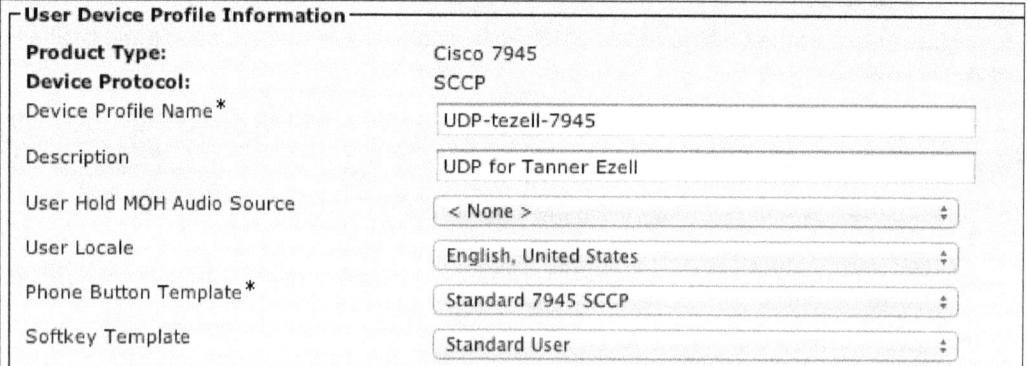

11. Under the section **Logged Out (Default) Profile Information**, we may specify the appropriate user under the **Login User Id** drop-down:

12. Click on **Save**.

>  For the purpose of this recipe we will not detail the configuration of the line(s).

13. On the top-right corner, under the **Related Links** drop-down, select **Subscribe/Unsubscribe Services**:

14. Click on **Go**.
15. Select the appropriate IP Phone Service from the **Select a Service** drop-down:

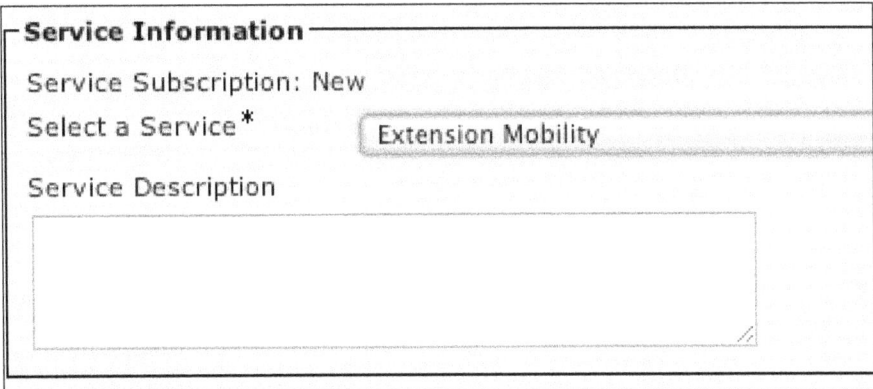

16. Click on **Next**.

Advanced Features

17. If desired, change the **Service Name**:

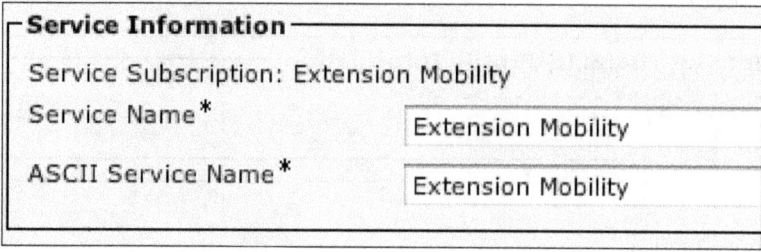

18. Click on **Subscribe**.

The service should now appear under the section **Subscribed Services,** as shown in the following screenshot:

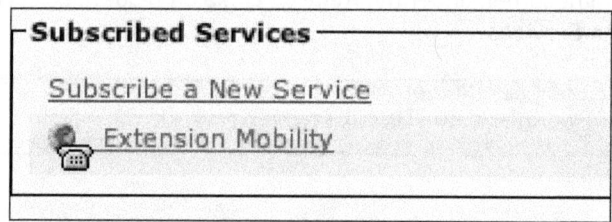

Next, we must associate the device profile to the end user's account.

1. Navigate to the **End User** page (**User Management | End User**).
2. Navigate to the **Device Information** section.
3. Select the appropriate device profile from the **Available Profiles** box, then click the down arrow. The device profile should then appear under the **CTI Controlled Device Profiles** box:

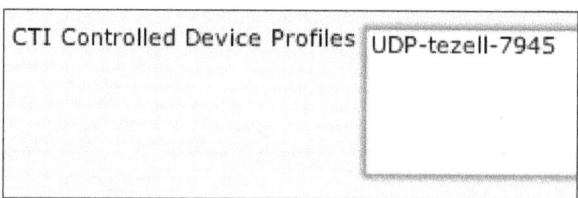

4. Under the **Extension Mobility** section, select the device profile from the **Available Profiles** box, then click the down arrow. The device profile should then appear under the **Controlled Profiles** box.

5. If desired, specify the **Default Profile**:

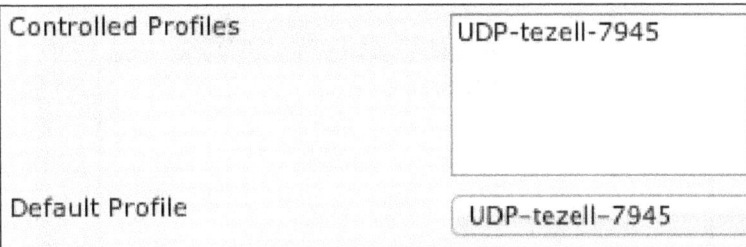

6. Ensure the **Allow Control of Device from CTI** box is checked.
7. Click on **Save**.

After having done all that, we can now log in to Extension Mobility on our device:

1. Click the **Services** button.

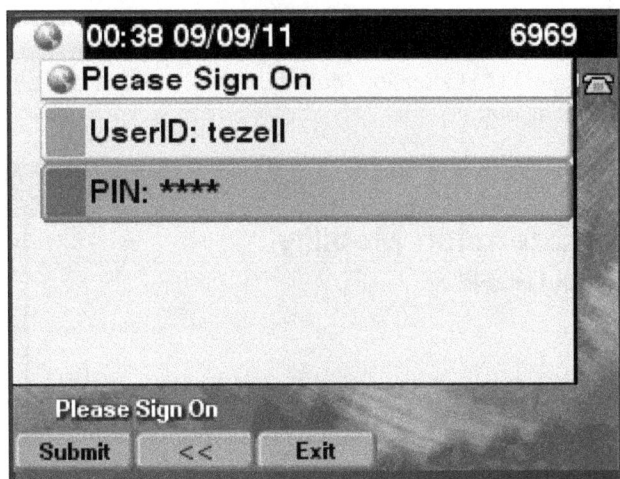

2. Enter the **UserID** and **PIN**, and then select **Submit**.

Advanced Features

3. Upon successful log in, we should see the following screenshot:

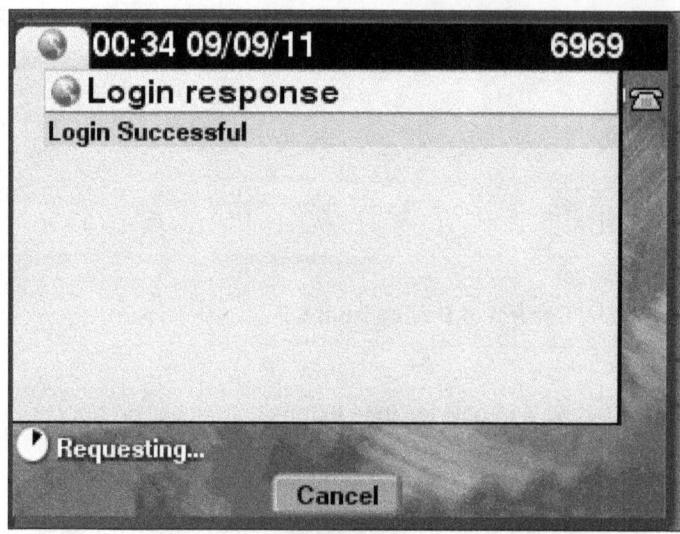

4. After having logged in to Extension Mobility, hitting the services button again will give us the option to log out:

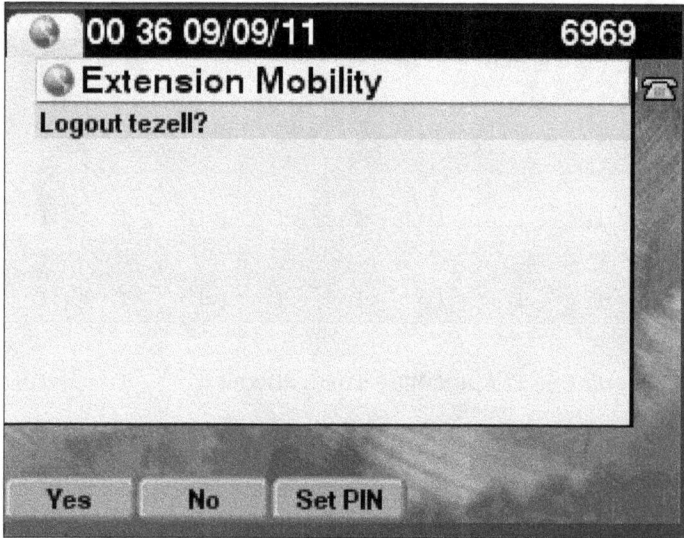

5. If we forgot to subscribe the IP Phone Service to the Device Profile, we would see the following on our device:

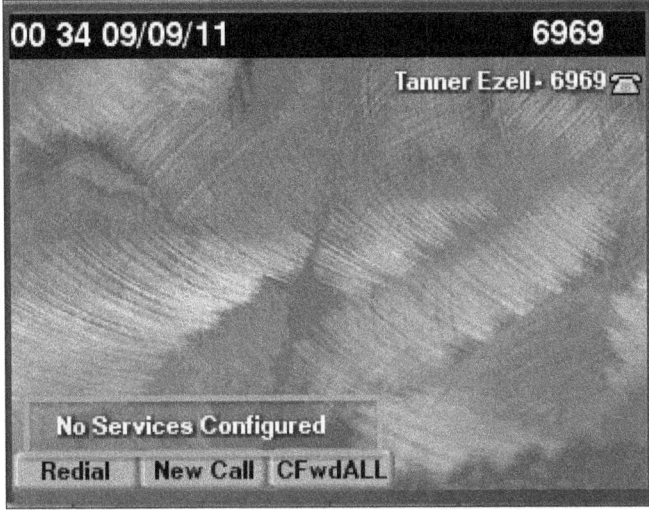

How it works...

One of the most important steps in this procedure is associating the device profile with the end user account. Without this, there would be no way to associate the end user/pin with a profile, and would return an error.

After associating the device profile, the system will check the credentials. If successful, the phone will return either the success message, or if multiple device profiles are assigned to the end user, it will present an option to select one. This is where the default device profile comes into play.

After the user selects the profile (if necessary) the information configured on that profile will be downloaded to the phone device. If we forgot to subscribe the IP Phone Service to the device profile, we'll receive the error message **No Services Configured**, or if multiple services are programmed it will simply not appear in the list.

Configuring Extension Mobility service parameters

There are various Extension Mobility related service parameters that can be configured for the cluster. In this recipe, we will attempt to detail some of them and what they do.

Advanced Features

How to do it...

To configure Extension Mobility specific service parameters, perform the following:

1. Navigate to the service parameters configuration page (**System | Service Parameters**).
2. Specify the appropriate **Server**.
3. Under the **Service** drop-down menu, select **Cisco Extension Mobility**.
4. Select **Advanced**.

The following is a brief description of each field:

- **Enforce Intra-cluster Maximum Login Time**: If set to **True,** the device will unregister from extension mobility after the time set by the **Intra-cluster Maximum Login Time** and **Inter-cluster Maximum Login Time** fields, respectively.

- **Intra-cluster Maximum Login Time**: The maximum amount of time a user may be logged into a device of the same cluster. This field is ignored unless **Enforce Intra-cluster Maximum Login Time** is set to **True**.

- **Inter-cluster Maximum Login Time**: The maximum amount of time a user may be logged in remotely to a device of a different cluster. This field is ignored unless **Enforce Intra-cluster Maximum Login Time** is set to **True**.

- **Maximum Concurrent Requests**: This field specifies the number of simultaneous login and logout operations the Unified Communications Manager will perform.

- **Intra-cluster Multiple Login Behavior**:
    - **Multiple Logins Allowed**: This allows a user to login to more than one device at a time.
    - **Multiple Logins Not Allowed**: Second and subsequent login attempts after a user is already logged in will fail.
    - **Auto Logout**: If a user logs in to a second device, the Unified Communications Manager automatically logs the user out of the first device.

- **Alphanumeric User ID**: If **True,** this allows the user ID to contain numbers and letters, otherwise only numeric IDs will be accepted.

- **Remember the Last User Logged In**: If **True**, the phone device will retain the User ID in the Extension Mobility service, allowing the user to only require the PIN to log in.

- **Clear Call Logs on Intra-cluster EM**: If **True** the call logs are cleared upon login and logout.

- **Validate IP Address**: If **True**, the Unified Communications Manager will attempt to validate the IP Address to ensure it is a trusted device.

- **Trusted List of IPs**: This field contains IP address or host names of devices trusted, separated by a semi-colon. This field is only used if **Validate IP Address** is set to **True**.
- **Allow Proxy**: If **True**, this will allow the Extension Mobility login/log out operations to use a proxy. This setting is only used if **Validate IP Address** is set to **True**.
- **EMCC Allow Proxy**: Same as **Allow Proxy** but applies to Cross Cluster Extension Mobility. This setting is only used if **Validate IP Address** is set to **True**.
- **Extension Mobility Cache Size**: Determines how many devices are cached by the system. This setting is only used if **Validate IP Address** is set to **True**.

5. Click on **Save**.

How it works...

The Unified Communications Manager will use these parameter settings when performing Extension Mobility login and log out operations.

Enabling the Cross Cluster Extension Mobility services

Before we can begin configuring and setting up Cross Cluster Extension Mobility, we must first activate the necessary services.

How to do it...

To activate the necessary services, perform the following:

1. First navigate to the **Unified Serviceability** page (`https://cucm/ccmservice`).
2. Navigate to the **Services Activation** page (**Tools | Service Activation**).
3. Activate the following services:
    - Cisco CallManager
    - Cisco Tftp
    - Cisco Extension Mobility
    - Cisco Bulk Provisioning Service
4. Click on **Save**.

How it works...

Just as with regular extension mobility, these services are required so that the Unified Communications Manager can serve out configurations as well as have the extension mobility service active.

Configuring the Cross Cluster Extension Mobility phone service

Similar to Extension Mobility, we must first create the service. This service would then be assigned to the appropriate devices and device profiles.

Getting ready

This recipe assumes the Extension Mobility service is already active.

How to do it...

To create the Cross Cluster Extension Mobility phone service, perform the following:

1. Navigate to the **Phone Services** configuration page (**Device | Device Settings | Phone Services**).
2. Click on **Add New**.
3. Specify a **Service Name**.
4. Specify the **Service URL**, substitute **192.168.1.5** with the appropriate IP address.

>  http://192.168.1.5:8080/emapp/EMAppServlet?device=#DEVICENAME#&EMCC=#EMCC#.

5. Check **Enable**.

6. If we are to enable this service for all devices, check **Enterprise Subscription**.

```
Service Information
  Service Name*        Cross Cluster Extension Mobility
  ASCII Service Name*  Cross Cluster Extension Mobility
  Service Description
  Service URL          http://192.168.1.5:8080/emapp/EMAppServlet?devi
  Secure-Service URL
  Service Category*    XML Service
  Service Type*        Standard IP Phone Service
  Service Vendor
  Service Version
  ☑ Enable
  ☐ Enterprise Subscription
```

7. Click on **Save**.

How it works...

This service, when applied to a device or device profile, will allow the user the access to and use of the Cross Cluster Extension Mobility service.

Configure users for Cross Cluster Extension Mobility

Before a user can be allowed to use the cross cluster extension mobility features, they must first be configured for it.

Getting Ready

This recipe assumes the device profile has already been created for the user and associated with that user.

Advanced Features

How to do it...

To configure a user for Cross Cluster Extension Mobility, perform the following:

1. Navigate to the **End User** configuration page (**User Management | End User**).
2. Locate the user we are to configure and access their page.
3. Under the **Extension Mobility** section, check **Enable Extension Mobility Cross Cluster**:

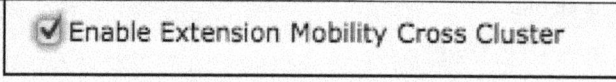

4. Click on **Save**.

How it works...

The enable Extension Mobility Cross Cluster check box is required; it tells the Unified Communications Manager that this user can use this feature.

Preparing certificates for Cross Cluster Extension Mobility

In order for the clusters to talk to each other securely, they must have the certificate information of each cluster that is participating in the Cross Cluster Extension Mobility.

Getting ready

This recipe assumes the SFTP server required has already been setup, and access details are known.

How to do it...

First, we must configure the bulk certificate management; this specifies the SFTP server that will store the certificates.

1. First navigate to the **OS Administration** page (https://cucm/cmplatform).
2. Navigate to the **Bulk Certificate Management** page (**Security | Bulk Certificate Management**).
3. Specify the **IP Address** of the SFTP server.
4. Specify the **Port**, if different.

5. Specify the **User ID** that can access the SFTP server.
6. Specify the **Password** for the user in step 5.
7. Specify the **Directory.**

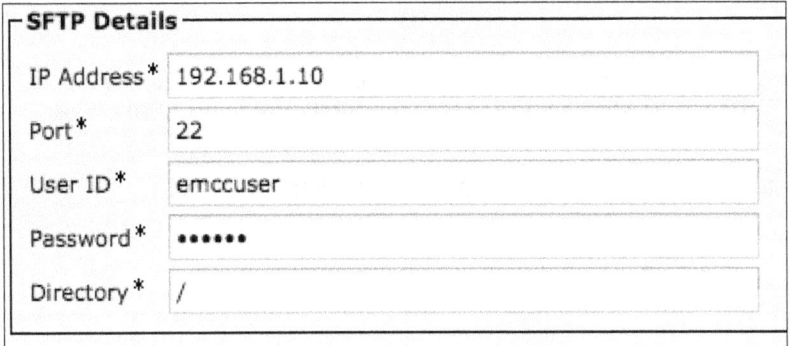

8. Click on **Save**.

 After clicking **Save**, the server will attempt to access the server with the details provided.

Next, we export the certificates to the SFTP server:

1. Navigate to the **Bulk Certificate Management** page (**Security | Bulk Certificate Management**).
2. Click **Export**.
3. For the **Certificate Type**, select **All** from the drop-down box.

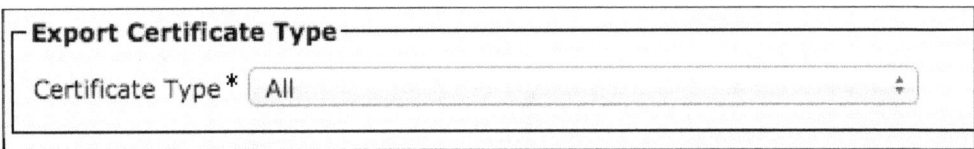

4. Click on **Export**.
5. Click on **Close**.

Advanced Features

Next, we consolidate the certificates into a single certificate; this certificate will be distributed to each cluster participating in Cross Cluster Extension Mobility:

1. Navigate to the **Bulk Certificate Consolidation** page (**Security | Bulk Certificate Management | Consolidate | Bulk Certificate Consolidate**).

    This menu option is only available after a minimum of two clusters have exported their certificates to the SFTP server.

2. For the **Certificate Type**, select **All** from the drop-down box:

3. Click on **Consolidate**.

    If new certificates are later exported, we must run the consolidation process again or communication may fail between the clusters.

Finally, we import the bulk certificate:

1. Navigate to the **Bulk Certificate Consolidation** page (**Security | Bulk Certificate Management | Import | Bulk Certificate Import**).
2. For the **Certificate Type**, select **All** from the drop-down box:

   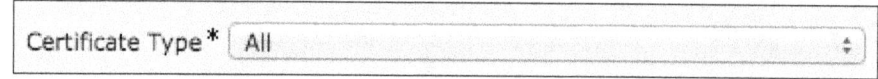

3. Click on **Import**.

How it works...

This process first exports the security certificates of each cluster into the SFTP server; those certificates are then consolidated into a single certificate. The generated certificate is then used by each of the clusters when communicating in the Cross Cluster Extension Mobility process.

Creating a template for Cross Cluster Extension Mobility devices

When a user remotely logs in to the cluster, the settings from this template will be applied to that device.

How to do it...

To create the template, perform the following:

1. Navigate to the Extension Mobility Cross Cluster (**EMCC**) **Template Configuration** page (**Bulk Administration | EMCC | EMCC Template**).
2. Click **Add New**.
3. Specify a **Template Name**.
4. Specify the **Device Pool**.
5. Specify the **SIP Profile**.
6. Specify a **Common Device Configuration**.

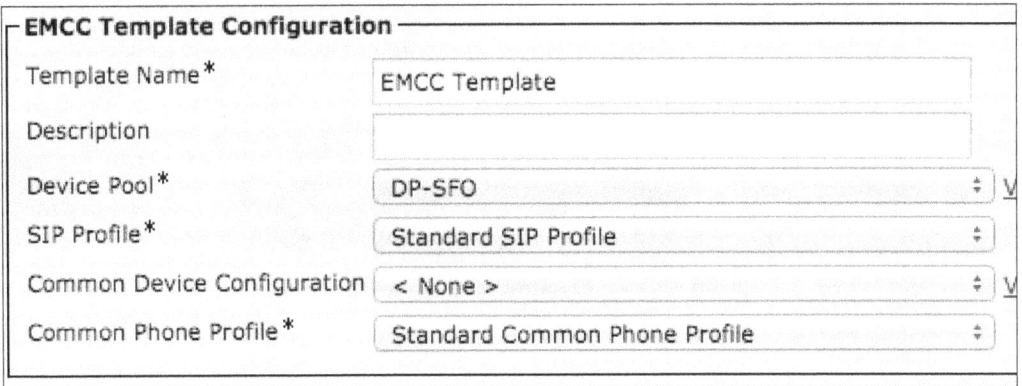

7. Click on **Save**.

Next, we can update the devices using the created template:

1. Navigate to the **Insert/Update EMCC** configuration page (**Bulk Administration | EMCC | Insert/Update EMCC**).
2. Under the **Insert/Update EMCC** section, select **Update EMCC Devices**.
3. From the **Default EMCC Template** drop-down, select the **EMCC Template** previously created.

Advanced Features

4. Select **Run Immediately**, or, if necessary, **Run Later**.

[form image showing: Update EMCC Devices (selected), Default EMCC Template* [EMCC Template], Don't Reset (selected); Job Information – Job Description: Update EMCC Devices; Run Immediately (selected), Run Later (To schedule and activate this job, use Job Sch...)]

5. Click on **Submit**.

>  We may also insert devices by selecting Insert EMCC Devices at step 2 and specifying the number of devices we are to insert.

How it works...

The **EMCC Template** details the configuration information that will be passed along to the remote (also known as "visiting") device.

Configuring Cross Cluster Extension Mobility parameters

Before Cross Cluster Extension Mobility can function, there are a few parameters that must first be set.

How to do it...

To configure the enterprise parameters, perform the following:

1. Navigate to the **Enterprise Parameters** page (**System | Enterprise Parameters**).
2. For each cluster participating in cross cluster extension mobility, specify a unique **Cluster ID**.

Parameter Name	Parameter Value
Cluster ID *	EMCC-SFO-Cluster

3. Click on **Save**.

Next, we will configure the EMCC Feature parameters:

1. Navigate to the **EMCC Feature Configuration** page (**Advanced Features | EMCC | EMCC Feature Configuration**).
2. From the **Default TFTP Server for EMCC Login Device** drop-down box, select the desired server:

Default TFTP Server for EMCC Login Device	192.168.1.5

3. From the **Default Server for Remote Cluster Update** drop-down box, select the desired server:

Default Server For Remote Cluster Update	192.168.1.5

4. Click on **Save**.

How it works...

The cluster ID must be unique between the clusters participating in Cross Cluster Extension Mobility, otherwise this process will fail. Additionally, we must specify which server will act as the default TFTP server, which will serve the configuration information to the device after it logs in.

Configuring intercluster trunks for Cross Cluster Extension Mobility

Cross Cluster Extension Mobility requires the use of SIP trunks to communicate between the clusters. However there are some specific settings that must be configured.

How to do it...

To configure a SIP trunk for Cross Cluster Extension Mobility, perform the following:

1. Navigate to the **Trunk** configuration page (**Device | Trunk**).
2. Click on **Add New**.
3. From the **Trunk Type** drop-down box, specify **SIP Trunk.**
4. From the **Trunk Service Type** drop-down box, specify **Extension Mobility Cross Cluster**.

Advanced Features

5. Click on **Next**.
6. Configure the appropriate settings for the trunk including:
   - **Name**
   - **Device Pool**
   - **SIP Trunk Security Profile**
   - **SIP Profile**
7. Check **Send Geolocation Information**.
8. Ensure that both **Unattended Port** and **Media Termination Point Required** are not checked.
9. Click on **Save**.

How it works...

When using Cross Cluster Extension Mobility, we must send the geolocation information; without this, the feature will fail. Additionally, we must ensure that the **Unattended Port** and **Media Termination Point Required** are not checked, as this can also cause the feature to fail.

Configuring the intercluster service profile for Cross Cluster Extension Mobility

The intercluster service profile is where we activate our Cross Cluster Extension Mobility feature; this must be done after all other configurations have been performed.

Getting ready

This recipe assumes that the certificates, SIP trunks, and if desired, RSVP, have already been created and are in place.

How to do it...

To configure the intercluster service profile, perform the following:

1. Navigate to the **EMCC Intercluster Service Profile** page (**Advanced Features | EMCC | EMCC Intercluster Service Profile**).
2. Under the **EMCC** section, check **Active**.
3. Under the **PSTN Access** section, check **Active** and specify the **SIP Trunk**.

4. Under the **RSVP Agent** section, check **Active** and specify the **SIP Trunk**.

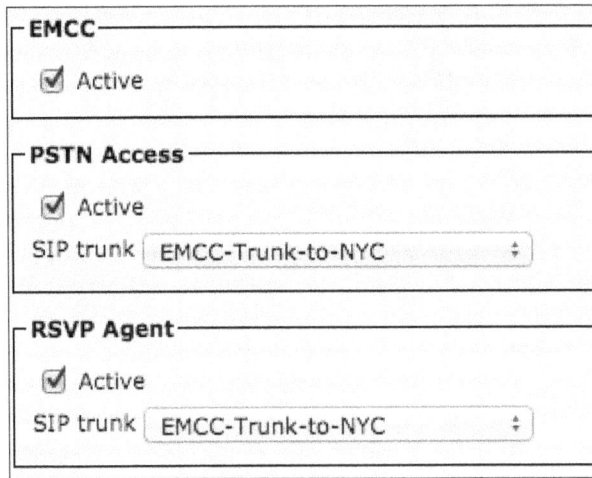

5. Click on **Validate**.
6. When there are no errors, click on **Save**.

Finally, configure the remote cluster for Cross Cluster Extension Mobility:

1. Navigate to the **EMCC Remote Cluster** page (**Advanced Features** | **EMCC** | **EMCC Remote Cluster**).
2. Click **Add New**.
3. Specify the **Cluster Id**.
4. If desired, specify a **Description**.
5. Specify the **Fully Qualified Name**.

> It is generally a good idea to use the IP Address instead of the domain name here.

6. Click on **Save**.

Repeat steps 2 to 6 for each cluster that will participate in Cross Cluster Extension Mobility.

How it works...

First, we activate the Cross Cluster Extension Mobility feature and specify the SIP Trunk between the clusters. We then add the remote clusters by specifying the cluster ID and fully qualified name, which in general should be the IP address of the remote device.

Advanced Features

Configuring monitoring and recording

In call center type environments, call recording and monitoring is a vital feature for quality assurance and legal reasons. In this recipe, we will configure all the necessary aspects to get this feature working.

Getting ready

This recipe assumes the necessary calling search spaces have already been created.

How to do it...

To configure monitoring and recording, perform the following:

1. First, we must create the Application user that will be responsible for monitoring and recording (**User Management | Application User**).
2. Click on **Add New**.
3. Specify a **User ID**.
4. From the **Available Devices** listbox, select the devices we want to monitor and record, click the down arrow, and they will appear in the **Controlled Devices** listbox.
5. Click **Add User to Group**.
6. Add the user to the following groups:
    - Standard CTI Allow Call Monitoring
    - Standard CTI Allow Call Recording
    - Standard CTI Enabled
7. Click **Add Selected**.
8. Click **Save** to save the application user.

Next we will create a recording profile:

1. Navigate to the **Recording Profile** page (**Device | Device Settings | Recording Profile**).
2. Click **Add New**.
3. Specify a **Name**.
4. Specify the **Recording Calling Search Space**.

5. Specify the **Recording Destination Address**.

6. Click on **Save**.

Next, we will create the route point that will send the call to our recording software:

 We must make sure that we have already created a SIP Trunk to the recording software before creating the route point.

1. Navigate to the **Route Pattern** configuration page (**Call Routing | Route/Hunt | Route Pattern**).
2. Click **Add New**.
3. Specify the **Route Pattern**; this will be the same one we specified for the **Recording Destination** previously.
4. From the **Gateway/Route List** drop-down menu, select the SIP trunk to the recording software.
5. Click on **Save**.

Now we must enable the device and line settings for recording.

1. Navigate to the desired device (**Device | Phone**).
2. Set **Built In Bridge** to **On.**

3. Click on **Save**.
4. Next, navigate to the directory number we want to enable for recording.

Advanced Features

5. Select the desired option from the **Recording Option** drop-down box.
6. Select the appropriate **Recording Profile** from the drop-down box.
7. From the **Monitoring Calling Search Space** drop-down box, select a calling search space that has access to all partitions:

Recording Option*	Automatic Call Recording Enabled
Recording Profile	RecordingProfile
Monitoring Calling Search Space	CSS-AllCSS

8. Click on **Save**.

How it works...

Depending on the software used for monitoring and recording, and the recording option chosen, a recorded or monitored call is sent to the destination specified in the recording profile. That destination is a route point that points to the recording software.

There's more...

With service parameters, we have the option to specify if a tone will be played alerting the agent, customer, or both. We can configure that behavior by performing the following steps:

1. Navigate to the Service Parameters page (**System | Service Parameters**).
2. Select the appropriate **Server**.
3. Select **Cisco CallManager** from the **Service** drop-down box.

4. Specify the desired settings for call recording and monitoring under the **Clusterwide Parameters (Feature - Call Recording)** and **Clusterwide Parameters (Feature - Monitoring)** sections:

Clusterwide Parameters (Feature - Call Recording)	
Play Recording Notification Tone To Observed Target *	True
Play Recording Notification Tone To Observed Connected Parties *	False

Clusterwide Parameters (Feature - Monitoring)	
Play Monitoring Notification Tone To Observed Target *	True
Play Monitoring Notification Tone To Observed Connected Parties *	False

5. Click on **Save**.

Configuring geolocations and filters

Geolocations and filters are generally necessary only when there is a legal requirement to prevent features such as Tail End Hop Off (TEHO).

Getting ready

This recipe assumes the device pools, devices, trunks, and so on have already been configured and exist in the system.

Advanced Features

How to do it...

To configure geolocations and filters, perform the following:

1. Navigate to the **Geolocation Configuration** page (**System | Geolocation Configuration**).
2. Click on **Add New**.
3. Specify a **Name**.
4. Specify any additional desired details:

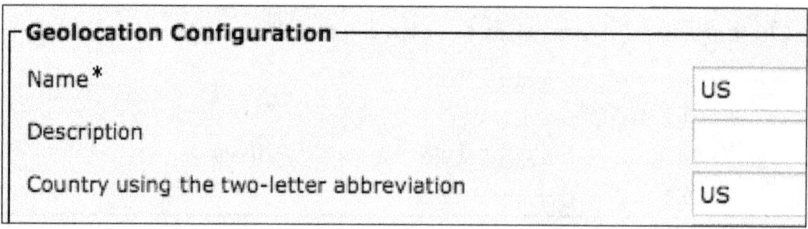

5. Click on **Save**.

Repeat steps 2 to 5 for each location as desired.

If desired, to configure a geolocation filter, perform the following steps:

1. Navigate to the **Geolocation Filter Configuration** page (**System | Geolocation Filter**).
2. Click **Add New**.
3. Specify a **Name**.
4. Check the box appropriate to the criteria by which you wish to filter:

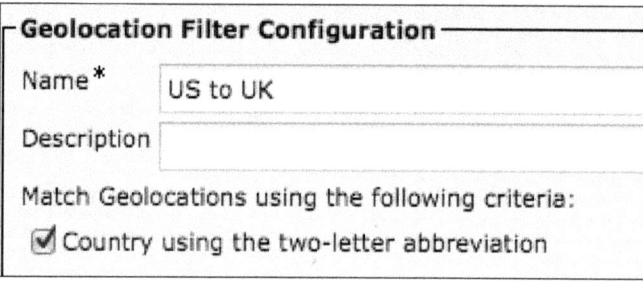

5. Click on **Save**.

Repeat steps 2 to 5 for each filter as desired.

Finally, apply the geolocation and filters to the appropriate devices, device pool, and so on.

An example of the geolocation and filter on a device pool:

```
Geolocation Configuration
Geolocation        US
Geolocation Filter US to UK
```

On a phone device:

```
Geolocation        US
```

How it works...

By themselves, geolocation and filters don't do much of anything. Instead, they are a way of marking devices so the programming behind logical partitioning can function.

Implementing logical partitioning

Logical partitioning uses geolocation information and filters to deny or allow calls between locations; for instance, TEHO calls between two countries may need to be denied due to legal requirements.

Getting ready

This recipe assumes geolocations and filters have already been configured and applied to the appropriate devices.

How to do it...

To implement logical partition, perform the following:

1. **First,** enable the **logical partitioning enterprise parameter**.
2. Navigate to the **Enterprise parameters** page (**System | Enterprise Parameters**).

Advanced Features

3. Under the **Logical Partitioning Configuration** section, set **Enable Logical Partitioning** to **True**.

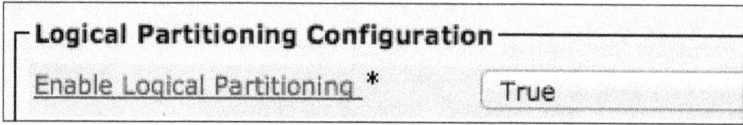

4. Click on **Save**.

Next, to configure a logical partitioning policy, perform the following steps:

1. Navigate to the **Logical Partitioning Policy Configuration** page (**Call Routing | Logical Partition Policy Configuration**).
2. Click **Add New**.
3. Specify a **Name**.
4. Select the desired fields to filter by.

5. Click on **Save**.

The page will refresh and then we can set our policies.

6. Select a **Device Type**.
7. Select a **Geolocation Policy**.
8. Select the **Other Device Type**.
9. Specify the desired **Policy**.
10. Click on **Save**.

We must then repeat steps 6 to 10 for each relationship we wish to define.

Chapter 8

How it works...

Logical partitioning works by combining policy information with geolocation information. When we create a logical partition policy, we are defining which type of devices can make calls, generally between two countries or regions. This is done largely by specifying the device type, which can be border or interior.

Border devices are generally gateways or devices that reach the PSTN.

Interior devices are devices such as phones, cti route points and cti ports.

This distinction is necessary so that we may allow calls over the IP WAN to others on cluster devices (interior), but do not allow calls over the IP WAN to TEHO out the other side (border).

Configuring hotline service parameters

Hotline service parameters will have to be configured to match what the far-end switch expects to receive during signaling.

How to do it...

The hotline service parameters must first be configured before configuring the hotline feature.

   In general, the defaults selected here are sufficient.

To configure the hotline service parameters, perform the following:

1. Navigate to the **Service Parameters Configuration** page (**System | Service Parameters**).
2. Specify the appropriate **Server**.
3. Under the **Service** drop-down menu, select **Cisco CallManager**.
4. Click **Advanced**.
5. Navigate down to the section **Clusterwide Parameters (Route Class Signaling)**.
6. For **Route Class Trunk Signaling Enabled** select **True** from the drop-down menu:

7. Specify a text label for the **SIP Hotline Voice Route Class Label** field.

Advanced Features

8. Specify a text label for **SIP Hotline Data Route Class Label** field.

SIP Hotline Voice Route Class Label *	hotline
SIP Hotline Data Route Class Label *	hotline-ccdata

9. Click on **Save**.

How it works...

There are three primary service parameters for the hotline feature; their functions are described as follows:

- **Route Class Trunk Signaling Enabled**: This enables interworking between IP and TDM switches that use route classes.

- **SIP Hotline Voice Route Class Label**: This label represents the hotline voice route class and proves useful when interworking with TDM networks that make routing decisions based on hotline voice route class. Make sure that the far-end switch expects the same value that you configure in this parameter.

- **SIP Hotline Data Route Class Label**: This label represents the hotline data route class and proves useful when interworking with TDM networks that make routing decisions based on hotline voice route class. Make sure that the far-end switch expects the same value that you configure in this parameter.

Configuring a hotline device

A hotline device functions in a similar manner to a device that is configured for Private Line Automatic Ringdown (PLAR), in that once the phone goes off hook, it will dial a preconfigured number. Hotline extends this functionality by limiting hotline devices from talking to non-hotline devices.

Getting ready

This recipe assumes the relevant hotline service parameters have been configured.

How to do it...

To configure a hotline device, perform the following:

1. Create a partition for the hotline device (**Call Routing | Class of Control | Partition**).

2. Create a calling search space for the hotline device (**Call Routing | Class of Control | Calling Search Space**):

   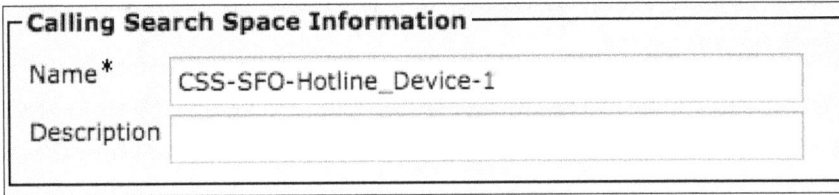

   Select the partition:

Selected Partitions	PT-SFO-Hotline_Device-1

3. Now we create a **Translation Pattern** using the previously created partition and calling search space (**Call Routing | Translation Pattern**).
4. Leave the **Translation Pattern** field blank.
5. Specify the **Partition** created in step 1.

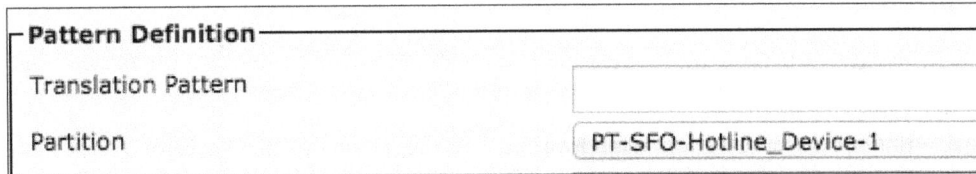

6. Specify the **Calling Search Space** created in step 2.

Calling Search Space	CSS-SFO-Hotline_Device-1

Advanced Features

7. Specify the destination the hotline device will dial in the **Called Party Transform Mask** field.

8. Click **Save** to save the translation pattern.
9. Next, locate and configure the hotline device (**Device | Phone**).
10. From the **Calling Search Space** drop-down, select the one created in step 2.
11. Check **Hot line Device**.

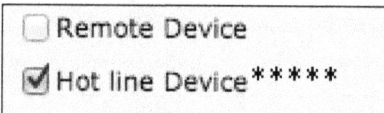

12. Click on **Save**.
13. Now, assign the partition created in step 1 to the directory number that we specified in step 7 (**Call Routing | Directory Number**).

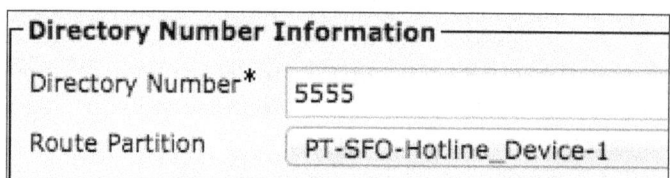

14. Click on **Save**.

Next, to configure the route patterns/translation patterns to enable sending the route class hotline voice, perform the following steps:

1. Under the Route Pattern (**Call Routing | Route/Hunt | Route Pattern**) or Translation Pattern (**Call Routing | Translation Pattern**), select **Hotline Voice** from the **Route Class** drop-down menu:

2. Click on **Save**.

Finally, to enable the use of route classes on the gateway or trunk device, perform the following steps:

1. Under the gateway (**Device | Gateway**) or Trunk (**Device | Trunk**) device select **On** from the **Route Class Signaling Enabled** drop-down:

Route Class Signaling Enabled*	On

2. Click on **Reset**.
3. Click on **Save**.

How it works...

Hotline functions much the same as PLAR configured devices do. In addition to dialing the hotline feature, it will send specific signals informing that the originating device is a hotline device, and will either accept or reject that device, depending on configuration.

In this recipe, we create a partition and calling search space, which contains the created partition. This is applied to a translation pattern and is configured with the same partition. The effect of this is that when a device configured with the calling search space picks up the call, the only possible match is a null match, thus immediately dialing the number configured in the translation pattern.

By checking **Hotline Device** on the phone, the Unified Communications manager will send the appropriate information in the form of signaling and route classes. To this end, the route patterns and/or translation patterns must be configured to send the hotline voice route class.

In order for the route class information to reach the destination intact, the **Route Class Signaling Enabled** option must be set to **On**.

Configuring barge for devices and users

The barge feature allows users to barge into an already active call, during which the user can be notified the call has been barged into, by way of a barge tone. Additionally, the conference barge feature can be used to place all parties into an active conference.

How to do it...

To configure a phone for barge, perform the following:

1. Navigate to the device that will be configured for the barge feature (**Device | Phone**).

Advanced Features

2. Under **Device Information** section, select **On** from the **Built In Bridge** drop-down:

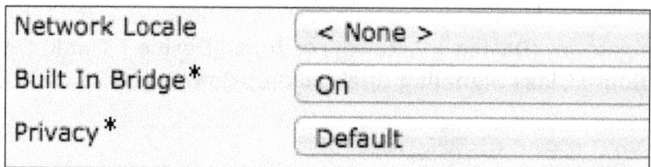

3. Click on **Save**.
4. Next, navigate to the **End User** page of the user that will use the barge feature (**User Management | End User**).
5. Under the **Device Information** section, click **Device Association**.
6. Search for the device previously configured in Step 2. Check the box to the left of the device as shown in the following screenshot:

7. Click **Save Selected/Changes**.
8. In the top-right hand area of the window, select **Back to User** from the **Related Links** drop-down:

9. Click on **Go**.
10. Verify that the device shows up under **Controlled Devices**; if it does not, repeat steps 5 to 9 again.
11. Repeat these steps for each device and user to be configured for the barge feature.

How it works...

The barge feature allows a user to be connected to a call already in progress on a shared line. To facilitate this, a feature known as the built in bridge must be enabled for the device. This can be done locally per phone, or globally for all devices through enterprise parameters.

When the user selects the barge softkey, they are added to the active call with the other parties; depending on configuration there may or may not be an entrance tone.

There's more...

There are two types of barges, the standard barge and the conference barge. Conference barge adds all parties to a conference (the device will read and act exactly like a conference call). This feature requires a conference bridge to be configured.

Conference barge

To configure conference barge, perform the following:

1. First, create a new softkey template (**Device | Phone Settings | Softkey Template**), and add the **cBarge** softkey to the **Remote In Use** call state:

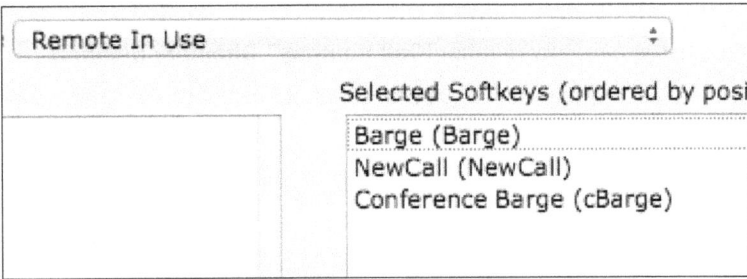

2. Apply the newly created softkey template to the desired device (**Device | Phone**).

Configuring barge tones

Whenever a call is barged, whether standard barge or conference barge, a tone can be heard depending on the configuration of the device and service parameters.

To configure barge tones globally, perform the following:

1. Navigate to the service parameters configuration page (**System | Service Parameters**).
2. Specify the appropriate **Server**.
3. Under the **Service** drop-down menu, select **Cisco CallManager**.

Advanced Features

4. Under the **Clusterwide Parameters (Feature - General)** section, select the desired option from the **Party Entrance Tone** drop-down menu:

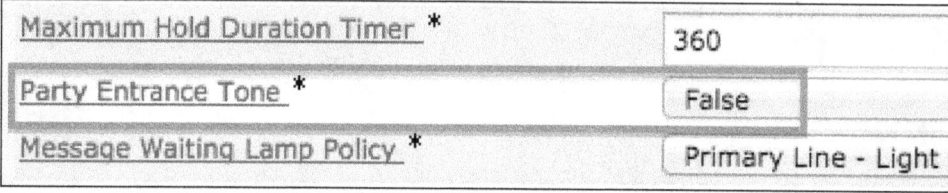

5. Click on **Save**.

To configure barge tones on a per number basis, perform the following:

1. Navigate to the directory number (**Call Routing | Directory Number**).
2. Under the **Line Settings for All Devices** section, select the desired option from the **Party Entrance Tone** drop-down menu:

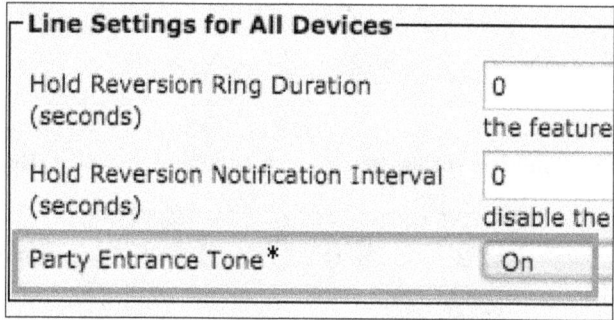

3. Click on **Save**.

Configuring privacy for devices and users

The privacy feature allows the user to mark a call as private, preventing other users of the shared line to view with whom the user is on a call.

Getting ready

Before we can use the privacy feature, we must first enable it in the system parameters.

To enable the privacy feature, perform the following:

1. Navigate to the **Service Parameters Configuration** page (**System | Service Parameters**).

Chapter 8

2. Specify the appropriate **Server.**
3. Under the **Service** drop-down menu, select **Cisco CallManager**.
4. Under the **Clusterwide Parameters (Device - Phone)** section, select **True** from the **Privacy Setting** drop-down menu:

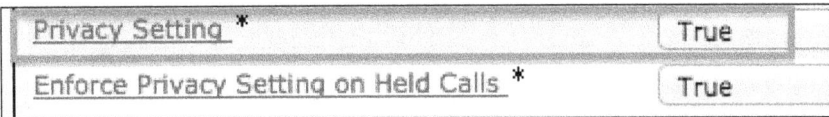

5. Click on **Save**.

How to do it...

To configure the privacy feature, perform the following:

1. Navigate to the device that will be configured for the privacy feature (**Device | Phone**).
2. Under **Device Information** section, select **On** from the **Privacy** drop-down:

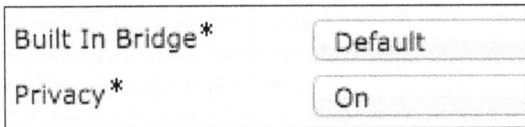

3. Click on **Save**.
4. Next, configure a phone button template (**Device | Phone Settings | Phone Button Template**) and add **Privacy** as one of the button items:

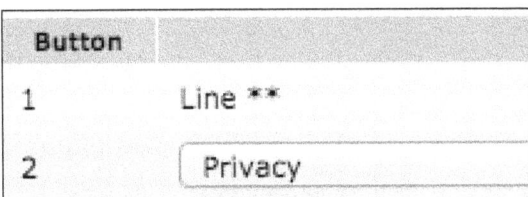

5. Save the phone button template by clicking **Save**.

Advanced Features

6. Next, apply the newly created phone button template to the device (**Device | Phone**):

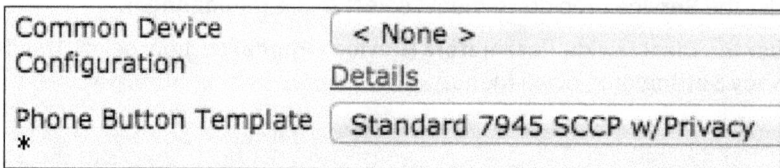

7. Save the changes to the device and soft reset it by clicking **Save**, then **Apply Config**.
8. Next, associate the previously configured device to the end user who will be using the privacy feature (**User Management | End User**).
9. Under the **Device Information** section, click **Device Association**.
10. Search for the device previously configured in step 2 and step 6. Check the box to the left of the device, as shown in the following screenshot:

11. Click on **Save Selected/Changes**.
12. In the top-right hand area of the window, select **Back to User** from the **Related Links** drop-down menu:

13. Click on **Go**.

How it works...

Privacy works on shared lines by preventing other users of that shared line viewing the caller ID information of the person the user is connected to. When pressing the privacy button, the caller ID information will no longer be available to other users.

There's more...

In addition to the privacy feature, there is another feature called Privacy on Hold. This retains the privacy information when the caller is placed on hold.

To enable Privacy on Hold, perform the following:

1. Navigate to the service parameters configuration page (**System | Service Parameters**).
2. Specify the appropriate **Server.**
3. Under the **Service** drop-down menu, select **Cisco CallManager.**
4. Under the **Clusterwide Parameters (Device - Phone)** section, select **True** from the **Enforce Privacy Setting on Held Calls** drop-down menu:

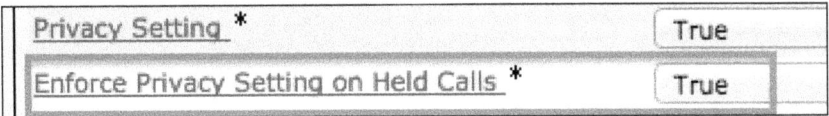

5. Click on **Save**.

9
Securing Unified Communications

In this chapter, we will cover:

- Configuring phone security profiles
- Configuring devices for secure tone
- Configuring Certificate Authority Proxy Function
- Configuring digest authentication
- Implementing endpoint hardening
- Implementing a secure conference bridge
- Implementing secure Meet-Me conferences
- Configuring VPN for Cisco IP phones
- Configuring application users for secure communication

Introduction

This chapter will provide common configuration information for securing a Unified Communications Manager cluster.

We will configure phones to communicate over the secure real time protocol, configure conference resources to use SRTP and prevent Meet-Me conferences from allowing unsecured devices, and configure the Unified Communications Manager for remote VPNs by IP phones.

Configuring phone security profiles

Phone security profiles allow us to group security-related settings for a phone type and protocol that we can then assign to a device. The device will then be required to enforce those settings.

How to do it...

To configure a phone security profile, perform the following:

1. First navigate to the phone security profile page (**System | Security | Phone Security Profile**).
2. Click on **Add New**.
3. From the **Product Type** drop-down, select the appropriate device type.
4. Click on **Next**.
5. Select the appropriate protocol from the drop-down.

> Select the type of device profile you would like to create
>
> Product Type: Cisco 7945
> Select the phone security profile protocol: * SCCP

6. Click on **Next**.
7. Specify a **Name**.
8. From the **Device Security Mode** drop-down, select the desired mode.
9. If desired, check **TFTP Encrypted Config**.
10. Specify the **Authentication Mode**.

11. If desired, change the **Key Size**:

```
┌─Phone Security Profile Information─────────────────────────────┐
│  Product Type:      Cisco 7945                                 │
│  Device Protocol:   SCCP                                       │
│  Name*              Secure 7945                                │
│  Description                                                   │
│  Device Security Mode   Authenticated                       ▼  │
│     ☐ TFTP Encrypted Config                                    │
└────────────────────────────────────────────────────────────────┘
┌─Phone Security Profile CAPF Information────────────────────────┐
│  Authentication Mode*    By Authentication String           ▼  │
│  Key Size (Bits)*        1024                               ▼  │
│  Note: These fields are related to the CAPF Information settings on the Phone Configu│
└────────────────────────────────────────────────────────────────┘
```

For SIP devices:

1. Specify the **Transport Type**.
2. If desired, check **Enable Digest Authentication**.
3. If using digest authentication and if desired, check **Exclude Digest Credentials in Configuration File**.
4. If necessary, change the **SIP Phone Port**.
5. Click on **Save**.

How it works...

The phone security profile is applied to a phone device and added to its configuration. This requires the device to be reset. After the phone security profile is applied, the phone will enforce the settings as specified in the security profile.

Configuring devices for secure tone

Secure tone allows a user of a secure phone to hear audible confirmation that the communication with the other caller is either secure or non-secure. This happens immediately after the phone connects with the remote phone.

Getting ready

Before we configure a phone device to allow secure tones to play, we need to select the appropriate server and activate the secure tone:

1. Navigate to the service parameters configuration page (**System | Service Parameters**).
2. Specify the appropriate **Server**.
3. Under the **Service** drop-down menu, select **Cisco CallManager**.
4. Under the **Clusterwide Parameters (Feature - Secure Tone)** section, select **True** from the secure tone drop-down:

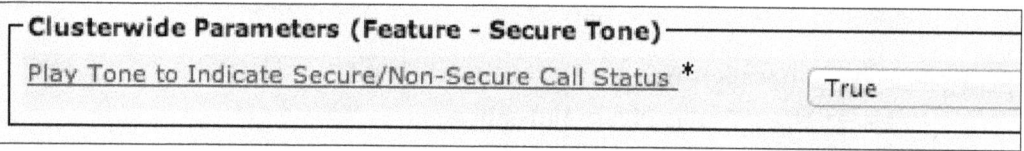

5. Click on **Save**.

This recipe also requires a phone security profile to have already been created.

> Shared lines and the Extension Mobility service are not supported for protected phones!

How to do it...

To configure a phone device to allow secure tones to play, perform the following:

1. Navigate to the desired device (**Device | Phone**).

2. From the **Softkey Template** drop-down, select **Standard Protected Phone**:

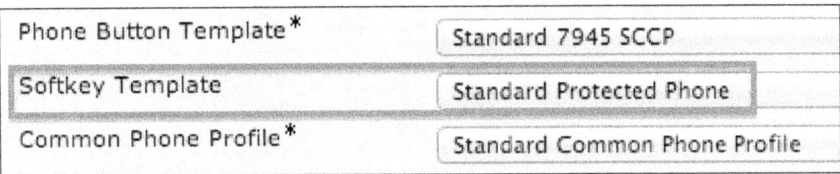

3. From the **Join Across Lines** drop-down, select **Off**:

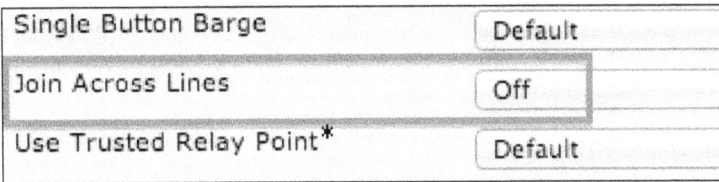

4. Check the box next to **Protected Device**:

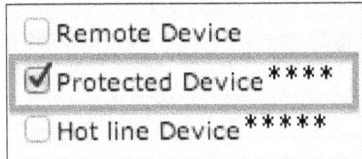

5. From the **Device Security Profile** drop-down, in the **Protocol Specific Information** section, select a secure phone profile:

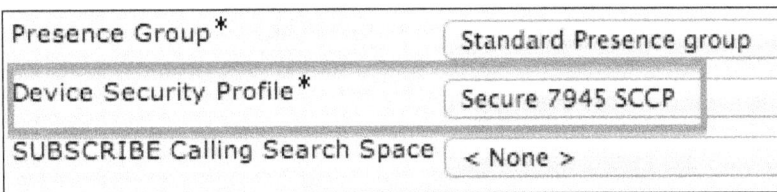

6. Click on **Save**.
7. From the Device configuration page, select the **Directory Number**.
8. Under the **Multiple Call/Call Waiting Settings** section (near the bottom) specify the value of 1 for the following fields:
    - **Maximum Number of Calls**
    - **Busy Trigger**
9. Click on **Save**.

Securing Unified Communications

How it works...

There are a few limitations when configuring a protected phone for secure tone. Firstly, the softkey template must be the Standard Protected Phone template. This prevents access to unprotected features. Secondly, Join Across Lines is not supported on protected phones, nor are shared lines. Therefore, these must be disabled.

By checking the **Protected Device** checkbox, we inform the Unified Communications Manager that this device will use the secure tone feature (which must be set to **True** in the service parameters).

When a protected phone initiates a call with another secure phone, three long beeps will be heard. When a protected phone initiates a call with an unprotected phone, six short beeps will be heard.

There's more...

When configuring secure tone with an MGCP E1 gateway, we must perform the following:

1. Navigate to the appropriate MGCP gateway (**Device | Gateway**).
2. From the **Global ISDN Switch Type** drop-down, select **EURO**:

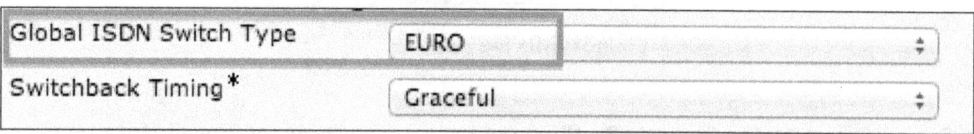

3. Click on **Save**.
4. Next, from the E1 Port configuration, check the **Enable Protected Facility IE** box:

5. Click on **Save**.

This is necessary to allow the system to pass protected status of the call between the IP phone and the protected PBX that is connected to the gateway.

> When using a MGCP E1 gateway, it must be configured for SRTP. This is done using the `mgcp package-capability srtp-package` command.

Configuring Certificate Authority Proxy Function

The **Certificate Authority Proxy Function** (**CAPF**) automatically authenticates using certificates and authentication strings, and can issue local certificates to endpoint devices.

Getting ready

Before we can configure the CAPF functionality, we must first activate the services. To activate the appropriate services, perform the following:

1. Navigate to the Unified Serviceability configuration page (https://192.168.1.5/ccmservice).
2. Navigate to the service activate page (**Tools | Service Activation**).
3. Under the **Security Services** section check the box next to these services:
   - **Cisco CTL Provider**
   - **Cisco Certificate Authority Proxy Function**

Security Services	
	Service Name
☑	Cisco CTL Provider
☑	Cisco Certificate Authority Proxy Function

4. Click on **Save**.

 Certificate tokens must be obtained from Cisco prior to implementing CAPF.

How to do it...

Prior to configuring the CAPF functionality, the Cisco CTL client must be run and configured. Doing so sets the Unified Communication Manager cluster security mode.

Running the CTL client is not documented here. Obtain the appropriate software from CCO and then follow the on-screen instructions.

Securing Unified Communications

First, we must configure and install the CAPF certificate on the phone device. To do so, perform the following:

1. Navigate to the device configuration page (**Device | Phone**).
2. The following configurations are under the **Certification Authority Proxy Function (CAPF) Information** section.
3. From the **Certificate Operation** drop-down, select **Install/Upgrade**.
4. From the **Authenticate Mode** drop-down, select **By Authentication String**.
5. Click on **Generate String**.

>  Generating a string is optional. If desired, specify an authentication string manually.

6. If desired, change the **Key Size** by selecting the appropriate option from the drop-down.
7. If desired, change the **Operation Completes By** date, by entering the date and time in the specified format.

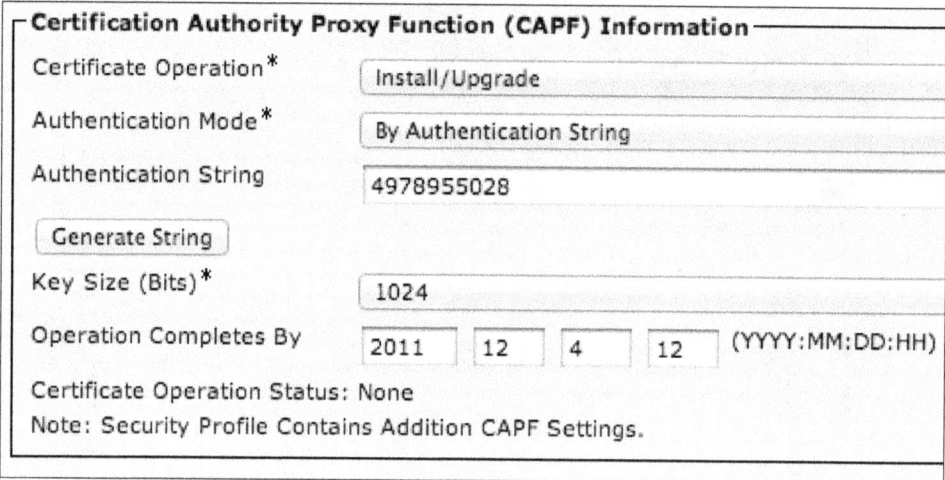

8. Click on **Save**.
9. Click on **Reset**.

   Next, enter the authentication string on the phone itself by performing the following:

10. Press the *Settings* button on the phone.
11. Press ****#** to unlock the settings.
12. Scroll down and select the **Security Configuration** option.

13. Scroll down to the **LSC** option and select **Update**.
14. Enter the **Authentication String** as configured on the device configuration page. In this example, we would enter 4978955028.
15. Press **Submit**.
16. Repeat Steps 1 to 15 for each device to have the CAPF certificate installed.

How it works...

When an IP phone interacts with CAPF, the phone authenticates against an authentication string or a certificate. CAPF then signs the phone certificate and sends a certificate back to the phone in a secure message. The private key as used by the phone is never exposed during communication and as a result allows secure communication between the phone and other CAPF-enabled devices.

Configuring digest authentication

Digest authentication causes the Unified Communications Manager to challenge all request messages for phones that are running SIP.

Getting ready

This recipe assumes the phone security profile has already been created for SIP devices with **Enable Digest Authentication** checked.

How to do it...

To configure digest authentication for an end user and device, perform the following:

1. Navigate to the end user configuration page for the appropriate end user (**User Management | End User**).
2. Under the **User Information** section, specify the **Digest Credentials**.
3. Enter the credential again in the **Confirm Digestion Credentials** field:

Digest Credentials	••••••••
Confirm Digest Credentials	••••••••

4. Click on **Save**.
5. Next, we configure the digest information for the SIP phone device.

Securing Unified Communications

6. Navigate to the phone configuration page (**Device | Phone**).
7. Under the **Protocol Specific Information** section, select a security profile that uses digest authentication under the **Device Security Profile** drop-down:

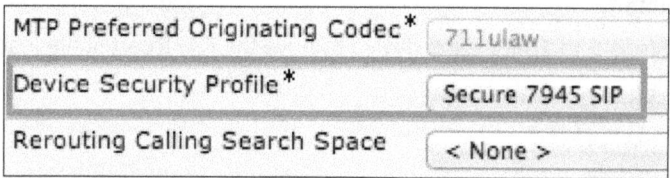

8. From the **Digest User** drop-down, select the end user that was configured in steps 1 to 4:

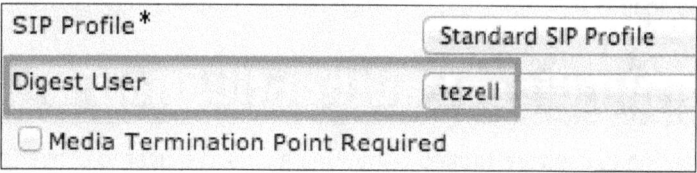

9. Click on **Save**.

For 7940 and 7960, manually enter the digest credentials.

How it works...

Digest authentication works by using challenges for all messages sent between the phone and the Unified Communications Manager. The End User digest information is sent as authentication to the Unified Communications Manager. If the challenge is successful (that is, if the digest authentication information matches with what is in the configuration), the system will act upon the messages it receives (such as to initiate a call, hold, transfer, and so on).

Implementing endpoint hardening

Endpoint hardening is a supplementary step that can provide greater protection from various forms of attacks. It may also make it difficult for users to gain information about the system by preventing the phone from relaying certain information.

Getting ready

Determine from business requirements the fields and options required, and those that will not be required. Those that are not required can be disabled as part of endpoint hardening.

How to do it...

To harden an endpoint from various forms of attacks and vulnerabilities, perform the following:

1. Navigate to the endpoint to be hardened (**Device | Phone**).
2. Under the **Product Specific Configuration Layout** section, enable or disable the following fields as required:
   - **PC Port**
   - **Settings Access**
   - **Gratuitous ARP**
   - **PC Voice VLAN Access**
   - **Web Access**

3. Click on **Save**.
4. Click on **Reset**.
5. Repeat these steps for each endpoint that requires hardening.

How it works...

By disabling certain services, we can increase the security of our setup and prevent our phones from attacks such as Gratuitous ARP poisoning.

Disabling the PC Port prevents a user from connecting a computer to the network by way of this port. This is particularly useful for common place (that is, lobby) phones.

Disabling access to the settings menu prevents a user from gathering information about the networking, including relevant IP addresses and VLAN information.

Securing Unified Communications

By disabling the PC Port VLAN access, we effectively prevent users connected to the phone from sniffing voice traffic. This feature can be useful for administrators when troubleshooting, but in general should be disabled and enabled on an as-needed basis.

Implementing a secure conference bridge

Secure conferencing allows a conference resource to be set up that uses encryption (SRTP).

How to do it...

To configure a conference resource for secure conferencing, perform the following:

1. Navigate to the conference bridge configuration page (**Media Resources | Conference Bridge**).
2. Click on **Add New**.
3. From the **Conference Bridge Type** drop-down, select **Cisco IOS Enhanced Conference Bridge**.
4. Specify the **Conference Bridge Name**.
5. Specify the **Device Pool**.
6. From the **Device Security Mode** drop-down, select **Encrypted Conference Bridge**.

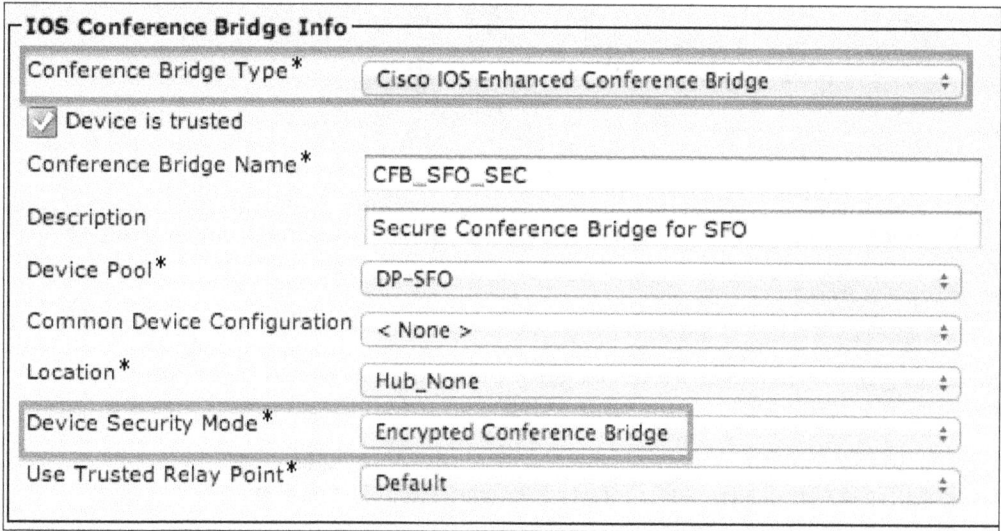

7. Click on **Save**.

How it works...

Secure conferencing requires configuration on both the Unified Communications Manager and the IOS device itself. However, once configured, the Unified Communications Manager will set up encrypted RTP traffic for all devices connected to the conference. It is important that the conference bridge type is IOS Enhanced with the security mode set to **Encrypted**.

Implementing secure Meet-Me conferences

Meet-Me conferences too can be secured by way of preventing non-secure devices from initiating a conference.

How to do it...

To configure a secure Meet-Me conference, perform the following:

1. Navigate to the Meet-Me number configuration page (**Call Routing | Meet-Me Number/Pattern**).
2. Click on **Add New**.
3. Specify the **Directory Number or Pattern**.
4. Specify a **Partition** if necessary.
5. From the **Minimum Security Level** drop-down, select **Authenticated** or **Encrypted** depending on business requirements:

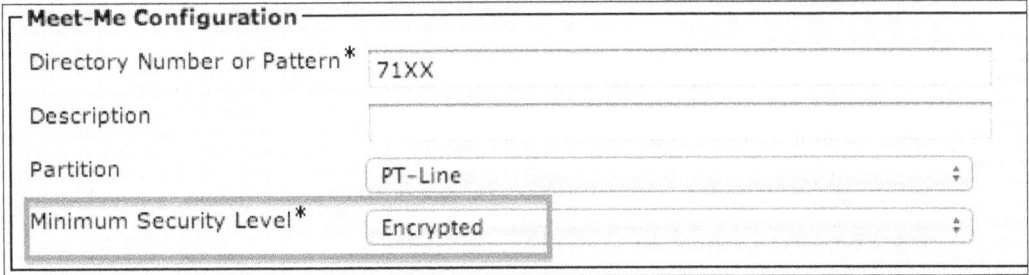

6. Click on **Save**.

How it works...

Secure Meet-Me conferencing works by limiting access to Meet-Me conferences to devices that are secured. The security level configured will determine the types of devices, such as secured phones or non-secured phones, which can join a conference.

Securing Unified Communications

Configuring VPN for Cisco IP phones

The VPN client for IP phones allows remote users and telecommuters to have a physical phone that securely communicates with the cluster.

How to do it...

Implementing VPN support for Cisco IP phones requires multiple configurations to be completed both on the ASA/IOS device as well as the Unified Communications Manager. This recipe covers the Unified Communications Manager side of the configuration.

First we upload the VPN certificate from the IOS/ASA device by performing the following:

1. Navigate to the operating system administration page (http://192.168.1.5/cmplatform).
2. Navigate to certificate management (**Security | Certificate Management**).
3. Click on **Upload Certificate**.
4. From the **Certificate Name** drop-down select **Phone-VPN-trust**:

5. Select the certificate.
6. Click on **Upload File**.

Next we must configure a VPN gateway corresponding to the certificate we just uploaded:

1. Navigate to the Unified CM administration page (http://192.168.1.5/ccmadmin).
2. Navigate to the VPN Gateway configuration page (**Advanced Features | VPN | VPN Gateway**).
3. Click on **Add New**.
4. Specify the **VPN Gateway Name**.
5. Specify the **VPN Gateway URL**.
6. From the **VPN Certificates in your Truststore** list, select the previously uploaded certificate and select the **Down Arrow**.
7. Verify that the selected certificate shows in the **VPN Certificates in this Location** box.
8. Click on **Save**.

Next we configure a VPN group for the VPN Gateway that we just created:

1. Navigate to the VPN Group configuration page (**Advanced Features | VPN | VPN Group**).
2. Click on **Add New**.
3. Specify a **VPN Group Name**.
4. From the **All Available VPN Gateways** list select the previously created VPN Gateway and select the **Down Arrow**.
5. Verify that the VPN Gateway appears in the **Selected VPN Gateways in this VPN Group** list.
6. Click on **Save**.

With the VPN Group set up, we can now create the VPN profile:

1. Navigate to the VPN Profile configuration page (**Advanced Features | VPN | VPN Profile**).
2. Click on **Add New**.
3. Specify a **Name**.
4. If necessary, change the default values for **MTU** and **Fail to Connect**.
5. From the **Client Authentication Method** drop-down, select the desired method.
6. If desired, check **Enable Password Persistence**:

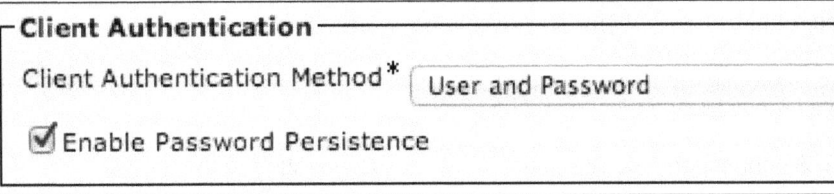

7. Click on **Save**.

Finally we can add the previously created VPN profile and VPN group to the common phone profiles.

1. Navigate to the common phone profile configuration page (**Device | Device Settings | Common Phone Profile**).
2. Select the phone profile to update.
3. Under the **VPN Information** section, specify the appropriate **VPN Group** and **VPN Profile** from the drop-down.
4. Click on **Save**.
5. Click on **Reset**.

The phone devices should update with the appropriate firmware, and can now use the VPN functionality.

How it works...

Certificates from the IOS or ASA device are added to the Unified Communications Manager. These certificates are then associated with a VPN gateway (the one that issued the certificate). The gateway can then be added to a VPN group.

The VPN profile specifies how a device must authenticate itself to the network. The profile and group are then added to a common phone profile configuration. Devices associated with this common phone profile are then updated to install secure versions of the firmware, along with certificate information that can be used to connect to the IOS/ASA device.

Configuring application users for secure communication

Some third party applications support the use of secure JTAPI and CTI Port communication. To enable those features we must configure the application or appropriate end users with the user groups necessary to allow communication.

Getting ready

This recipe requires the CAPF functionality to have already been configured.

Determine which user groups your application user (or end user) requires based on the functionality required.

To use a TLS connection, add Standard CTI Secure Connection to the group.

For SRTP connection, add Standard CTI Enabled, Standard CTI Secure Connection, and Standard CTI Allow Reception of SRTP Key Material to the group..

How to do it...

To configure the application (or end user) for secure communication, perform the following:

1. Navigate to the application user configuration page (**User Management | Application User**).
2. Select the desired application user.

3. Under the **Permissions Information** section, click on **Add User Group**.
4. Select the appropriate user groups to add.
5. Click on **Add Selected**.
6. Verify the user groups shown under the **Groups** pane.

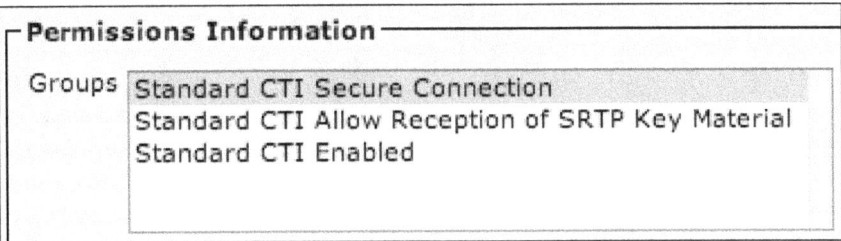

7. Click on **Save**.

Next, configure a CAPF profile for an application user (or end user) by performing the following:

1. Navigate to the **Application User CAPF Profile** configuration page (**User Management | Application User CAPF Profile Configuration**).
2. Click on **Add New**.
3. Specify the **Application User** from the drop-down.
4. Specify an **Instance Id**.

5. Specify the appropriate **Certificate Operation** from the drop-down. In this case it is **Install/Upgrade**.
6. Specify the **Authentication Mode** from the drop-down.
7. If necessary, specify the **Authentication String** or click on **Generate String**.

Securing Unified Communications

8. If necessary, change the **Key Size** by selecting the appropriate value from the drop-down.

```
┌─Certification Authority Proxy Function (CAPF) Information─────────────────┐
│ Certificate Operation*    [Install/Upgrade                    ▼]          │
│ Authentication Mode*      [By Authentication String           ▼]          │
│ Authentication String     [8213001501                          ]  [Generate String] │
│ Key Size (bits)*          [1024                               ▼]          │
│ Operation Completes By    [2011]:[12]:[7]:[12]  (YYYY:MM:DD:HH)           │
│ Certificate Operation Status: Operation Pending                           │
└────────────────────────────────────────────────────────────────────────────┘
```

9. Click on **Save**.
10. Verify that the CAPF profile shows under the application user.

```
┌─CAPF Information────────────────────────┐
│ Associated CAPF Profiles  [42318571]    │
│                                         │
└─────────────────────────────────────────┘
```

The third party application can now be configured for secure communication.

How it works...

Third party applications rely on end user and application users as their interface to the Unified Communications Manager. By associating the necessary user groups to these integration users, we allow the third party applications permission to use those features. This can allow said applications to create TLS connections to the Unified Communications Manager and communicate voice information over secure RTP (SRTP).

10
Serviceability, Upgrades, and Disaster Recovery

In this chapter, we will cover:

- Configuring alarms
- Configuring traces
- Configuring SNMP versions 1 and 2
- Configuring SNMP Version 3
- Applying patches and upgrades
- Configuring a backup device
- Configuring a backup schedule
- Performing a manual backup
- Restoring from backup

Introduction

This chapter aims to cover configuration of alarms and tracing. With alarms in particular, SNMP becomes an important factor in the maintenance and troubleshooting of a Unified Communications cluster. This chapter covers configuration of SNMP Version 1 and 2, as well as version 3, for Unified Communications Manager.

Finally we will cover the backup and restore process for the Unified Communications Manager publisher.

Configuring alarms

Alarms notify us when events that could have (or already have had) effects on the system occur. By configuring alarms, we can receive notifications and act upon them.

How to do it...

To configure alarms, perform the following:

1. First, navigate to the Unified Serviceability page (https://cucm/ccmservice).
2. Next, navigate to the alarm configuration page (**Alarm | Configuration**)
3. Select the server from the **Server** drop-down and click on **Go**.
4. Select the desired **Service Group** from the drop-down and click on **Go**.
5. Finally select the desired **Service** from the drop-down and click on **Go**:

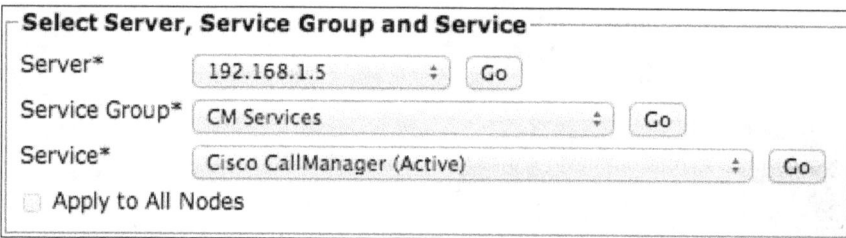

6. If desired, check **Enable Alarm** under the **Local Syslogs** section. Set the **Alarm Event Level** as necessary.
7. If desired, check **Enable Alarm** under the **Remote Syslogs** section.
8. Specify the **Server Name**.
9. Select the appropriate alarm level from the **Alarm Event Level** drop-down.
10. To prevent excessive logging, optionally check **Exclude End Point Alarms**.
11. If desired, check **Enable Alarm** under the **SDI Trace** section. Set the **Alarm Event Level** as necessary.

12. If desired, check **Enable Alarm** under the **SDL Trace** section. Ensure to set the **Alarm Event Level** as necessary:

```
Local Syslogs
☑ Enable Alarm                                    Alarm Event Level  [ Informational ⇅ ]

Remote Syslogs
☑ Enable Alarm                                    Alarm Event Level  [ Error ⇅ ]
Server Name1  192.168.1.99
☑ Exclude End Point Alarms

SDI Trace
☑ Enable Alarm                                    Alarm Event Level  [ Error ⇅ ]

SDL Trace
☑ Enable Alarm                                    Alarm Event Level  [ Error ⇅ ]
```

13. Click on **Save**.

How it works...

Alarms allow us to receive notifications of certain events as they happen on the system. This can be particularly useful when troubleshooting system problems, and for collecting information to send to Cisco TAC. Alternatively, for developers developing applications for the system, DEBUG level alarms can provide great insight as to why an error may be occurring.

It is import to understand which service you need to collect information from, so as to limit any unnecessary time spent looking at logs. For instance, the following services use the Cisco Tomcat Service for logging purposes:

- Cisco Extension Mobility application
- Cisco IP Manager Assistant
- Cisco Extension Mobility
- Cisco Web Dialer Web

Make sure to choose the appropriate service.

The alarm event level will determine the amount and type of information to log. The levels are defined as:

- **Emergency**: This level designates system as unusable
- **Alert**: This level indicates that immediate action is needed
- **Critical**: The system detects a critical condition
- **Error**: This level signifies that an error condition exists

Serviceability, Upgrades, and Disaster Recovery

- **Warning**: This level indicates that a warning condition is detected
- **Notice**: This level designates a normal but significant condition
- **Informational**: This level designates information messages only
- **Debug**: This level designates detailed event information that Cisco TAC engineers use for debugging

See also

For a complete listing of alarm services and what they do, visit the Serviceability Administration Guide for more information (`http://www.cisco.com/en/US/docs/voice_ip_comm/cucm/service/8_0_2/admin/sasrvdes.html#wpxref81578`).

Configuring traces

Traces provide valuable insight into specific feature sets of services. Traces are often useful to Cisco TAC and to developers.

How to do it...

To configure traces, perform the following:

1. First, navigate to the Unified Serviceability page (`https://cucm/ccmservice`).
2. Next, navigate to the trace configuration page (**Trace | Configuration**).
3. Select the server from the **Server** drop-down and click on **Go**.
4. Select the desired **Service Group** from the drop-down and click on **Go**.
5. Finally select the desired **Service** from the drop-down and click on **Go**:

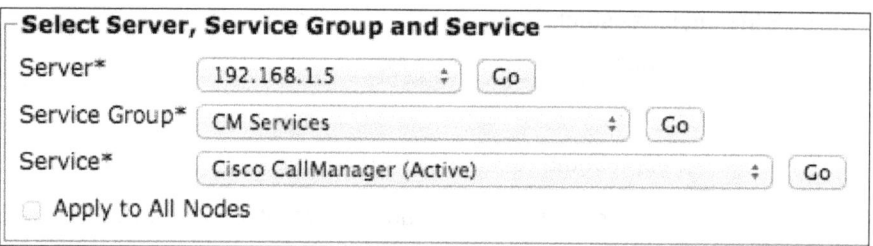

6. To enable the trace, check **Trace On**:

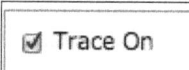

7. Under the **Trace Filter Settings**, specify the desired **Debug Trace Level** from the drop-down.

8. Depending on the trace we are configuring, there will be multiple options that can be enabled; we must check the boxes next to each feature from which trace information is to be collected. In the following screenshot, the trace settings are configured for debugging conference resources on an SIP gateway:

```
Trace Filter Settings
Debug Trace Level  [ Error            ▼ ]
☑ Cisco CallManager Trace Fields
      ☐ Enable H245 Message Trace                            ☐ Enable CDR Trace
      ☐ Enable DT-24+/DE-30+ Trace                           ☐ Enable Analog Trunk Trace
      ☐ Enable PRI Trace                                     ☐ Enable All Phone Device Trace
      ☐ Enable ISDN Translation Trace                        ☑ Enable MTP Trace
      ☐ Enable H225 & Gatekeeper Trace                       ☐ Enable All GateWay Trace
      ☐ Enable Miscellaneous Trace                           ☐ Enable Forward & Miscellaneous Trace
      ☑ Enable Conference Bridge Trace                       ☐ Enable MGCP Trace
      ☐ Enable Music On Hold Trace                           ☑ Enable Media Resource Manager Trace
      ☐ Enable CM Real-Time Information Server Trace         ☑ Enable SIP Call Processing Trace
      ☐ Enable SIP Stack Trace                               ☐ Enable SCCP Keep Alive Trace
      ☐ Enable Annunciator Trace                             ☐ Enable SpeedDial Trace
      ☐ Enable SoftKey Trace                                 ☐ Enable SIP Keep Alive (REGISTER Refresh) Trace
      ☐ Enable Route or Hunt List Trace
☐ Device Name Based Trace Monitoring
```

9. Click on **Save**.

How it works...

Traces provide detailed information about specific services, and functions of services, that can be useful for troubleshooting problems on the system.

Each service has its own unique set of fields which can be enabled or disabled for providing trace information. In this recipe we used the CallManager service as an example, and selected the fields necessary to troubleshoot a problem with an SIP-based conference resource that happens to act as a Media Termination Point.

To ensure that the most relevant information is present in trace files, configure the traces to include only the desired information at the desired debug trace level.

See also

For a complete listing of the trace fields for each service, visit the Serviceability Administration Guide available at http://www.cisco.com/en/US/docs/voice_ip_comm/cucm/service/8_0_2/admin/satrace.html#wp1183442.

Serviceability, Upgrades, and Disaster Recovery

Configuring SNMP versions 1 and 2

By configuring SNMP on the Unified Communications Manager, we can configure where we will receive notifications of alarms and other events. This recipe covers the configuration of SNMP servers prior to Version 3 of the protocol.

Getting ready

This recipe assumes the SNMP server information is already known and available.

How to do it...

To configure SNMP (versions 1 and 2), perform the following:

1. First navigate to the Unified Serviceability page (`https://cucm/ccmservice`).
2. Navigate to the community string configuration page (**SNMP | V1/V2c | Community String**).
3. Click on **Find**.
4. Click on **Add New**.
5. Specify the **Community String Name**:

6. To allow SNMP from any host, select **Accept SNMP Packets** from any host. Skip to step 12.
7. Otherwise, select **Accept SNMP Packets only from these hosts**.
8. Specify the IP address in the **Host IP Address** field:

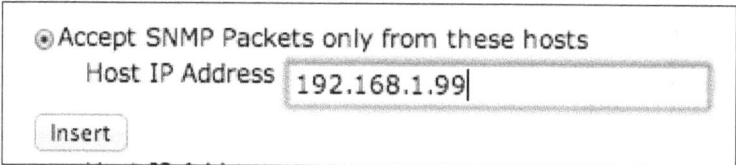

9. Click on **Insert**.

10. Verify that the SNMP server appears in the **Host IP Addresses** list:

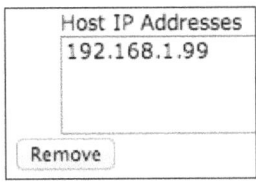

11. Optionally, to remove a server from the list, select the desired server and click on **Remove**.
12. From the **Access Privileges** drop-down, select the desired privileges for the SNMP server:

13. Click on **Save**.
14. A message box will inform you that the SNMP master agent will need to be restarted for the changes to take effect. If we are adding additional community strings or configurations, click on **Cancel**, otherwise click on **OK** to restart the service:

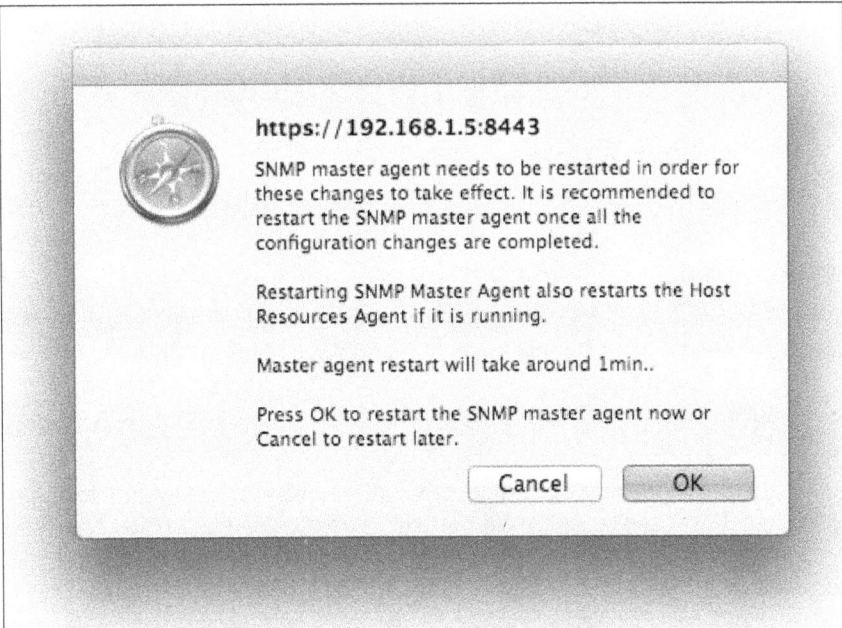

Serviceability, Upgrades, and Disaster Recovery

15. Next, navigate to the notification destination configuration page (**SNMP | V1/V2c | Notification Destination**).
16. Click on **Find**.
17. Click on **Add New**.
18. From the **Host IP Addresses** drop-down, select **Add New**.
19. Specify the **Host IP Address** of the SNMP sever.
20. Optionally, change the **Port Number** as appropriate.
21. Select the version of the SNMP server from the **SNMP Version** options.
22. Depending on which version of SNMP is being used, a new option will present itself.
23. For Version 1 servers, specify the **Community String** (as previously created):

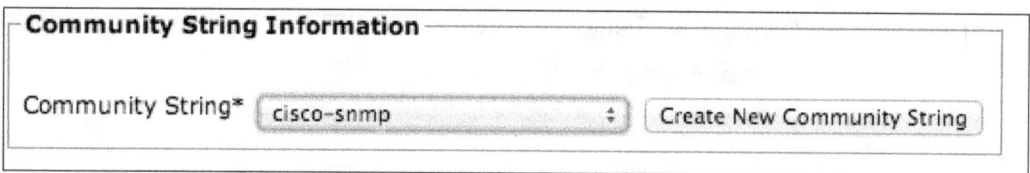

24. For Version 2 servers, specify the **Notification Type** from the drop-down and then specify the **Community String**:

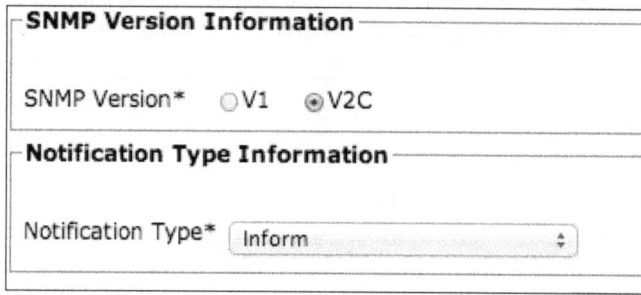

25. Click on **Insert**.
26. We will be presented with a message box again informing us to restart the SNMP master agent. Click on **Cancel** to do so manually, or click on **OK** to do so immediately.

How it works...

By configuring the community string and destination, we allow for the system to communicate to the appropriate SNMP server. Alarms in particular are sent across to the SNMP server for monitoring. The detail that is sent depends on how the alarm was configured and the alarm event level selected.

See also

For more information on how SNMP works with Unified Communications Manager see `http://www.cisco.com/en/US/docs/voice_ip_comm/cucm/service/8_0_2/admin/sasnmdes.html`.

Configuring SNMP Version 3

By configuring SNMP on the Unified Communications Manager, we can configure where we will receive notifications of alarms and other events.

Getting ready

This recipe assumes the SNMP server information is available and known, including IP address information, user information, and so on.

How to do it...

To configure SNMP Version 3, perform the following:

1. First, navigate to the Unified Serviceability page (`https://cucm/ccmservice`).
2. Navigate to the SNMP user configuration page (**SNMP | V3 | User**).
3. Click on **Find**.
4. Click on **Add New**.
5. Specify the **User Name**:

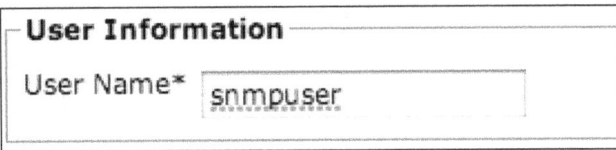

6. If necessary, specify the **Authentication Information**. Check **Authentication Required**. Enter the password in the **Password** and **Reenter Password** fields. Select the appropriate **Protocol**:

Serviceability, Upgrades, and Disaster Recovery

7. If necessary, specify the **Privacy Information** and check **Privacy Required**. Enter the password in the **Password** and **ReenterPassword** fields. Select the appropriate **Protocol**.

8. To allow SNMP from any host, select **Accept SNMP Packets from any host**. Skip to step 14.

9. Otherwise, select **Accept SNMP Packets only from these hosts**:

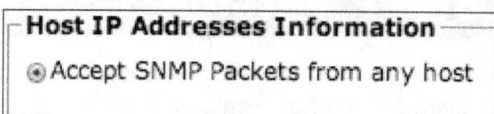

10. Specify the IP address in the **Host IP Address** field:

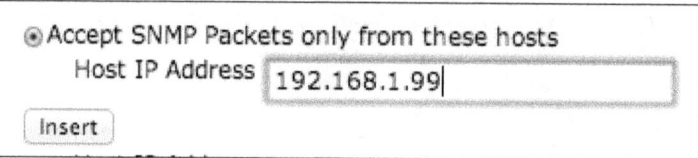

11. Click on **Insert**.

12. Verify that the SNMP server appears in the **Host IP Addresses** list:

13. Optionally, to remove a server from the list, select the desired server and click on **Remove**.

14. From the **Access Privileges** drop-down, select the desired privileges for the SNMP server:

15. Click on **Save**.

16. A message box will inform you the SNMP master agent will need to be restarted for the changes to take effect. If we are adding additional community strings or configurations, click on **Cancel**, otherwise click on **OK** to restart the service.
17. Next, navigate to the notification destination configuration page (**SNMP | V3 | Notification Destination**).
18. Click on **Find**.
19. Click on **Add New**.
20. From the **Host IP Addresses** drop-down, select **Add New**.
21. Specify the **Host IP Address** of the SNMP sever.
22. Optionally, change the **Port Number** as appropriate.
23. Specify the **Notification Type** from the drop-down.
24. If **Inform** is selected as the **Notification Type**, specify the **Remote SNMP Engine Id** by selecting **Add New** from the drop-down. Then specify the **Remote SNMP Engine Id**:

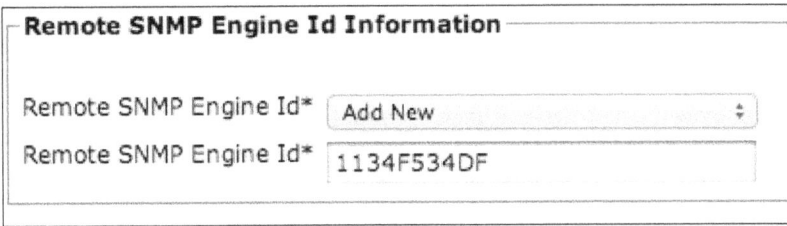

25. From the **Security Level** drop-down, select the appropriate entry:

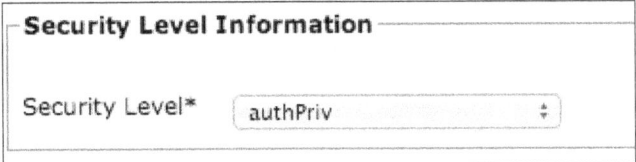

26. Click on **Create New User**.
27. Specify the appropriate **User Name**.
28. If necessary, specify the **Authentication Information**. Check **Authentication Required**. Enter the password in the **Password** and **Reenter Password** fields. Select the appropriate **Protocol**.
29. If necessary, specify the **Privacy Information** and check **Privacy Required**. Enter the password in the **Password** and **Reenter Password** fields. Select the appropriate **Protocol.**
30. Specify the appropriate **Access Privileges** from the drop-down.

31. Click on **Save**.
32. The user should now appear under the **User Information** section.
33. Select the created user:

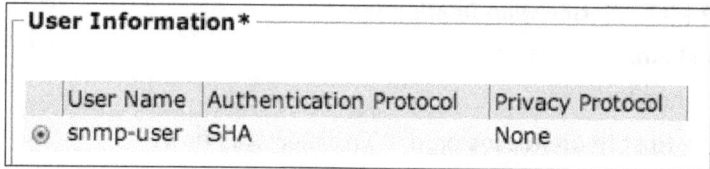

34. Click on **Insert**.
35. We will be presented with a message box again informing us to restart the SNMP master agent. Click on **Cancel** to do so manually, or click on **OK** to do so immediately.

How it works...

Unlike SNMP versions prior to Version 3, Version 3 uses users. By configuring users and destinations, we allow for the system to communicate to the appropriate SNMP server. Alarms in particular are sent across to the SNMP server for monitoring. The detail that is sent depends on how the alarm was configured and the alarm event level selected.

See also

For more information on how SNMP works with Unified Communications Manager see `http://www.cisco.com/en/US/docs/voice_ip_comm/cucm/service/8_0_2/admin/sasnmdes.html`.

Applying patches and upgrades

Patches and upgrades follow the same essential process which is detailed in the following sections.

Getting ready

Verify the patch or upgrade is downloaded and loaded onto the appropriate medium. If possible, verify that the image matches the MD5 sum provided by Cisco.

Chapter 10

How to do it...

To perform an upgrade or apply a patch, perform the following:

1. Navigate to the OS admin page (https://192.168.1.5/cmplatform).
2. Next, navigate to the install page (**Software Updates | Install/Upgrade**).
3. Specify the **Source** from the drop-down list.
4. Specify the **Directory**. If using a DVD/CD skip to step 9.
5. Specify the **Server**.
6. Specify the **User Name**.
7. Specify the **Password**.
8. Specify the appropriate protocol from the **Transfer Protocol** drop-down:

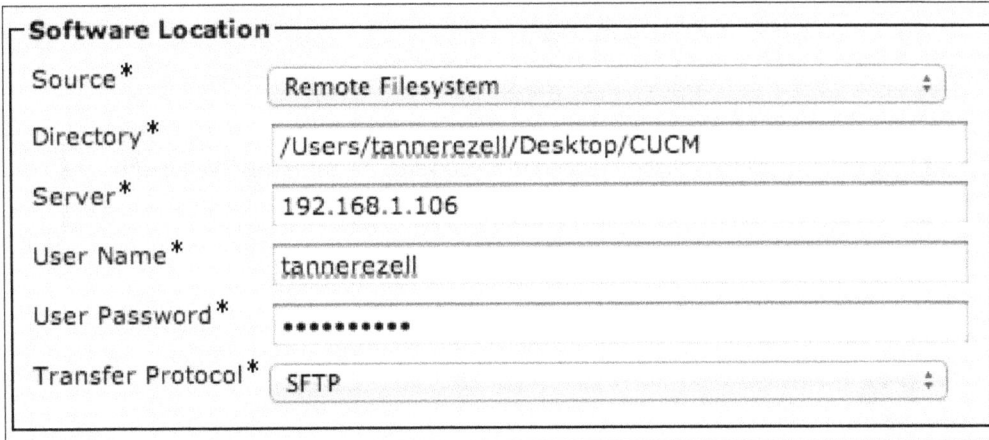

9. Click on **Next**.
10. Select the patch/upgrade to apply from the **Options/Upgrades** drop-down:

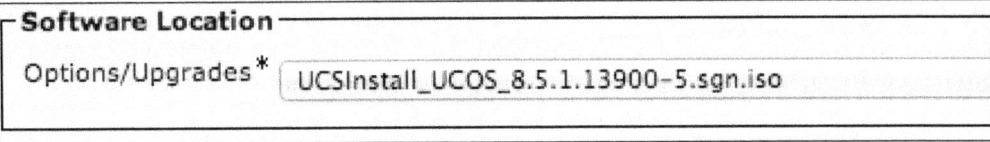

11. Click on **Next**.
12. After the software is downloaded locally to the server, we are presented with a screen that displaces the MD5 hash, Current Version, and Upgrade Version.

13. Select the desired reboot option:

```
┌─ File Checksum Details ──────────────────────────────────┐
│  File              UCSInstall_UCOS_8.5.1.13900-5.sgn.iso │
│  MD5 Hash Value    22:cb:5a:d5:bf:e7:8e:18:4e:93:b2:33:72:12:11:a1 │
├─ Version Information ────────────────────────────────────┤
│  Current Version   8.5.1.10000-26                        │
│  Upgrade Version   8.5.1.13900-5                         │
├─ Reboot Options ─────────────────────────────────────────┤
│  ◉ Reboot to upgraded partition                          │
│  ○ Do not reboot after upgrade                           │
└──────────────────────────────────────────────────────────┘
```

 It is highly recommended that you verify the MD5 Hash Value with the one provided by Cisco.

14. Click on **Next**.
15. The software upgrade/patch will now be applied to the system.

How it works...

The patch/upgrade is first downloaded to the system from the media that was used, be it CD/DVD or a network storage device. From there, the system will then unpack the contents of the patch/upgrade and apply it to the system. The install process creates logs that can be downloaded via the real-time monitoring tool. This is particularly useful if an error occurs.

When upgrading a cluster, it is important to first upgrade the publisher. After the publisher is upgraded, the subscribers can then be upgraded. Verify with the compatibility matrix that the currently operating version you are upgrading from is a version you can upgrade to.

Chapter 10

Configuring a backup device

Before we can perform a backup, we must have a device we can back up to. This can be a tape drive or a network share running SFTP.

Getting ready

We must have the backup device already configured and ready to go. For network devices, ensure we have the username and password as well as the path where the backup will be stored.

How to do it...

To configure the Unified Communications Manager for backups, perform the following:

1. Navigate to the disaster recovery system (`https://cucm/drf`).
2. Next, navigate to the backup device configuration page (**Backup | Backup Device**).
3. Click on **Add New**.
4. Specify a **Backup device name**:

```
Backup device name
Backup device name*                              backup-server
```

5. If using tape as a backup, select the **Tape Device** option and configure it appropriately. Skip to step 12.
6. If using a network share as a backup medium, specify **Network Directory**.
7. Specify a **Host name/IP address**.
8. Specify the **Path Name**.
9. Specify the **User Name**.
10. Specify the **Password**.

Serviceability, Upgrades, and Disaster Recovery

11. Specify the **Number of backups to store on the Network Directory**:

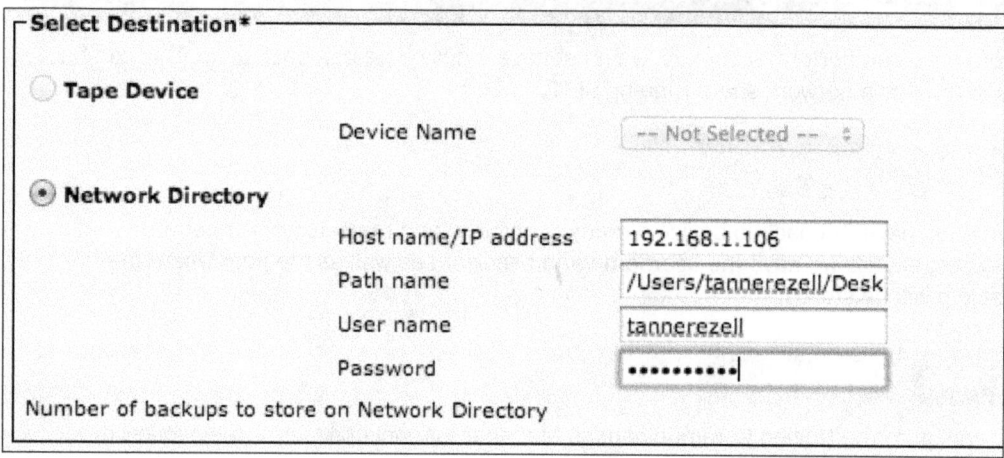

12. Click on **Save**.

>  The path name will vary depending on the operating system being used. In the previous example, we are using a Unix-based operating system. Make sure the path entered is appropriate to the chosen operating system.

13. Repeat this process for each backup device as desired.

How it works...

When we add a backup device, the Unified Communications Manager will attempt to communicate with the device to verify that it can be reached. Assuming it can, the device is then successfully added to the database as a backup device. After a backup device has been created, backup schedules and manual backups can be performed.

>  With the recent releases of UCM, SFTP is required for backup devices. This requirement is in part due to the virtualization of the appliance model.

Chapter 10

Configuring a backup schedule

To automate how often and when the Unified Communications Manager publisher is backed up, we create a schedule.

Getting ready

This recipe assumes a backup device has already been created and added to the system.

How to do it...

To configure the Unified Communications Manager for backups, perform the following:

1. Navigate to the disaster recovery system (https://cucm/drf).
2. Next, navigate to the backup schedule configuration page (**Backup | Scheduler**).
3. Click on **Add New**.
4. Specify a **Schedule Name**:

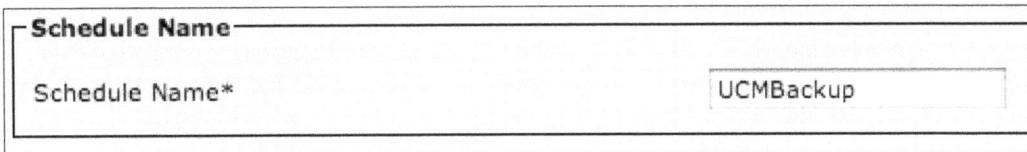

5. Specify the backup device from the **Device Name** drop-down:

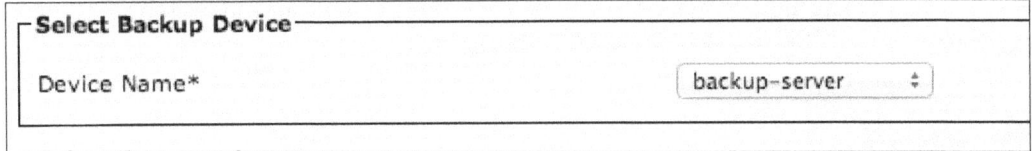

6. Select the features to back up:

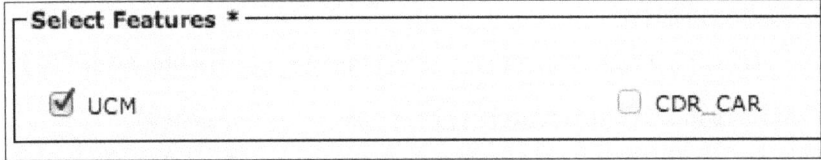

7. Specify the **Date** and **Time** to start the back up.

8. Specify the **Frequency** the backup will run at:

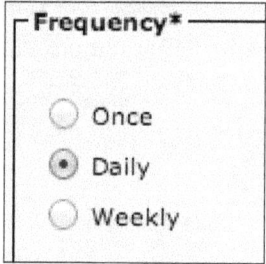

9. Click on **Save**.
10. To enable the schedule, click **Enable Schedule**.

 If desired we may select a schedule as a default by clicking on **Set Default Schedule**.

How it works...

By creating a schedule, we are telling the Unified Communications Manager publisher when, where, and what to back up. We do this by specifying the backup device, which features (UCM or CDR/CAR) to backup, at what time to start the backup, and how often to run it.

Performing a manual backup

Sometimes we need to perform a backup prior to a scheduled time for various reasons, often right before an upgrade or patch is applied to the system.

Getting ready

This recipe assumes a backup device has already been added to the system.

How to do it...

To manually back up the Unified Communications Manager, perform the following:

1. Navigate to the disaster recovery system (`https://cucm/drf`).
2. Next, navigate to the manual backup page (**Backup | Manual Backup**).
3. Select the backup device from the **Device Name** drop-down.

4. Specify the features to be backed up:

Select Backup Device

Device Name*   backup-server

Select Features *

☑ UCM
☐ CDR_CAR

5. Click on **Start Backup**.

How it works...

This simple process starts to back up the selected features to the device specified. During the backup process, we will see a status indication and access to logs of each item being backed up as seen in the following screenshot.

Backup details

Tar Filename: 2011-11-30-11-35-50.tar
Backup Device: NETWORK
Operation: BACKUP
Percentage Complete: 81%

Feature	Server	Component	Status	Result **
UCM	SFOCUCMPUB01	CDPAGT	100	SUCCESS
UCM	SFOCUCMPUB01	SYSLOGAGT	100	SUCCESS
UCM	SFOCUCMPUB01	PLATFORM	100	SUCCESS
UCM	SFOCUCMPUB01	CLM	100	SUCCESS
UCM	SFOCUCMPUB01	BAT	100	SUCCESS
UCM	SFOCUCMPUB01	ANN	100	SUCCESS
UCM	SFOCUCMPUB01	MOH	100	SUCCESS
UCM	SFOCUCMPUB01	TCT	100	SUCCESS
UCM	SFOCUCMPUB01	CCMPREFS	100	SUCCESS
UCM	SFOCUCMPUB01	CCMDB	0	Active
UCM	SFOCUCMPUB01	TFTP	0	---

Serviceability, Upgrades, and Disaster Recovery

Restoring from backup

There may come a time when the system and its configuration are corrupted. Restoring the system to a known good configuration can quickly bring the cluster back online.

How to do it...

To restore from a backup, perform the following:

1. Navigate to the disaster recovery system (`https://cucm/drf`).
2. Next navigate to the manual backup page (**Restore | Restore Wizard**).
3. Select the backup device from the **Device Name** drop-down:

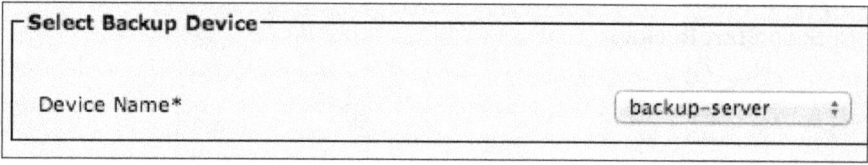

4. Click on **Next**.
5. Select the desired backup to restore from (sorted by date and time):

6. Click on **Next**.
7. Select the features from the backup to be restored:

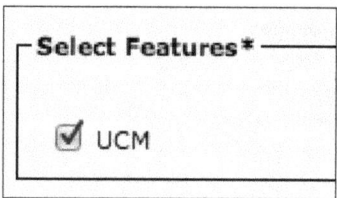

8. Click on **Next**.
9. Select the **Server** to be restored.
10. Click on **Restore**.

How it works...

The restore wizard works by finding backups made to the selected backup device, and prompting the user to choose from which backup they wish to restore the system. After selecting the appropriate backup device and backup, we must select the appropriate features to restore from the backup (UCM and CDR/CAR). Finally, that information is restored to the Unified Communications Manager.

After restoring, the system will reboot.

11
Bulk Administration Tool

In this chapter, we will cover:

- Introducing the Bulk Administration Tool
- Enabling the Bulk Provisioning Service
- Creating and using a custom file
- Bulk provisioning phones
- Bulk provisioning users
- Bulk provisioning user device profiles
- Bulk provisioning gateways
- Bulk provisioning Forced Authorization Codes
- Bulk provisioning Client Matter Codes
- Bulk provisioning call pickup groups
- Bulk provisioning access lists
- Bulk provisioning remote destination profiles
- Bulk provisioning remote destinations
- Bulk provisioning mobility profiles
- Exporting data

Introduction

In this chapter, we will introduce the Bulk Administration Tool. We will take a look at how to use the `bat.xls` spreadsheet to generate CSV files, how to create a custom CSV file without the `bat.xls` spreadsheet, and cover the fields required for some of the most common items that are bulk provisioned, including devices, user device profiles, analog gateways, and mobility users.

Introducing the Bulk Administration Tool

The **Bulk Administration Tool** (**BAT**) can be a huge asset to new deployments or when we need to add numerous devices of identical configuration. In the specific case of phones, it is common to create a bat template file to use.

Getting ready

When using a custom file we typically use the `bat.xlt` provided by the Unified Communications Manager. This file can be downloaded by navigating to **Bulk Administration | Upload/Download Files**, checking the box next to **bat.xlt** and then clicking on **Download Selected**.

Open this file in Excel. If we are prompted to enable macros, make sure to do so.

After the bat file is open, click on the **Phones** tab. We are greeted with a few cells and some buttons.

How to do it...

Normally, if we were bulk creating devices we would perform the following:

1. Click on the **Create Format** button after which a new window will open.
2. From the **Device Fields** list, select the appropriate items (**Mac Address** and **Description** will be pre-populated). For media related fields we would specify:
    - **Media Resource Group List**
    - **Network Hold MOH Audio Source**
    - **User Hold MOH Audio Source**

3. After the fields have been added, click on **Create**:

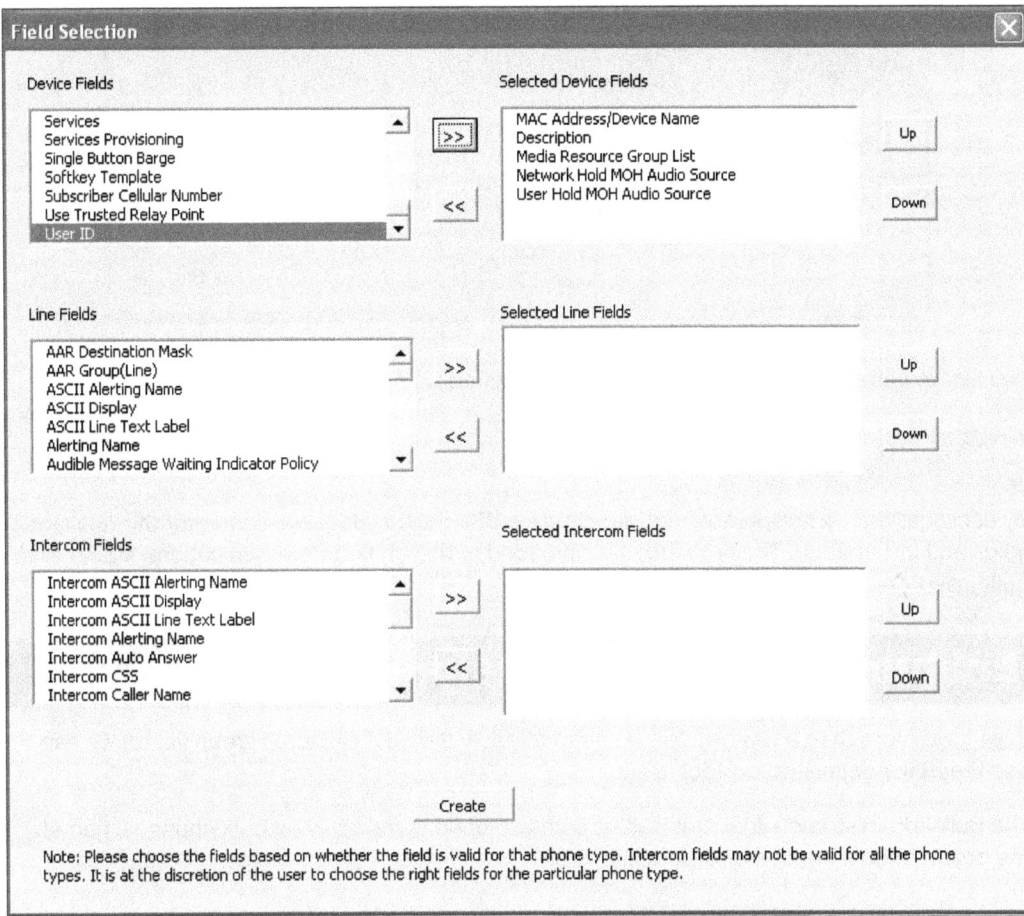

4. The structure of the spreadsheet will change to reflect the fields we selected.
5. Populate the fields with their appropriate data and then click on **Export to BAT Format**.

MAC Address/Device Name (String[12/50] MANDATORY)	Description (String [128] OPTIONAL)	Media Resource Group List (String[50] OPTIONAL)	Network Hold MOH Audio Source (Integer[2] OPTIONAL)	User Hold MOH Audio Source (Integer[2] OPTIONAL)
SEP002155A4A12F	7925	MRGL-SFO	1	1
SEP001BD4546BB0	7945	MRGL-SFO	1	1

Bulk Administration Tool

6. We are prompted with a dialog box. Specify the location and filename then click on **OK**:

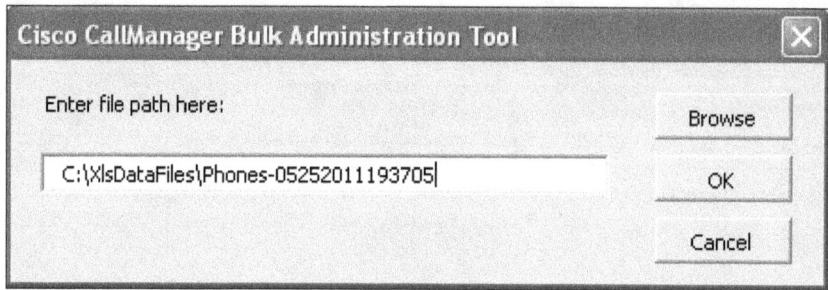

The file we generated can now be uploaded to Unified Communications Manager.

How it works...

By using the `bat.xls` spreadsheet, we create a CSV file for which we can enter the relevant fields and information. These in turn are uploaded to the Unified Communications Manager to bulk insert devices.

Enabling the Bulk Provisioning Service

If we have more than a few devices we need to apply a media resource group list to, we can use the Bulk Administration Tool (BAT).

The Bulk Administration Tool provides us with two options for applying bulk changes, namely, the option to query or use a custom file.

How to do it...

Before we can use the BAT tool, we must first ensure the service is active:

1. Navigate to Cisco Unified Serviceability (`https://192.168.1.5/ccmservice`).
2. After logging in, go to **Service Activation** (**Tools | Service Activation**).
3. Under **Database and Admin Services**, check the box next to **Cisco Bulk Provisioning Service**.
4. Click on **Save**.
5. After the page reloads, verify if the service started successfully by navigating to **Tools | Control Center – Feature Services**.

6. The service is located under the section titled **Database and Admin Services**:

Database and Admin Services				
	Service Name	Status	Activation Status	Start Time
○	Cisco AXL Web Service	Started	Activated	Sun May 22 1
○	Cisco UXL Web Service	Not Running	Deactivated	
○	Cisco Bulk Provisioning Service	Started	Activated	Wed May 25 1
○	Cisco TAPS Service	Not Running	Deactivated	

Once we have verified the Bulk Provisioning Service, we can continue to bulk provision endpoints, users, and so on.

How it works...

The Bulk Provisioning Service is the portion of Unified Communications Manager that turns CSV files and templates into devices, and users and the like into meaningful objects in the configuration database.

Creating and using a custom file

In general, when performing updates using the Custom File format, we can typically get away with the **MAC ADDRESS** or **DEVICE NAME** field. The file might look something like:

```
MAC ADDRESS
SEP001BD4546BB0
SEP00215554F98F
```

How to do it...

To upload the custom update file to Unified Communications Manager, navigate to **Bulk Administration | Upload/Download Files**.

1. Click on **Add New** to upload a new file.
2. Specify the **File** we previously created.
3. From the **Select The Target** drop-down, select **Phones**.

4. From the **Select Transaction Type** drop-down, select **Update Phones – Custom File**:

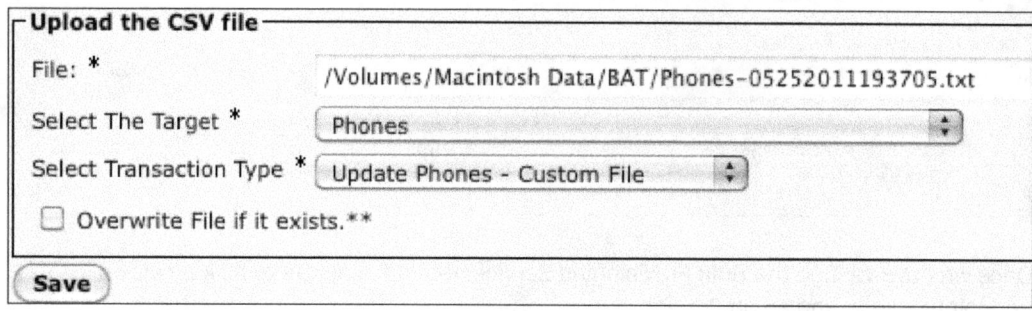

5. Click on **Save**.
6. Navigate to the **Update Phone | Custom File** page under **Bulk Administration | Phones**.
7. From the **Custom File** drop-down, select the file we just uploaded and click on **Find**.
8. Click on **Next**.
9. Under the section **Logout/Reset/Restart**, select **Apply Config**.
10. Under the **Device Information** section, check the boxes next to:
    - **Media Resource Group List**
    - **User Hold MOH Audio Source**
    - **Network Hold MOH Audio Source**

    Select the appropriate setting from the respective drop-down boxes.

11. Under the **Job Information** section, select either **Run Immediately** to run the job, or **Run Later** to schedule a time to run it.

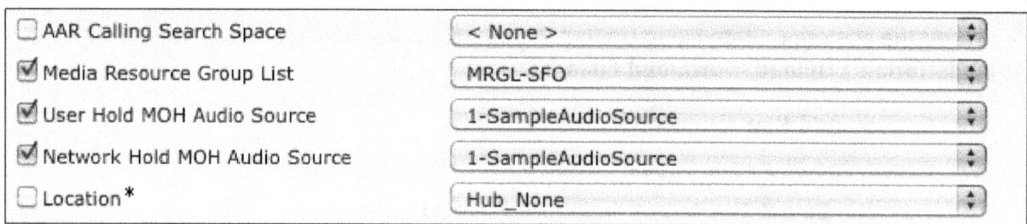

12. Click on **Submit**.

After a job has been submitted, we can check the status by going to **Bulk Administration | Job Scheduler**.

After locating the job, we can activate the job if we haven't done so already. After the job has completed, we will see a screen detailing the success/failure, and a link to the log file. The log file will also contain information on devices that failed to be updated, if any.

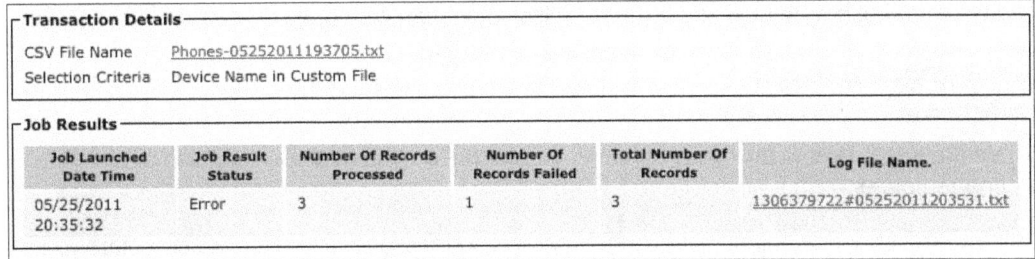

In this particular case, one of our lines contained a device that didn't exist in the system and caused the error.

How it works...

Using a custom created CSV file (as opposed to using one that is created by the `bat.xls` file demonstrated earlier) works identically to those created by the spreadsheet. Once the file is uploaded to the system, it can be used and applied to run specific tasks. In this case, we updated the phones specified in the CSV for media related settings. This procedure is nearly identical to all operations that use the BAT tool.

There's more...

In some cases we may want to update devices on a common setting or attribute such as the device pool, or even the device name. We can accomplish this using a query.

Bulk updating using a query is nearly identical to using a custom file. The only difference is that we can construct a query to return a list of devices to update.

As shown in the following screenshot, we can create custom queries to match a wide range of parameters:

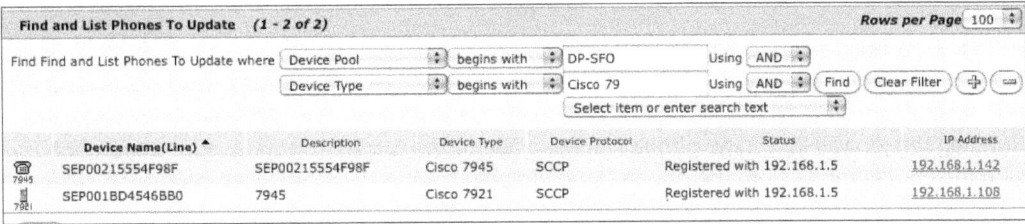

The BAT process is identical to using a custom file after this step.

Bulk provisioning phones

Phone devices in general make up the bulk of the endpoints on a Unified Communications cluster. Knowing how to bulk add/update/delete them can be a huge time saver.

How to do it...

There are a few ways to bulk insert phones. In my opinion, the best way is to use a Phone Template.

1. The phone template is pretty much how it sounds, a template for devices. Here you configure the template just as you would configure any phone device by providing CSS information, device pools, and so on. You can even specify the line configuration.

2. This is done by adding a new phone template (**Bulk Administration | Phones | Phone Template**) and configuring it just as you would configure a phone device.

3. After the template has been created, a CSV file with phone information can be uploaded (when uploading this file select **Phones | Insert Phones – Specific Details**):

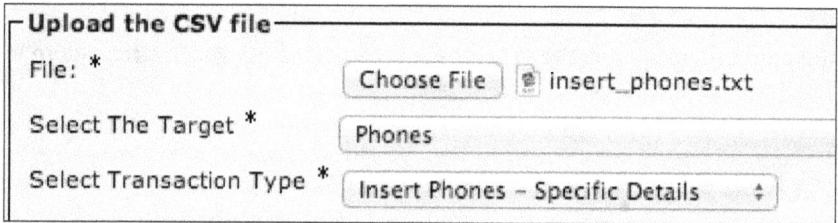

4. The file is finally available under the **Insert Phones** submenu (**Bulk Administration | Phones | Insert Phones**):

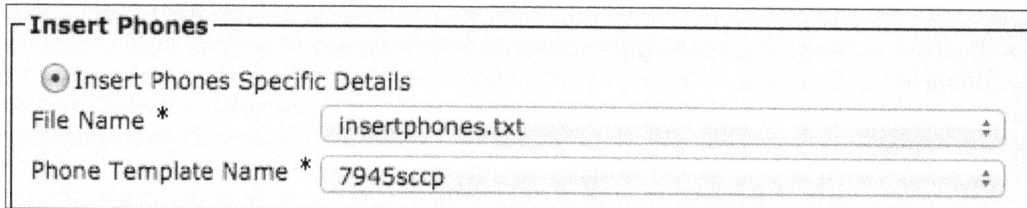

Running the job will insert the phones as specified in the `insertphones.txt` document with the configuration from the phone template specified.

The CSV file in general will have the following fields:

- **MAC ADDRESS**
- **DESCRIPTION**
- **LOCATION**
- **DIRECTORY NUMBER n**
- **DISPLAY n**
- **LINE TEXT LABEL n**

For line specific configurations, the following fields can also be applied:

- **FORWARD BUSY EXTERNAL DESTINATION n**
- **FORWARD BUSY INTERNAL DESTINATION n**
- **FORWARD NO ANSWER INTERNAL DESTINATION n**
- **FORWARD NO ANSWER EXTERNAL DESTINATION n**
- **FORWARD NO COVERAGE EXTERNAL DESTINATION n**
- **FORWARD NO COVERAGE INTERNAL DESTINATION n**
- **CALL PICKUP GROUP n**

How it works...

Information from the CSV file is matched with the fields specified and applied to the selected template, thus creating devices merging information from both.

Bulk provisioning users

As bulk provisioning devices save time, bulk provisioning users can also save time for systems that are not LDAP integrated.

How to do it...

The bulk provisioning of users works very similarly to the provisioning of devices:

1. Create a user template (**Bulk Provisioning | Users | User Template**).

2. Create a CSV file with the desired information with which to populate the user page, and upload it using the **Users**, **Insert Users** settings:

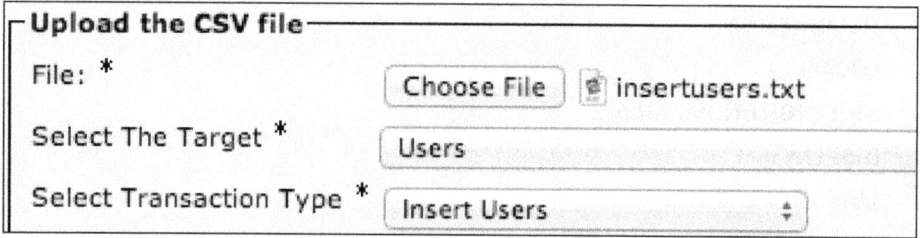

3. After the file is uploaded, it will be available under the **Insert Users** submenu (**Bulk Administration | Users | Insert Users**). It can be selected with the user template to create users in the system:

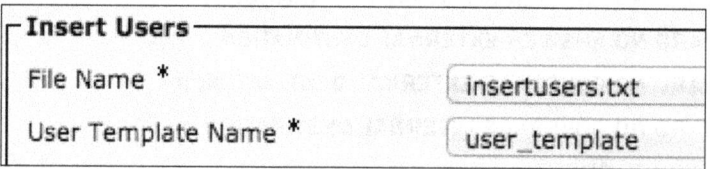

4. Clicking on **Submit** will begin the job.

The following fields can be included in the CSV file. Not all fields are required or are relevant to every setup:

- **FIRST NAME**
- **MIDDLE NAME**
- **LAST NAME**
- **USER ID**
- **PASSWORD**
- **MANAGER USER ID**
- **DEPARTMENT**
- **PIN**
- **DEFAULT PROFILE**
- **USER LOCALE**
- **TELEPHONE NUMBER**
- **PRIMARY EXTENSION**
- **ASSOCIATED PC**
- **IPCC EXTENSION**

- MAIL ID
- PRESENCE GROUP
- SUBSCRIBE CALLING SEARCH SPACE
- DIGEST CREDENTIALS
- REMOTE DESTINATION LIMIT
- MAXIMUM WAIT TIME FOR DESK PICKUP
- ALLOW CONTROL OF DEVICE FROM CTI
- ENABLE MOBILITY
- ENABLE VOICE MAIL ACCESS
- ENABLE EMCC
- PRIMARY USER DEVICE
- USER GROUP n
- CONTROLLED PROFILE n
- CONTROLLED DEVICE n
- CTI CONTROLLED PROFILE n

How it works...

When bulk provisioning, users information from the CSV file is merged with the settings specified in the templates. The resulting users are added to the database.

This only applies to systems that are not LDAP integrated.

Bulk provisioning user device profiles

If using the Extension Mobility feature, bulk provisioning the user device profiles can be a big time saver.

How to do it...

The bulk provisioning of user device profiles works very similarly to the provisioning of devices.

1. Create a UDP template (**Bulk Provisioning | User Device Profiles | UDP Template**). Configure the UDP template just as you would configure a phone device.

Bulk Administration Tool

2. Create a CSV file with the desired information with which to create the profiles, and upload it using the **UDP**, **Insert UDP – Specific Details** settings:

```
Upload the CSV file
File: *                        [ Choose File ]  insertudp.txt
Select The Target *            [ UDP ]
Select Transaction Type *      [ Insert UDP – Specific Details  ▾ ]
```

3. After the file is uploaded it will be available under the Insert UDP submenu (**Bulk Administration | User Device Profiles | Insert UDP**). It can be selected with the UDP template to create the users in the system:

```
Insert User Device Profiles
 ● Insert User Device Profiles Specific Details
File Name *                                       [ insertudp.txt ]
User Device Profiles Template Name *              [ udptemplate 7945 ]
```

The CSV file in general will have the following fields:

- **DEVICE PROFILE NAME**
- **DESCRIPTION**
- **DIRECTORY NUMBER n**
- **DISPLAY n**
- **LINE TEXT LABEL n**

Additionally, the following fields can be supplied for each line:

- **FORWARD BUSY EXTERNAL DESTINATION n**
- **FORWARD BUSY INTERNAL DESTINATION n**
- **FORWARD NO ANSWER EXTERNAL DESTINATION n**
- **FORWARD NO ANSWER INTERNAL DESTINATION n**
- **FORWARD NO COVERAGE EXTERNAL DESTINATION n**
- **FORWARD NO COVERAGE INTERNAL DESTINATION n**
- **CALL PICKUP GROUP**

How it works...

The information contained in the CSV file is merged with the configuration of the UDP template to create the user device profiles. Remember, if you have different models of UDP profiles to create, you'll need a separate CSV file as well as a separate UDP template.

Bulk provisioning gateways

Configuring analog voice gateways with multiple analog ports by hand can be extremely tedious. Use the BAT tool to make this process easier.

How to do it...

The bulk provisioning of gateways works very similarly to the provisioning of devices.

1. Create a gateway template (**Bulk Provisioning | Gateways | Gateway Template**). Configure the gateway template just as you would a gateway device by specifying the type, modules and sub modules. Protocol is important here as it will affect the CSV fields.
2. Create a CSV File with the desired information with which to create the profiles, and upload it using the **Gateways**, **Insert Gateways** setting:

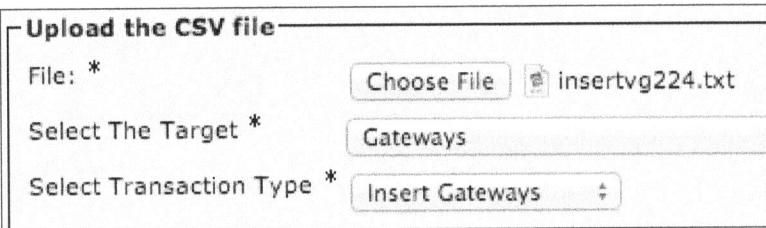

3. After the file is uploaded, it will be available under the Insert UDP submenu (**Bulk Administration | User Device Profiles | Insert UDP**). It can be selected with the UDP template to create the users in the system:

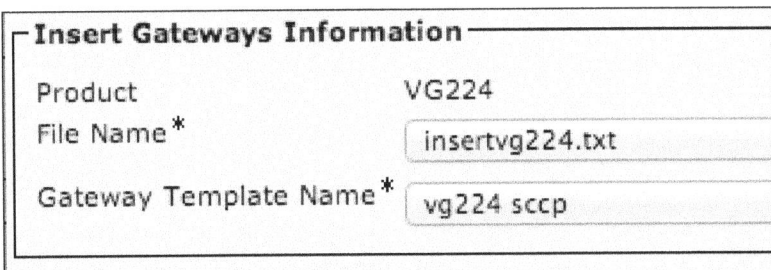

For SCCP gateways, the following fields are generally used:

- **DOMAIN NAME**
- **DESCRIPTION**
- **SLOT**
- **SUBUNIT**
- **PORT NUMBER**
- **PORT DESCRIPTION**
- **PORT DIRECTORY NUMBER**
- **CSS**
- **ROUTE PARTITION**
- **DISPLAY**

For MGCP gateways the following fields are used:

- **DOMAIN NAME**
- **DESCRIPTION**
- **SLOT**
- **SUBUNIT**
- **PORT NUMBER**
- **PORT DESCRIPTION**
- **PORT DIRECTORY NUMBER**

How it works...

The information contained in the CSV file is merged with the configuration of the gateway template, to configure the Analog Voice Gateway. Remember to use the appropriate fields for the appropriate protocol type.

Unlike UDP profiles or phone devices, when configuring multiple ports, there will be one line per port. For instance:

DOMAIN NAME,DESCRIPTION,SLOT,SUBUNIT,PORT NUMBER,PORT DESCRIPTION,PORT DIRECTORY NUMBER

SKIGW6969696969,VG224,2,0,0,,1234

SKIGW6969696969,VG224,2,0,1,,1235

SKIGW6969696969,VG224,2,0,2,,1236

SKIGW6969696969,VG224,2,0,3,,1237

SKIGW6969696969,VG224,2,0,4,,1238

Bulk provisioning Forced Authorization Codes

If using Forced Authorization Codes in quantity, it may be beneficial to bulk provision them.

How to do it...

1. First we must prepare the CSV file. The CSV file will generally have the following fields:
   - **FORCED AUTHORIZATION CODE**
   - **AUTHORIZATION CODE NAME**
   - **AUTHORIZATION LEVEL**

2. Next upload the CSV file by selecting **Forced Authorization Codes** and **Insert Forced Authorization Codes,** as shown in the following screenshot:

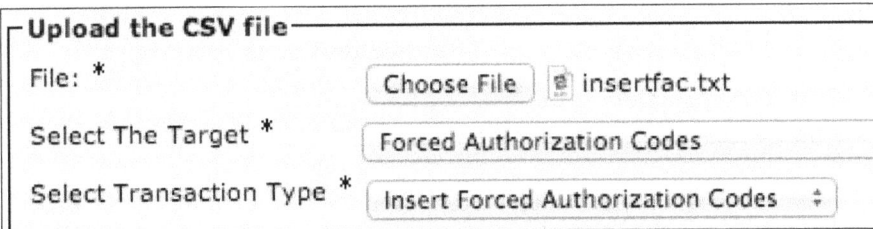

3. Finally, after the file is uploaded we can insert the Forced Authorization Codes (**Bulk Administration** | **Forced Authorization Codes** | **Insert Forced Authorization Codes**):

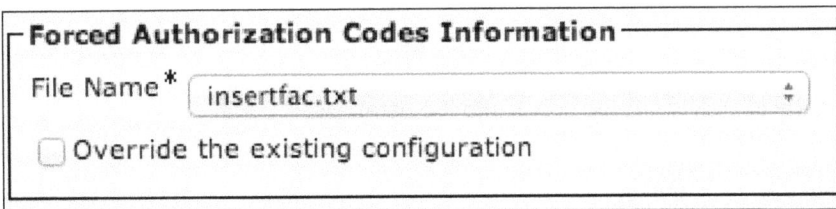

Submitting the job will insert the codes into the database.

How it works...

The Bulk Administration Tool will take the information contained in the CSV file and create the corresponding Forced Authorization Codes.

Bulk Administration Tool

Bulk provisioning Client Matter Codes

If using Client Matter Codes in quantity, it may be beneficial to bulk provision them.

How to do it...

1. First we must prepare the CSV file. The CSV file will have the following fields:
   - **CLIENT MATTER CODE**
   - **DESCRIPTION**

2. Next upload the CSV file by selecting **Client Matter Codes** and **Insert Client Matter Codes** as shown in the following screenshot:

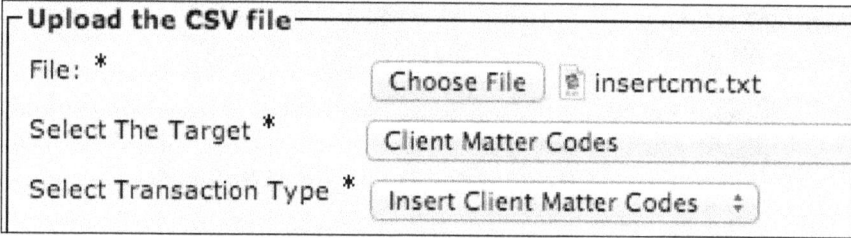

3. Finally, after the file is uploaded we can insert the Client Matter Codes (**Bulk Administration | Client Matter Codes | Insert Client Matter Codes**):

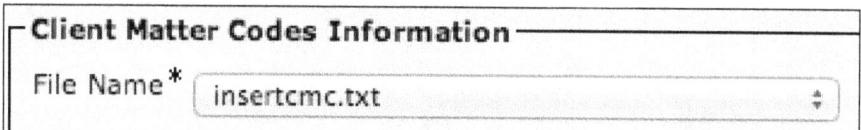

Submitting the job will insert the codes into the database.

How it works...

The Bulk Administration Tool will take the information contained in the CSV file and create the corresponding Client Matter Codes.

Chapter 11

Bulk provisioning call pickup groups

If using numerous call pickup groups, it may be beneficial to bulk provision them.

How to do it...

1. First we must prepare the CSV file. The CSV file will have the following fields:
   - **PICKUP GROUP NAME**
   - **PICKUP GROUP NUMBER**
   - **PARTITION**
   - **OTHER PICKUP GROUP NAME 1**
   - **OTHER PICKUP GROUP NAME 2**
   - **OTHER PICKUP GROUP NAME 3**

2. Next upload the CSV file by selecting **Pickup Groups** and **Insert Pickup Groups** as shown in the following screenshot:

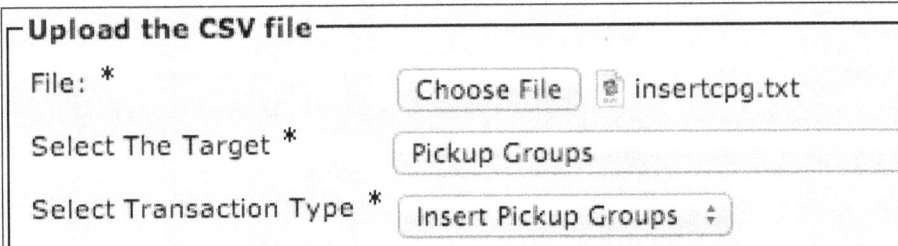

3. Finally, after the file is uploaded we can insert the Pickup Groups (**Bulk Administration | Call Pickup Groups | Insert Call Pickup Groups**):

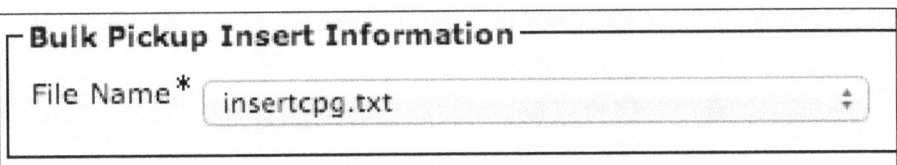

Additionally, configure the **Call Pickup Group Notification Settings** as desired:

```
Call Pickup Group Notification Settings
   Call Pickup Group Notification Policy*        Visual Alert
   Call Pickup Group Notification Timer (seconds)*   8

   Call Information Display For Call Pickup Group Notification
   ☑ Calling Party Information    ☐ Called Party Information
```

Submitting the job will insert the pickup groups into the database.

How it works...

The Bulk Administration Tool will take the information contained in the CSV file, combined with the settings on the **Insert Call Pickup Groups** page, to create the corresponding pickup groups.

Bulk provisioning access lists

When using the mobility feature and access lists, bulk provisioning can save us time.

How to do it...

1. First we must prepare the CSV file; the CSV file will have the following fields:
   - **ACCESS LIST NAME**
   - **ACCESS LIST DESCRIPTION**
   - **ACCESS LIST ALLOWED**
   - **ACCESS LIST OWNER**
   - **ACCESS LIST MEMBER 1**
   - **DN MASK 1**
   - **ACCESS LIST MEMBER 2**
   - **DN MASK 2**
   - **ACCESS LIST MEMBER 3**
   - **DN MASK 3**

2. Next upload the CSV file by selecting **Access Lists** and **Insert Access List,** as shown in the following screenshot:

Upload the CSV file

File: *   [Choose File] insertacl.txt

Select The Target *   [Access Lists]

Select Transaction Type *   [Insert Access List ⇕]

3. Finally, after the file is uploaded we can insert the access lists (**Bulk Administration | Mobility | Access List | Access List Insert**):

Bulk Access List Information

File Name*   [insertacl.txt]

☐ Override the existing configuration

Submitting the job will insert the access control lists into the database.

How it works...

The Bulk Administration Tool will take the information contained in the CSV file and insert the appropriate access lists into the system.

Bulk provisioning remote destination profiles

When using the mobility feature, bulk provisioning the remote destination profiles can save us a lot of time.

How to do it...

1. First, we create a remote destination profile template (**Bulk Administration | Mobility | Remote Destination Profiles | Remote Destination Profile Template**) and configure it with the appropriate information.

Bulk Administration Tool

2. Next we must prepare the CSV file. The CSV file will have the following fields; remember that not all fields will need to be populated:
   - **REMOTE DESTINATION PROFILE NAME**
   - **DESCRIPTION**
   - **DIRECTORY NUMBER 1**
   - **ROUTE PARTITION 1**

3. Now we upload the CSV file by selecting **Remote Destination Profiles** and **Insert Remote Destination Profiles** as shown in the following screenshot:

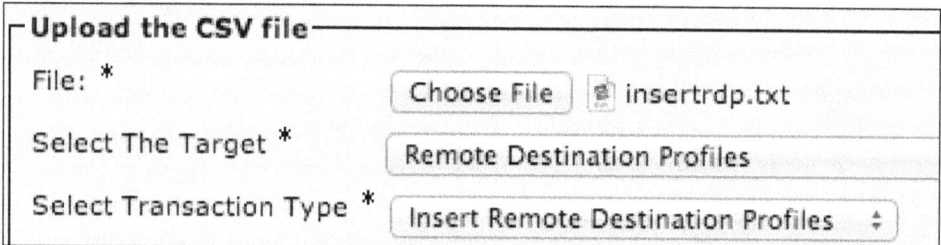

4. Finally, after the file is uploaded we can insert the remote destination files (**Bulk Administration | Mobility | Remote Destination Profile | Remote Destination Profile Insert**):

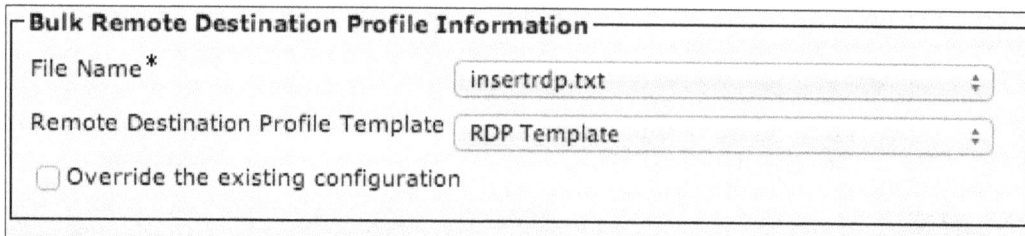

Submitting the job will insert the remote destination profiles into the database.

How it works...

The Bulk Administration Tool will take the information contained in the CSV file and insert the appropriate access lists into the system.

Bulk provisioning remote destinations

When using the mobility feature, bulk provisioning the remote destinations can save us a lot of time.

How to do it...

1. First we must prepare the CSV file. The CSV file will have the following fields, but remember that not all fields will need to be populated:
   - **NAME**
   - **DESTINATION**
   - **ANSWER TOO SOON TIMER**
   - **ANSWER TOO LATE TIMER**
   - **DELAY BEFORE RINGING TIMER**
   - **REMOTE DESTINATION PROFILE**
   - **TIME ZONE**
   - **IS MOBILE PHONE**
   - **DUAL MODE DEVICE**
   - **MOBILE SMART CLIENT**
   - **ENABLE MOBILE CONNECT 1**
   - **DAY OF WEEK 1**
   - **START TIME 1**
   - **END TIME 1**
   - **DAY OF WEEK 2**
   - **START TIME 2**
   - **END TIME 2**
   - **DAY OF WEEK 3**
   - **START TIME 3**
   - **END TIME 3**
   - **DAY OF WEEK 4**
   - **START TIME 4**
   - **END TIME 4**
   - **DAY OF WEEK 5**
   - **START TIME 5**
   - **END TIME 5**
   - **DAY OF WEEK 6**
   - **START TIME 6**
   - **END TIME 6**
   - **DAY OF WEEK 7**
   - **START TIME 7**
   - **END TIME 7**
   - **ACCESS LIST 1**
   - **ASSOCIATED LINE NUMBER 1**
   - **ROUTE PARTITION 1**
   - **MOBILITY PROFILE**

Bulk Administration Tool

2. Next upload the CSV file by selecting **Remote Destination, Insert Remote Destination** as shown in the following screenshot:

3. Finally, after the file is uploaded we can insert the remote destinations (**Bulk Administration | Mobility | Remote Destination | Remote Destination Insert**):

Submitting the job will insert the remote destinations into the database.

How it works...

The Bulk Administration Tool will take the information contained in the CSV file and insert the appropriate access lists into the system.

Bulk provisioning mobility profiles

When using the mobility feature, bulk provisioning the mobility profiles can save time.

How to do it...

1. First we must prepare the CSV file. The CSV file will have the following fields:
    - **MOBILITY PROFILE NAME**
    - **DESCRIPTION**
    - **SERVICE ACCESS NUMBER**
    - **ENTERPRISE FEATURE ACCESS NUMBER/PARTITION**
    - **CALLBACK CALLER ID**
    - **MOBILE CLIENT CALLING OPTION**

2. Next upload the CSV file by selecting **Mobility Profile, Insert Mobility Profile** as shown in the following screenshot:

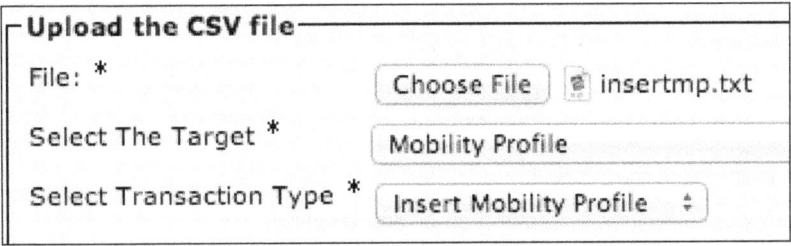

3. Finally, after the file is uploaded, we can insert the mobility profiles (**Bulk Administration | Mobility | Mobility Profile | Insert Mobility Profile**):

Submitting the job will insert the mobility profiles into the database.

How it works...

The Bulk Administration Tool will take the information contained in the CSV file and insert the appropriate access lists into the system.

Exporting data

There are many reasons why one might want to export data from the Unified Communications Manager database, perhaps to fix data before re-importing it, or to perform inventory. Whatever the reason, the export feature can provide us with a wealth of information about the configuration of the system.

How to do it...

To export data from the database, perform the following:

1. Navigate to the export page (**Bulk Administration | Import/Export | Export**):

Bulk Administration Tool

2. Specify a **Tar File Name**:

Job Information

Tar File Name* `ucm-callrouting-export`

---

3. We then check the boxes for each item we wish to have exported.
4. Verify dependencies by clicking on **Check Dependency.**

Select Items to Export

System Data

☑ Cisco Unified Communications Manager	☑ Cisco Unified Communications Manager Group
☐ Enterprise Parameter	☐ Location
☑ Server	☐ Service Parameter
☐ Physical Location	☐ Device Mobility group
☐ Device Mobility Info	☐ DHCP Server
☐ LDAP Directory	☐ LDAP Authentication
☐ Resource Priority Namespace List	☐ CUMA Server Security Profile
☐ Enterprise Phone Configuration	☐ Certificate

Call Routing Data

☐ Application Dial Rules	☑ CSS (Class of Control)
☐ Time Period (Class of Control)	☐ Time Schedule (Class of Control)
☐ Forced Authorization Codes	☐ Directory Lookup Dial Rules
☐ Call Pickup Group	☐ Directory Number (Unassigned)
☐ SIP Dial Rules	☐ Line Group
☑ Route List	☐ Hunt Pilot
☐ Access List	☑ Route Pattern

---

5. Click on **Submit**.
6. After the job finishes, navigate to the upload/download page (**Bulk Administration | Upload/Download Files**).

Chapter 11

7. Locate the file, check the box next to the filename:

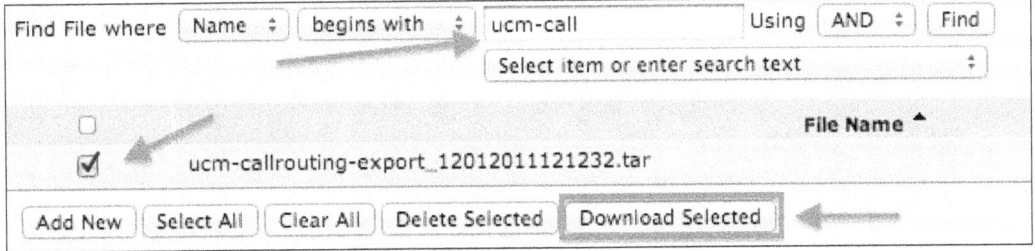

8. Click on **Download Selected**.

How it works...

By selecting the items we wish to export and then verifying the dependencies, the Bulk Administration Tool will prepare a tar file with CSV files for each item selected. Untarring (separating the combined .tar file out to show its contained files) the tar file will reveal these files.

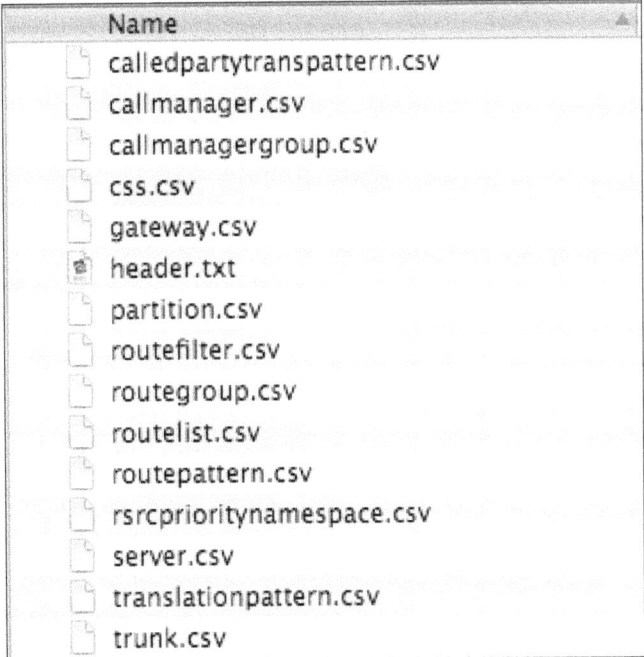

Index

A

AAR
  about 37, 48
  enabling 49
  implementing 50-52
  partitions 54
  route patterns 54
  search spaces, calling 54
  working 49, 53
AAR Destination Mask 53
AAR Groups
  AAR Destination Mask 53
  about 53
AAR partitions 54
access lists, BAT
  bulk provisioning 278, 279
alarm event level 241
  alert 241
  critical 241
  debug 242
  emergency 241
  error 241
  informational 242
  notice 242
  warning 242
alarms
  configuring 240
  working 241, 242
application user, RTMT
  creating 75, 76
application users, for secure communication
  configuring 236, 237
authorization levels, FAC 35
Automated Alternate Routing. *See* **AAR**

B

backup
  restoring, from 258
backup and restore process, UCM
  alarms, configuring 240
  backup device, configuring 253, 254
  backup schedule, configuring 255
  manual backup, performing 256
  patches and upgrades, applying 250, 251
  restoring, from backup 258
  SNMP Version 3, configuring 247-249
  SNMP (Versions 1 and 2), configuring 244, 245, 246
  traces, configuring 242, 243
backup device
  configuring 253, 254
  working 254
backup schedule
  configuring 255, 256
  working 256
bandwidth requirements
  calculating 40
barge, for devices and users
  conference barge 215
  configuring 213, 214
  standard barge 215
  types 215
  working 214
barge tones
  configuring 215, 216
BAT. *See* **Bulk Administration Tool**
Bulk Administration Tool
  about 262
  access lists, bulk provisioning 278
  bat template file, creating 262

Bulk Provisioning Service, enabling 264
bulk provisioning users 269, 271
call pickup groups, bulk provisioning 277
Client Matter Codes, bulk provisioning 276
custom file, creating 265
data, exporting 283, 284
Forced Authorization Codes, bulk provisioning 275
gateways, bulk provisioning 273
mobility profiles, bulk provisioning 282
phones 268
remote destination profiles, bulk provisioning 279
remote destinations, bulk provisioning 280
user device profiles, bulk provisioning 271
using 262, 263
working 264
Bulk Provisioning Service
  enabling 264, 265
  working 265
bulk provisioning users 269, 271

C

CAC 37
CAC technologies
  about 37
  Automated Alternate Routing, enabling 48
  Automated Alternate Routing, implementing 50
  location-based call admission control 37
  regions 43
  RSVP 45
call admission control. *See* **CAC**
called party transformation patterns 15
calling party transformation patterns 15
calling restrictions
  classes, determining 22
  fraud, mitigating 25
  implementing, partitions and calling search spaces used 20, 22
  patterns 23
  working 22
calling search spaces, Client Matter Codes 36
calling search spaces, FAC
  about 34

device calling search space 34
line calling search space 34
call park
  about 154
  configuring 154, 155
  implementing 154, 156
  working 156
call pickup groups, BAT
  about 277
  bulk provisioning 277, 278
call routing
  working with, short dial numbers 28
call routing considerations, FAC
  E.164 call routing 34
  traditional call routing 34
CAPF
  about 227
  configuring 227
  working 229
CCMUser web interface 137
centralized call processing 40
Certificate Authority Proxy Function. *See* **CAPF**
certificates, Cross Cluster Extension Mobility
  preparing 194-196
Cisco Extension Mobility 241
Cisco Extension Mobility application 241
Cisco IP Manager Assistant 241
Cisco IP Voice Media Streaming App Service parameters 57
Cisco TAC 241
Cisco Web Dialer Web 241
Client Matter Codes
  about 35
  calling search spaces 36
  design considerations 36
  implementing 35
  partitions 36
  route patterns 36
  working 36
Client Matter Codes, BAT
  bulk provisioning 276
CM Services 178
Codec selection 69
conference barge
  about 215
  configuring 215

credential policies
  assigning 138
  configuring 132, 133
  working 134, 140, 141
Cross Cluster Extension Mobility
  certificates, preparing 194-196
  intercluster service profile, configuring 200, 201
  intercluster trunks, configuring 199, 200
  parameters, configuring 198, 199
  template, creating 197
  users, configuring 193
Cross Cluster Extension Mobility phone service
  configuring 192
Cross Cluster Extension Mobility services
  enabling 191
CTI route point 151
CUCM 71
custom alert actions, RTMT
  configuring 86, 88
custom alerts, RTMT
  creating 82-85
  working 86
custom background image
  adding 169-172
custom file, Bulk Administration Tool
  creating 265-267
  using 267
  working 267
custom LDAP filters
  configuring 131
  working 131
custom media files
  adding, for Music On Hold 72
custom ringtone
  adding 166-168
  working 169

D

data export, Bulk Administration Tool
  about 283, 284
  working 285
DEBUG level alarms 241
decentralized call processing 40

default credential policies
  configuring 135, 136
  working 137, 138
design considerations, FAC 34
dest addr 91
device and unified mobility
  configuring 102
  device mobility, enabling 106, 107
  device mobility groups, configuring 103
  device mobility info, configuring 104-106
  device pools, configuring for device mobility 103, 104
  Enterprise Feature Access, enabling 122
  Intelligent Session Control, enabling 110, 111
  mid-call feature access codes, configuring 108, 109
  Mobile Voice Access, implementing 118-120
  mobility access lists, implementing 111, 112
  Mobility softkey, adding 123
  physical locations, configuring 102
  remote destination profiles, configuring 113, 114
  remote destinations, configuring 115-117
  Session Handoff, configuring 109, 110
device mobility
  enabling 106
  working 107
device mobility groups
  configuring 103
  working 103
device mobility info
  configuring 104, 105
device pools, for device mobility
  configuring 103, 104
  working 104
device profiles, for Extension Mobility
  configuring 183-189
  working 189
devices, for secure tone
  configuring 224, 225
  working 226
Dialed Number Analyzer
  about 94
  using 94
  working 97

Dial Plan
  analyzing, with Dialed Number Analyzer 93-97
dial plan considerations and partitions
  about 10
  common system partitions 10
  partitioning, at local level 10
  partitioning, at national level 10
dial plan considerations and route patterns
  about 11
  seven digit dialing 11
  teven digit dialing 12
digest authentication
  about 229
  configuring 229
  working 230
directed call park
  about 156
  configuring 157
  working 157
direct transfer to voice mail
  implementing 148-151
  working 151
disaster recovery system
  URL 253
dual mode configuration, for iPhone
  about 173-175
  working 176

E

E.164 called and calling party transformations
  implementing 12-14
  partitions and calling search spaces 16, 17
  working 15
E.164 route partitions
  implementing 8, 9
E.164 route patterns
  implementing 8, 9
e-mail server, RTMT
  configuring 81
endpoint hardening
  about 230
  implementing 230
  working 231

Enterprise Feature Access
  about 122
  enabling 122
  working 122
Extension Mobility phone service
  configuring 179, 180
Extension Mobility service
  about 178
  device profiles, configuring 183-189
  enabling 178
  parameters, configuring 189
  phone devices, configuring 180-182
  working 179
Extension Mobility service parameters
  configuring 190

F

FAC
  about 32
  authorization levels 35
  calling search spaces 34
  call routing considerations 34
  design considerations 34
  implementing 32
  partitions 34
  working 33
Forced Authorization Codes. *See* **FAC**
Forced Authorization Codes, BAT
  bulk provisioning 275

G

gateways, BAT
  bulk provisioning 273, 274
geolocations and filters
  configuring 205-207

H

host protocol addr 91
hotline device
  configuring 210-213
  working 213
hotline service parameters
  configuring 209
  working 210

I

Intelligent Session Control
  about 110
  enabling 110
  working 111
intercluster service profile, Cross Cluster Extension Mobility
  configuring 200, 201
intercluster trunks, Cross Cluster Extension Mobility
  configuring 199, 200
Intercom feature
  about 158
  configuring 158-162
  working 163
IOS conference bridges
  configuring 58
  working 59

L

LCR
  about 17
  implementing 17-19
  working 20
LDAP authentication
  enabling 129, 130
  working 130
LDAP Directory
  configuring 126, 127
  working 129
LDAP synchronization
  enabling 126
  working 126
Least Cost Routing. *See* **LCR**
local route groups
  implementing, with device pools 6
  working 8
location-based call admission control
  bandwidth requirements, calculating 40
  centralized vs. decentralized 40
  implementing 37, 38
  quality of service 41
  single cluster 40
  strategies, implementing 41
  synchronization issues 42
  working 39

logical partitioning
  about 207
  implementing 207, 208
  working 209

M

Malicious Call Identification
  about 163
  configuring 163-165
  enabling 163
  working 165
manual backup
  performing 256
  working 257
media resource group lists
  applying, to devices 65
  configuring 63
  working 64
media resource groups
  configuring 62
  working 63
media termination points. *See* **MTPs**
meet-me conferencing
  about 151
  configuring 152
  implementing 151-153
  working 154
MeetMe softkey 152
mid-call feature access codes
  configuring 108
  working 109
Mobile Voice Access
  about 118
  implementing 118-121
  working 121
mobility access lists
  implementing 111, 113
mobility profiles, BAT
  bulk provisioning 282, 283
Mobility softkey
  adding 123
  working 124
monitoring
  configuring 202-204

MTPs
  about 60
  configuring 60
  working 61
multicast Music On Hold
  configuring 69, 70
  working 71
Music On Hold audio sources
  Network Hold MOH Audio Source 68
  User Hold MOH Audio Source 68
Music On Hold audio source selection process 71

N

Network Hold MOH Audio Source 68

O

OS admin page
  URL 251

P

packet capture logs
  collecting 91, 93
packet capture mechanism
  about 88
  working 90
packets, RTMT
  capturing 89, 90
parameters, Cross Cluster Extension Mobility
  configuring 198, 199
parameters, Extension Mobility service
  configuring 189, 190
Park softkey 154
partitions and calling search spaces
  CSS-SFO-Inbound-ANI 16
  CSS-SFO-Outbound-ANI 16
  CSS-SFO-Outbound-DNIS 16
  CSS-US-Inbound-ANI 17
partitions, calling restrictions
  about 24
  international 24
  national 24
  premium 25
partitions, Client Matter Codes 36
partitions, FAC 34

patches and upgrades
  applying 250-252
patterns, calling restrictions
  about 23
  blocking, in E.164 environments 23
  blocking, in traditional environments 23
  sdesign considerations, for preventing call restriction bypass 23
phone devices, BAT 268
phone devices, for Extension Mobility
  configuring 180-182
  working 183
phone security profiles
  configuring 222, 223
physical locations, device mobility
  configuring 102
Portable Network Graphics (PNG) 169
port num 91
privacy, for devices and users
  configuring 216-218

Q

quality of service 41
Query Wizard
  used, for collecting traces 76

R

recording
  configuring 202-204
regions, for call admission control
  configuring 43
  implementing 43
  working 44
remote destination profiles
  configuring 113, 114
  creating 113
  working 115
remote destination profiles, BAT
  bulk provisioning 279, 280
remote destinations
  configuring 115-117
  working 117
remote destinations, BAT
  bulk provisioning 280, 282

Resource Reservation Protocol. *See* **RSVP**
restore wizard
  working 259
route patterns, AAR
  calling 54
route patterns, Client Matter Codes 36
routing, on holidays 32
RSVP
  about 37, 45
  carrier support 48
  implementing 45, 46
  settings 47
  working 47
RSVP settings
  about 47
  No reservations 47
RTMT
  about 73
  custom alert actions, configuring 86-88
  custom alerts, creating 82-85
  Dial Plan, analyzing with dialed number analyzer 93, 94
  e-mail server, configuring 81
  packets, capturing 88, 89
  traces, collecting using Query Wizard 76-79
  user permissions, configuring 73, 74

S

search spaces, AAR
  calling 54
secure conference bridge
  about 232
  implementing 232
  working 233
secure Meet-Me conferences
  about 233
  configuring 233
  implementing 233
  working 233
Separate Music On Hold servers 69
Session Handoff
  about 109
  configuring 109
  working 110
seven digit dialing
  implementing 11

short dial numbers
  call routing, working with 28
  implementing 26, 27
  working 28
single cluster 40
Single Music On Hold server 69
Skinny Client Control Protocol (SCCP) 59
SNMP Version 3
  configuring 247-249
SNMP Versions 1 and 2
  configuring 244-246
software conference bridges
  Cisco IP Voice Media Streaming App Service parameters 57
  configuring 56
  design considerations 57
  working 57
Solution Reference Network Design guide
  reference link 121
src addr 91
standard barge 215
Standard RealtimeAndTraceCollection 74
Standard SERVICEABILITY 75
Standard SERVICEABILITY Administration 75
Standard SERVICEABILITY Read Only 75
strategies, location-based call admission control
  device pools, using 41
  implementing 41
  per device, configuring 41
synchronization issues, location-based call admission control 42

T

template, Cross Cluster Extension Mobility
  creating 197
ten digit dialing
  implementing 12
third party application
  about 236
  working 238
time-of-day routing
  about 28
  considerations 31
  holidays, implementing 32
  implementing 28-30

routing, on holidays 32
working 31
traces
configuring 242
enabling 242, 243
working 243
traces, RTMT
collecting, Query Wizard used 76-80
transcoders
configuring 59, 60
working 60
Transfer softkey 157

U

UCM
about 5
application users, configuring for secure communication 236-238
calling restrictions, implementing 20, 22
CAPF, configuring 227-229
Client Matter Codes, implementing 35
custom media files, adding for Music On Hold 72
devices for secure tone, configuring 224, 225
digest authentication, configuring 229
E.164 called and calling party transformations, implementing 12-14
E.164 route partitions, implementing 8, 9
E.164 route patterns, implementing 8, 9
endpoint hardening, implementing 230, 231
FAC, implementing 32
IOS conference bridges, configuring 58
LCR, implementing 17-19
local route groups, implementing with device pools 6, 7
media resource group lists, configuring 63, 64
media resource groups, configuring 62, 63
MTPs, configuring 60
multicast Music On Hold, configuring 69, 70
phone security profiles, configuring 222, 223
secure conference bridge, implementing 232
secure Meet-Me conferences, implementing 233
securing 221
short dial numbers, implementing 26, 27
software conference bridges, configuring 56
Time-of-Day routing, implementing 28-30
transcoders, configuring 59, 60
unicast Music On Hold, implementing 65, 67
user features 147
user management 125
VPN, configuring for Cisco IP phones 234-236
unicast and multicast Music On Hold 68
unicast Music On Hold
about 65
implementing 65, 67
working 68
Unified Communications Manager. *See* **UCM**
Unified Serviceability page
URL 240
user device, BAT
bulk provisioning 271, 273
user features
call park, implementing 154-156
custom background image, adding 169-172
custom ringtone, adding 166-168
directed call park, implementing 156
direct transfer to voice mail, implementing 148-151
dual mode configuration, for iPhone 173- 175
Intercom feature, configuring 158-162
Malicious Call Identification, configuring 163,-165
meet-me conferencing, implementing 151-153
user groups
assigning, to end users 145, 146
configuring 143, 144
working 145
User Hold MOH Audio Source 68
user management
credential policies, assigning 138-141
credential policies, configuring 132, 133
custom LDAP filters, configuring 131
default credential policies, configuring 135-138
LDAP authentication, enabling 129, 130
LDAP Directory, configuring 126-128
LDAP synchronization, enabling 126
user groups, assigning to end users 145, 146
user groups, configuring 143, 144
user roles, configuring 141

user permissions, RTMT
  configuring 73, 74
  custom user group 74
  working 74
user roles
  configuring 141
  working 142
users, Cross Cluster Extension Mobility
  configuring 193

V

VPN client for IP phones
  about 234
  configuring 234, 235
  working 236

Thank you for buying
Cisco Unified Communications Manager 8: Expert Administration Cookbook

About Packt Publishing

Packt, pronounced 'packed', published its first book "*Mastering phpMyAdmin for Effective MySQL Management*" in April 2004 and subsequently continued to specialize in publishing highly focused books on specific technologies and solutions.

Our books and publications share the experiences of your fellow IT professionals in adapting and customizing today's systems, applications, and frameworks. Our solution-based books give you the knowledge and power to customize the software and technologies you're using to get the job done. Packt books are more specific and less general than the IT books you have seen in the past. Our unique business model allows us to bring you more focused information, giving you more of what you need to know, and less of what you don't.

Packt is a modern, yet unique publishing company, which focuses on producing quality, cutting-edge books for communities of developers, administrators, and newbies alike. For more information, please visit our website: www.PacktPub.com.

About Packt Enterprise

In 2010, Packt launched two new brands, Packt Enterprise and Packt Open Source, in order to continue its focus on specialization. This book is part of the Packt Enterprise brand, home to books published on enterprise software – software created by major vendors, including (but not limited to) IBM, Microsoft and Oracle, often for use in other corporations. Its titles will offer information relevant to a range of users of this software, including administrators, developers, architects, and end users.

Writing for Packt

We welcome all inquiries from people who are interested in authoring. Book proposals should be sent to author@packtpub.com. If your book idea is still at an early stage and you would like to discuss it first before writing a formal book proposal, contact us; one of our commissioning editors will get in touch with you.

We're not just looking for published authors; if you have strong technical skills but no writing experience, our experienced editors can help you develop a writing career, or simply get some additional reward for your expertise.

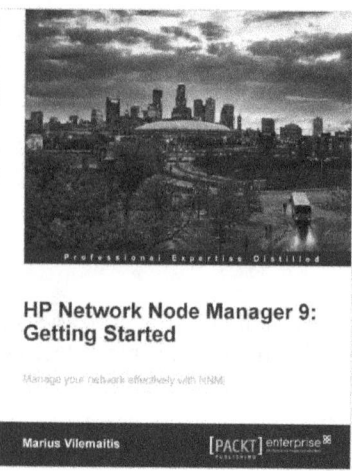

HP Network Node Manager 9: Getting Started

ISBN: 978-1-84968-084-4　　　Paperback: 584 pages

Manage your network effectively with NNMi

1. Install, customize, and expand NNMi functionality by developing custom features
2. Integrate NNMi with other management tools, such as HP SW Operations Manager, Network Automation, Cisco Works, Business Availability center, UCMDB, and many others
3. Navigate between incidents and maps to reduce troubleshooting time
4. Screenshots and step-by-step instructions to customize NNMi in the way you want

IBM Lotus Sametime 8 Essentials: A User's Guide

ISBN: 978-1-84968-060-8　　　Paperback: 284 pages

Mastering Online Enterprise Communication with this collaborative software

1. Collaborate securely with your colleagues and teammates both inside and outside your organization by using Sametime features such as instant messaging and online meetings
2. Make your instant messaging communication more interesting with the inclusion of graphics, images, and emoticons to convey more information in fewer words
3. Communicate with other instant messaging services and users, such as AOL Instant Messaging, Yahoo Instant Messaging, and Google Talk and know how someone's online status can help you communicate faster and more efficiently

Please check **www.PacktPub.com** for information on our titles

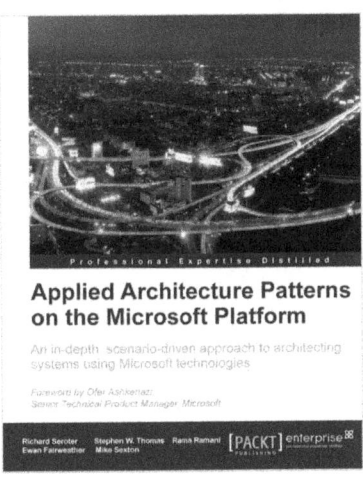

Applied Architecture Patterns on the Microsoft Platform

ISBN: 978-1-849680-54-7 Paperback: 544 pages

An in-depth, scenario-driven approach to architecting systems using Microsoft technologies

1. Provides an architectural methodology for choosing Microsoft application platform technologies to meet the requirements of your solution

2. Examines new technologies such as Windows Server AppFabric, StreamInsight, and Windows Azure Platform and provides examples of how they can be used in real-world solutions

3. Considers solutions for messaging, workflow, data processing, and performance scenarios

Oracle SOA Suite 11g R1 Developer's Guide

ISBN: 978-1-84968-018-9 Paperback: 720 pages

Develop Service-Oriented Architecture Solutions with the Oracle SOA Suite

1. A hands-on, best-practice guide to using and applying the Oracle SOA Suite in the delivery of real-world SOA applications

2. Detailed coverage of the Oracle Service Bus, BPEL PM, Rules, Human Workflow, Event Delivery Network, and Business Activity Monitoring

3. Master the best way to use and combine each of these different components in the implementation of a SOA solution

Please check www.PacktPub.com for information on our titles

www.ingramcontent.com/pod-product-compliance
Lightning Source LLC
Chambersburg PA
CBHW080935220326
41598CB00034B/5793